*These are the*
# MARITIMES

*These are the*

# MARITIMES

## Will R. Bird
Author of *This Is Nova Scotia*
and *Off-Trail in Nova Scotia*

**McGRAW-HILL RYERSON LIMITED**
Toronto • Montreal • New York • London • Sydney • Mexico
Johannesburg • Panama • Düsseldorf • Singapore • São Paulo
Kuala Lumpur • New Delhi

*Published 1959*
*Fourth Printing, 1969*
*First Paperback Edition 1974*

0-07-077697-0
2 3 4 5 6 7 8 9 10 - AP 74 - 10 9 8

PRINTED AND BOUND IN CANADA

# Contents

# Illustrations

| | |
|---|---|
| The Bell Museum at Baddeck | *Nova Scotia Film Bureau* |
| Festival of Arts, Tatamagouche | *Nova Scotia Film Bureau* |
| Louisburg National Historic Park | |
| | *Nova Scotia Film Bureau* |
| Fort Edward, in Victoria Park, Charlottetown | |
| | *National Film Board of Canada* |
| Queen Square, Charlottetown | |
| | *National Film Board of Canada* |
| Government House, Charlottetown | |
| | *National Film Board of Canada* |
| Tonging for Oysters | *National Film Board of Canada* |
| Hunter River | *National Film Board of Canada* |
| Col. E. W. Johnstone and one of his miniature castles, Burlington | *National Film Board of Canada* |
| Green Gables | *National Film Board of Canada* |
| Cavendish Beach | *National Film Board of Canada* |
| Christ Church Cathedral, Fredericton | |
| | *New Brunswick Travel Bureau* |
| Grand Falls | *The Smith Studio, Sackville* |
| Salmon angling in New Brunswick | |
| | *The Smith Studio, Sackville* |

*These are the*
# MARITIMES

# 1

## *Spruce Gum, Reversing Falls,*
## *Magnetic Hill, and Sea-Horse*

THE BEST SORT OF VACATION, many people say, is the one not planned to the final detail, the one in which you drive according to desire, and stop where night overtakes you. So we decided to be somewhat like Alice in Wonderland and leisurely explore the Maritimes without any pressure of itinerary, seeing everything as if for the first time and making friends where we could. On a lovely June morning we "entered" via St. Stephen, New Brunswick, as if we were from Boston or New York, parked on a side street and strolled near Customs with a camera at the ready, trying to look like tourists in a foreign land.

A pleasant-faced man of the Rotarian type, with a packet of official-looking papers in his hand, scanned us, paused and remarked that we had a fine day. We agreed, and he said he hoped we would take time enough to look around the town. We asked him what there was to see and he rose to the bait.

"There's nothing to match it for real friendliness along the whole border from here to the Pacific," he enthused. "I mean, between us and Calais. Many of our people are from Maine, and many in Calais were originally Canadians. We share our water supply with Calais, and that's one for Ripley. Calais firemen come here when they hear the alarm, and our lads go to Calais when there's a fire over there. Calais comes here and helps us put on a real humdinger of a July first, and we go back and help them with their Fourth of July."

We asked him what there was in the way of industry.

"I'm glad you asked that," he said. "For we've got the finest chocolates in North America, made right here in St. Stephen. There's four hundred and fifty people working in the plant, and that's pretty good when you think we have less than four thousand of a population. Ganong's is the name of the plant and chocolates, and they make a hundred different kinds of candy. Ganong's invented the nutbar back in 1905, and the people in the factory tell that the president of Ganong's, Arthur D. Ganong, eats a pound of candy every day. His son's our mayor and he eats a pound a day. Why they even write essays about candy in the school here, and birthdays mean a box of Ganong's no matter who has the birthday. I'll tell you, too, why Ganong's have the best chocolates. It's because they're the only big plant that sticks to hand-dipping. The others do it by machine, and lose part of the flavour. Dipping is quite a trick, too, and it takes a girl two or three years to be good at it, and five or six before she can really turn out a day's work."

We said we'd have to sample Ganong's before we left town, and asked if there were anything else unusual in town.

"Do you chew gum?" he quizzed.

"Not much," we said. "Why?"

"I mean nature's chewing gum," he grinned. "Not the rubber stuff that's flavoured for the first five or six minutes, but the natural pure spruce gum that's full of flavour no matter how long you use it. We put out the world's best here in St. Stephen, and nothing's added to it. Just pure gum, and we get most of it, about ninety per cent of it, from Nova Scotia, the most of it from Cumberland County. If you're down that way start asking around Bass River or Advocate and you may run into a man that makes a good living just walking around and picking gum off trees."

"Good living!" we echoed. "You couldn't find a pound in a day?"

"He can," grinned our friend. "He finds tons—not pounds."

The question was to believe him or not but he slipped a sample from his pocket and we read the label, and had to believe it was "unsweetened refined nature gum."

"Any unusual history?" we queried.

"Plenty," he came back. "They were mostly United Empire Loyalists who settled here, but nobody talks about it as we don't want to tramp on any corns. In the war of 1812 we had a mass meeting with Calais and shook hands on a deal that we would not fight, no matter what the rest of the country did. But the British thought we were in danger and sent us a supply of gunpowder. You know what became of it? We loaned it to Calais to celebrate with on the Fourth of July. And I've heard my old folks talk about the time there was a good bounty on bears over in Maine, and none here. So every bear that was trapped or shot around our way somehow turned up his toes over on the Calais side, and like good friends, all hands split the difference. You couldn't really call that illegal as who knows but what they were Maine bears just visiting on this side."

"What about local characters?" we asked.

"They're scarce now," said our friend. "But don't forget that we've had some mighty good baseball teams in this place. We've had the Maritime championship more than once. Speaking of characters, I remember when I was a young fellow forty-odd years ago there was an old chap who kept eight dogs as company and he used to make a blood purifier every spring that he sold for a dollar. It was supposed to prevent spring fever and drive away pimples and boils. He was a good talker and swore he got the recipe from the Indians, and mentioned a dozen herbs by Latin names. The women liked him and he sold the stuff more and more until at last he was peddling it the year around. The one old girl, his best customer, fell and broke her arm and the doctor found she was simply drunk. Her folks found she had a dozen bottles of the purifier on hand and it didn't need a specialist to find that each bottle was filled with water and West Indies rum. But they didn't catch the old boy. He'd stocked up every customer with a bargain sale, turned all his dogs loose, and left to live with a cousin in Kentucky. Years after we heard he'd become a colonel down there."

A strident voice called from a nearby shop and our informant asked us to excuse him and departed hastily. We started back to where we had parked and a fat little man with a bald head, seated in a new Buick, grinned at us. He was in the line waiting to go through Customs.

"You comin' or goin'?" he asked.

"Going into New Brunswick now," we said.

"Boy, you'll like it!" he said. "We've done the works. Nova Scotia and Prince Edward Island and New Brunswick. Last year we did Quebec and Maine. Next year we're going west. Nothing like it. We did the Island yesterday. When we started this touring we thought we'd take a camera and the wife bought one, but it was hard to get the right light and guess the distance and all that, and we saw we could gather up the travel books they issue and when we get home the wife cuts out the pictures and pastes them in a scrap book and we show folks where we've been. It's a lot easier that way."

A fat little woman beside the talker peered out at us. "We only started three years ago," she said in a soft voice. "We didn't have the means before that."

"So what!" said the man, rubbing his cheek against hers. "Lady luck give us the grin at last and that's all that really matters. Say, friend, don't miss that Magnetic Hill near Moncton. There ain't nothing like it in this world. You won't believe it till you're there. Your car really rolls backward uphill when you have it out of gear. We rolled back three times and just had to believe it. And if you're going to Prince Edward Island take the early ferry. There's a line-up for the second, and . . ."

The car behind him beeped an urgent signal to get going and the fat little man waved as he drove on. His car license read "Maryland."

We rolled along a smooth and inviting new highway and in no time at all saw signs pointing from the main way to St. Andrews. We turned right and soon were in the quaint narrow streets of a little town where hurry is forgotten. There wasn't a trace of it along the sidewalks or anywhere. People walked leisurely going from shop to shop or to the waterfront, gulls flapped lazily to roosting places by the pier and dogs rested in the shade. The Algonquin Inn's roof drew us and we saw it was a huge rambling hotel. People rested in easy chairs or were admiring the flowers. Some watched a gull seated on the tip of the flag pole. We went back to the main street and parked by a small open space fronting the water. A sign on a building attracted us and we entered the shop of the Charlotte County Cottage Craft and soon were inspecting the finest assortment of woven goods we had seen. The display was so unusually fine that we simply had to dig up the story, and it was most interesting.

Dr. Grace Helen Mowatt was born on an old farm in New Brunswick, a farm that had belonged to the family for generations. She showed a fondness for drawing and sketching while at school so she was sent to Women's Art School at Cooper Union, New York. This was back in the gay nineties. Howard Chandler Christie taught illustration, Frederic Deilman gave lectures in perspective, and John Henry Twatchman was the terror and inspiration of most young art students. He made Miss Mowatt work with frenzied zeal on block figures. She, like the other students, was forever copying patterns—Egyptian,

Greek, etc.—never had opportunity to do any drawing that would express her own feelings.

After graduation, Miss Mowatt taught art at a girl's boarding school but eventually returned to country life in New Brunswick and decided to establish a native art, an art that might express the farm life of the area. She began with hooked rugs, found that people could work out designs for themselves, and their very crudeness lent additional charm. She discovered that in every community there was at least one person with artistic ability, and encouraged such persons to work out designs dealing with the familiar in everyday life. Success attended every effort and soon the art of weaving homespun was revived, then embroidery was done on homespun with yarn and handbags were sold in quantities. The industry that had started in such a small way continued to grow and by 1920 between two and three thousand dollars a year was being paid to the farm women who were doing such good work. A shop was opened in St. Andrews, and examples of work sent to the British Empire Exhibition at Wembley. More attention was given to the homespun. Information was obtained from weavers on the Island of Harris and there were experiments in dyeing and in blending the wool to obtain more artistic shades. This gave a native touch that caught the fancy of visitors. The weavers became more expert, and the area was extended. The County has been likened to a huge factory covering an area of thirty square miles. But there is no smoke stack, no overhead expense for heating, lighting, insurance, no worries whatever, and the demand for the woven materials increased steadily. In 1945 Miss Mowatt turned over the operation of Cottage Craft to Kent and Bill Ross, two fine young business men who began expanding the work with emphasis on the production of tweeds in distinctive colours. The work is carried on through all phases from the raw wool to finished garments with the sale of skirts, suits, coats and men's sport jackets accounting for a major portion of the year's business. We watched the visitors flocking in, heard the continuous exclamations of delight, and saw the purchases that were being made.

"The demand is getting heavier all the time," smiled Bill Ross, "but our workers enjoy filling the demand. I don't think there's another factory like ours in the world. We only meet with the workers once in a while. They're in a hundred farm homes spread up the country roads, women who have become experts in production, who are forever trying to produce something just a little better than last year. They have a pride in their work that we've not seen matched anywhere, and that's why each year we have a better stock. It's really a pleasure to meet our customers and show them what we have."

There was a small building in the open space and two old men with the attitude of those alien to deadlines grinned and waved us a welcome as we sauntered over. Soon we learned that some wealthy citizens had built the place of idleness for the convenience of such oldsters as now occupied two seats by the door. In no time they were giving us a sort of history of St. Andrews.

"It was settled away back in 1783," said Checked Shirt, who had a large Adam's apple, "and not by them as were sent by Sir Guy Carleton, but by a group that called themselves the 'Penobscot Loyalist Association.' You see, back in that time this was all Nova Scotia and nobody had run a line to show where Maine began. So when the trouble started these Tories moved up and settled on what they thought was Nova Scotia, figuring the line would run by Penobscot. They had put up a lot of boxlike houses and were doing all right. Then word come that the St. Croix would be the boundary and down come them little houses and the framework, boards and all, with their furniture, dishes, livestock, everything, was put on vessels and moved over here. They even fetched their 'Coffee House' which was a sort of meeting-place and used as a tavern.

Well, ground was cleared and homes started again, ships were built and trade with the West Indies started. Everybody got a town lot and a strip of wild land out in the country, and them at Saint John raised such a howl over conditions that the powers at Halifax, not wanting to worry over places so far away, made this country into a new Province—New Brunswick. So that was the end of the northern part of Nova Scotia."

"It was a great little town back in the beginning," said Brown Shirt who held a pipe in his hand but rarely put it to his mouth. "Most of the people were quite religious and they had churches up in no time. Some from Connecticut had brought the Royal Coat of Arms from the town of Wallingford and they are over the west door of All Saints' Church. Take a look afore you leave town. The Anglicans run the place first but there were Scottish Presbyterians and it hurt them to have to use a hall in place of a kirk. There was a dinner party and at it one of the Anglicans made some remark about them having no kirk, and a merchant who was well to do offered to go ahead and finish one they had started and let lapse for want of funds. His name was Christopher Scott and he was a man of action. He sent to the West Indies for mahogany and got the best bird's-eye maple for pillars to support the gallery, got the best carpenters and plasterers money could fetch. He had them put a big Scotch thistle in plaster in each corner of the ceiling, and the pulpit is really a work of art, made of mahogany and bird's-eye maple and put together without nails or hammer. He put up a fine spire with a wind-vane at  the top, and on front of the tower had them paint a spreading oak tree, the emblem of Greenock, Scotland, his home. Around the tree they painted the name 'Greenock Church' and the date 'Finished June, 1824.' Go and have a look at it."

He paused for breath and Checked Shirt took up the story without a moment being lost. He told about the greats and near-greats who moved to St. Andrews. There was Sir William

Van Horne, President of the Canadian Pacific Railway, who bought Minister's Island and built a mansion, with stables, gardens and windmills, had an enormous barn stocked with Dutch cattle, made drives and pathways all over the place and often opened it to the public. At low tide you could cross over easily. There was an old blockhouse left as a relic of days of tension on the border. There was the famous author of 'Geordie' and other books, David Walker, choosing St. Andrews above all the rest of Canada, and the Sir James Dunn estate with a high fence around it. In fact there were VIP's anywhere you looked, and some of them were of the finest. They would meet with the regular loafers at the little building and chat about any subject under the sun. They said the early settlers were Loyalists who worshipped God and honoured the King and it has always been that way in the town, and the first-comers had really blessed Charlotte County with St. Stephens, St. Andrews, St. David, St. James, St. George and St. Patrick—all parishes. Even the river was St. Croix, and the little island we could see if we took the trouble was the one on which Champlain and his men had spent the first winter back in 1604 before moving to Port Royal.

"Probably the American visitors don't care much about your Loyalist history," we said. "And the settling of the old border line is forgotten."

"Likely," nodded Checked Shirt, "but now and then you meet with some American who must have had Tory ancestors. He'll tell you what he thinks of the doings in his own home state, and usually it's a grim story. Anyhow, we had our guns ready for them one time away back and now there's just that old blockhouse."

"And likely as good as that Dew Line they talk about," said Brown Shirt. "That one up north that should be gold-plated about now 'cording to the money they've spent on it. Say, did you know that Oliver Goldsmith, a grandnephew of the great Oliver, was born in this town. But don't let us keep you. You buy a book on the town, Miss Mowatt's story of St. Andrews and you'll find we've been giving you the truth. She's the smartest old woman in seven counties and you ought to meet her. Maybe you will—head on. If you see a car coming in the middle of the road, pull for the ditch. She's reckless."

"Never mind that part," broke in Checked Shirt. "She's done more for this town and county than any politician ever raised. There ain't many like her nowadays. She'd do more'n the ordinary woman at any job she tackled. She started something that's made work for the whole countryside."

It was later than we realized by the time we got away from our mines of information but we had a look at the blockhouse and around the shops that were attractive with displays intended to catch the eye of the visitor. Some large sport cars rolled by with passengers in bathing suits. We drove around and saw the Greenock Church with the painted oak on its tower, then went to the Algonquin Inn, had lunch and chatted with strangers who insisted on taking us to see the old cemetery with many quaint epitaphs. When, very late in the afternoon, we escaped, we drove only a few miles before stopping at Forest Lodge, Chamcook. We found it a delightful old home beautifully situated on a hillside with a huge champion moosehead in the hall, and a large living-room with the elegance of half a century ago. Miss Muriel Grimmer, the proprietor, is versed in the history of the countryside, a charming hostess; the food was wonderful, and the garden on the slope a delight. We wandered there in the evening and saw all kinds of bird life, heard a small owl as the dusk thickened and went to sleep with rustle of the great trees outside our window providing a sweet hush-hush to the end of the day.

In the morning we set off along Highway 1 and soon had reached St. George, a small place with the road its main street and a waterfall on the Magaguadavic River the only feature to interest the camera enthusiast. The inevitable

oldtimer was near the bridge, his thumbs under his braces
that held up very baggy trousers with three buttons and a
nail as fasteners for the frail support. We greeted him cheerfully and got a pleasant grin, then asked what there was that
we should see in the locality.

"Nothin', this time of morning," he announced. "Last
week I saw a moose come over the road right where you are,
but that was real early in the day. And I could take you back
a ways to a place where a woman feeds an old she raccoon and
her two young ones every morning reg'lar. They come to her
kitchen window and the old one's been fetchin' her family
there the last six, seven years."

Well, we said, that was interesting, but was there any
person of outstanding ability in the place. The thumbs
tightened their grip on the braces. "Yes, there is. We've got
a woman here's a champeen scrabbler if ever there was one.
You know the game? Well, she's licked every school teacher
and town visitor ever come here. Whenever she gets stuck
a bit she uses an Injun word. Her pa was a guide and taught
her a lot of them, and it ain't no use to argy with her 'cause
she says there's no rules ag'in such words, and she's willin' for
all hands to use 'em."

We drove on and saw on our left an abandoned airfield that
had been used as an Air Training Centre in World War Two.
Then there were woods, a fine sweep of beach at New River,
and more woods and dips and hills and American cars on
their way home, trailers and occasional trucks. The long
stretches of wooded country exhaled the breath of spruce and
pine and fir and there was quietness save for the whine of
tires on pavement. Sometimes there were small places with
schools and canteens and later we reached an area of motels
and overnight cabins and knew we were approaching Saint
John. There were several turns, well marked, and then we
were rolling downhill into the heart of the old city. Up steep

King Street and along the Square and we were at the Admiral
Beatty Hotel with time to see much before day's end.

Saint John is the oldest incorporated city in Canada, and
looks it from any angle. It rises from the water front and the
buildings somehow look as though they had been in place
when the upheaval occurred, and now rest where the disturb-
ance ended. We wandered down King Street and into stores
that opened from one department to another, only you moved
direct from the first floor into the second floor. There is an
air of yesterday about the biggest store, and it has been
purposely kept that way, a senior clerk told us. He said they
received mail orders from people who had moved away years
before but always felt they could buy anything from such
an unchanging establishment. We were told that the Royal
Hotel was very old, and that some of the shops had relics of
bygone days in loft storerooms.

Going on down the hill the way seems a bit rougher and it
makes you feel that wind and fog has washed Saint John with
salt spray until most of it has the same appearance. We were
taken to see the Reversing Falls, a turmoil of water and rock
that is fascinating. The Saint John River meets the sea at
the head of the harbour and at low tide boils over an eleven-
foot drop. The tide begins to return and for a time the water
almost stills. Then the rising tide forces its way upstream
through the chasm in a perfect turmoil of eddies. Our guide
told us the Indian legend of the place is that the beaver was
so great an animal that his dams were flooding the redmen
from their lodges. Then came the mighty Glooscap, the great
God of the Indians, and he tore away the beaver dams and
chased the beaver from the country. The biggest dam of all
was at the mouth of the Saint John River and part of it was
carried out a distance when Glooscap wrecked the structure.
That piece stayed where it grounded at low tide and became
Partridge Island.

Talk with any clerk in a shop or the man in the street of

Saint John and you'll get history by the hatful. They tell you that early French fur traders chose the spot and built there a strong wooden fort as wars were fought with rivals across the Bay of Fundy. Finally the Frenchmen from the Nova Scotian side arrived at a time when the Saint John trader was absent with many of his men. A siege began at once but the resourceful wife, Madame de la Tour, rallied her garrison and put on so bold a front that the attacker was held at bay until one renegade within the stronghold contrived to betray his fellows. Honourable terms of surrender were offered but once the invader was in charge he hanged every man of the garrison and forced Madame de la Tour to watch the grisly game. He did not long enjoy the fruits of such a victory but was drowned during a canoe trip and his widow married the man from Saint John.

Historians seeking to prove the exact location of the fort, unearthed parts of the old foundation, located the place where the main gate had been, brought to light many relics of the seventeenth century. And down below the evidence of the la Tour fort they found proof of ancient Indian graves, showing that the locality had long been favoured by those who knew the country. We spent the rest of our day strolling there and visualized the scene in the long ago when the redmen came with loads of fur to trade for trinkets and hatchets.

In the morning the sun seemed reluctant to appear and under the clouds the old Loyalist city looked more than ever a grizzled veteran. We were shown an old Martello Tower which commands the harbour from the heights of West Saint John, and Trinity Church that had its first service on Christmas Day, 1791. A communion service sent out to Trinity by King George the Third in 1790 is a prize possession and still in regular use. Those who have a special interest in things historical will see in this old church a hand-carved replica of the Royal Arms of the House of Hanover. Only six such pieces were rescued from the American Colonies at the time of the Revolution, and this particular specimen hung originally in the Council Chamber of the Colony of Massachusetts Bay.

We were next shown the Old Stone Church so called because it was for some time the only stone building in Saint John. It was built in 1824 and every stone in the old walls was quarried in Bristol, England, and brought across in ships. When we were outside again the sun was struggling through the clouds and we suggested that we be on our way but our friend insisted on taking us to what he called Canada's oldest museum. It is somewhat apart from the centre of the city, which is a help in parking, and after we saw the collections of Indian relics and old-time uniforms and pioneer utensils we were glad we had not missed the place.

"The man who invented kerosene, Abraham Gesner, began this museum," said our genial guide," and we hope some day to have a big neon sign to tell visitors that this is a museum. Not a third who come to the city find it. And don't forget that this is the home of Walter Pidgeon, that Arnold Benedict lived here until he was chased out, that we have the shortest, steepest, widest main street in any city, and the second largest drydock in the world."

"We'll not forget a thing," we promised. "We like every foot of your hilly, twisted city."

He began to glow and to pump our hands like a Rotary chairman, so we added, slyly. "A chap told us that fog from the Bay gives Saint John its sea-washed look, that you have a damp winter chill that goes to the bone, but we like it."

"Everybody who's jealous of us, like some lads up in Fredericton, tell that stuff," rejoined our friend. "We have no more fog than any other town or place on the sea coast and our winters are so mild the harbour never freezes. They're trying to rob us of winter trade with the St. Lawrence Seaway but they can't stop the ice from forming in the river. Nova

Scotia and we were seduced into Confederation at a time when we were getting along all right. Then they put on tariffs to protect Upper and Lower Canada and they've been protecting them ever since and paralyzing the Maritimes. We ought to leave them and join New England. I'm sorry." He saw our grins. "I really get hot under the collar and say more than I mean, but we won't have much to celebrate in 1967."

We were sorry we had teased him as he let us out at the Admiral Beatty but he was back before we were in our car and he had a publication that carried a story of New Brunswick that made it seem more or less unsettled with skeins of roads along the coastline and up river. We read that old United Empire Loyalists were still at the top of the social ladder in Saint John and it appeared that the biggest enterprize was to be seen at Gagetown where the Federal Government had built a huge military training camp as "a poultice to solace New Brunswick's aching need for jobs and cash."

Away we went and soon were on wonderful new paved roads. The map showed us that we bypassed Rothesay by the new highway but we had been long in Saint John so rolled along enjoying views of river scenery and soon were at Hampton where we stopped for gas. An elderly man in a faded blue shirt was standing by a half-ton truck and we asked him if Hampton had much history. "Just average," he commented. "It's one more place that moved over to get alongside the railroad. I guess it was a French village in the beginning but the English came in and by 1860 there was an inn and a jail and some stores. People got the idea to move and everyone packed up and came over here. They brought the Inn over and the jail was moved stone by stone. It was hard work and money was scarce so four-five fellows they had locked up were let go if they would work a week free. They say two of them kept on the job till it was finished. The undertaker here papered his house with Baptist papers back in the old days and half the history that's been written has been got from the walls of the old house."

There was some temptation to view the papers but the day had become beautiful, too nice to be inside, so we asked if there were any persons we should interview. He gave us directions to a house beyond the station and we found a delightful lady working in her garden. She was versed in the history of the countryside, had written much, had a gold mine of information for an ambitious investigator of things historical, and a most amazing story of rearing wild ducks. Some organization wondered if they could be raised like other birds and gave her a batch of eggs. Not only did she raise them but she treated them so well that when they were full grown and had taken wing up river she had only to beat her big spoon on the feeding pail to bring the flock on whistling wings.

It was a grand visit we had under the great shade trees and we hated to leave. A car horn tooted as we started away on main street and there was the half-ton truck and the man in the blue shirt wanted to know how we'd fared. We told him, and asked if he could direct us to any similar folk.

"No such luck," he shrugged. "I could send you to the reverse and no trouble. Right over yonder, inside the village limits, there's a woman that buys stale bread to feed to raccoons."

"How interesting!" we said. "Could we see them?"

"Interesting—hell!" he snorted. "There must be twenty-five of the . . . brutes there every night, and us tryin' to raise chickens and the like. I'd . . .'"

He drove away talking loudly, annoyed at our interest in coons, and we went on our way, taking in more river scenery, a village on our right, and pleasant vistas until suddenly we turned right at a bridge and were entering Sussex. There was a place on the right that served ice cream and soft drinks so in we went for a milk shake. A man on a stool beside us said Sussex had had a military camp as long as he could remember, that it was in the heart of a great dairy country, that Sussex had had a champion hockey team called the "Dairy Kings," that in the old days Sussex had the fastest half-mile racetrack in America and all the old squires in the region kept fast horses. Big bets were placed every summer when they brought horses from Prince Edward Island for summer racing, and one man had won more than ten thousand dollars in the days when a dollar was one hundred cents and no Income Tax men breathed down your neck.

He was a thin man with bony cheeks, and a willing talker.

"I belong three miles up on the new Fredericton road," he said, "and I have a good job but I'm taking the day off to go to a wedding. A cousin of mine is getting married."

He finished his coke with a gurgle, and shrugged. "He ain't got steady work and she ain't. They'll have to board with her people, and you know what that's like, but they're getting married all the same."

We murmured something inane about love finding a way. "Love!" he snorted. "They were at a dance and he just asked a foolish question and she give him a foolish answer. Then he daren't try to back out. He told me so himself."

A deluge of family history seemed in the offing so we hastily asked what interesting features could be found in Sussex. "The best in the world," declared the thin man. "Go and see the Deichmann's."

Soon we were driving up a slope toward a large white house with an imposing front, and in no time were inside and being greeted cordially. It is difficult to tell the story of the Deichmann pottery—the lamp bases, the bowls, the jugs, the tableware, the ash trays and plaques. Difficult to put in words the thrill of visiting their domain and seeing them in action, working their wizardry with clay and minerals and fire, transforming dull materials into objects of beauty and durability. Their name has become a household word in

Canada, and much of their famed product crosses the American border. Kjeld is a graduate of philosophy at the University of Copenhagen. He later studied art, particularly sculpture in France, Vienna and Italy. He married Erica, daughter of a Danish dean, Wisconsin born and Denmark bred, settled in New Brunswick and became interested in clay discovered on their property. Endless experimentation and progressive skill led to their fine stoneware after they had returned to Denmark for a year of study. They learned all the secrets of firing, how to obtain effects of special beauty by exposing the melting glazes in the kiln to oxygen or by excluding oxygen and exposing them only to carbonic gases, or by alternating these treatments. They share many of the processes of their craft but the potting is the work of Kjeld, and the modelling that of Erica.

They had many disappointments as they carried on their experiments but even when daily living was something of a problem with them they broke up any item that showed a flaw because they have set a high standard and nothing that is in any way an ordinary product is put before the public. Such methods have made the name "Deichmann's" signify the best that can be produced.

Visitors are welcome, whether or not they come to buy, but all should remember that time is money to an artist, and don't expect Kjeld to give you a complete course in pottery. It's fascinating enough just to watch him as he works on soft moist clay. It is a picture you retain, the potter at his wheel. Kjeld, beret on head, spins the wheel with his foot while his clever hands work with the clay and it grows into a shining flexible form ready to turn into a jug or old-time drinking mug. Erica has her work, too, and it is very important, the finishing. She has invented more than one thousand glazes, weighing out the specific chemicals with exacting care, mixing and straining, then dipping the object, which has been through the kiln once, into a bath of underglaze. When it is dried she brushes a freehand design inside the bowl, and some odd figure appears. Her lively imagination provides the most fascinating articles and all around, ranged on shelves and low tables are samples of Deichmann work, in all shades and sizes, unique, fantastic, curious, each with its own appeal. To own something in Deichmann is a real satisfaction.

It was an effort to tear away from that fairyland on the slope, and we hoped that every visitor along Highway 2 into Sussex would be fortunate to notice the sign and make a visit. Individual pottery, like other forms of creative expression, contains within itself endless technical and artistic possibilities. Kjeld and Erica Deichmann's handmade porcelain and stoneware is the result of years of tireless experimentation and concentration. The general public and critics alike have acclaimed their original pottery at museum exhibitions, and national and international competitions have given them many prizes and awards. Numerous articles, movies and films about their life and work have spread their fame, while quietly throughout the country appreciative people are building up collections of "Deichmann."

It was reaching toward the middle of the afternoon when we finished a lunch at an eating place on the way out of Sussex and June was at its best with shadows moving across the green hills and valleys like a tide rolling in. Buttercups and daisies splashed their beauty in pasture corners and we saw youngsters with tin cups filled with wild strawberries. Potatoes were up and we saw a woman in a wide straw hat hoeing in a garden. A sign pointed to Fundy Park and we could not resist an invitation to go and explore. Away we went on a fine road that became a roller coaster in some places and saw a fat woodchuck with two smaller ones sitting up in a clover patch. Swallows swooped and darted over a small brook and raced off to barn eaves with beaks filled with flies. High in the hot afternoon sky a hawk was circling on motionless wings.

We came to a small building where cars were parked alongside and people making reservations to go fishing and the like. But we rolled on and after soaring up some long grades and rolling down others arrived at a hilltop from which we could view the wide scope of the Park. Roads led to an eating place, to a handcraft building, to camping grounds, and to fine cottages of French chalet design. There was a salt-water swimming pool and a golf course, and people everywhere in vacation shorts and open shirts. Every cottage was taken but we got a place down in a small village just east of the park entrance. Then we drove up along a road leading to fishing places and campsites and swung back again and took many shots in colour for the scenery is exciting in every direction. We had a fine dinner and strolled around afterward and talked with people from New Hampshire and Illinois and Ontario, heard so many accounts of what there was to see and do that we resolved to go back there some day and have a real holiday. Fundy Park is something you have to see to comprehend, as the landscapes and seascapes are so unusual in variety and scope that they baffle description. There were tents high up on the slope and small lights twinkled there like stars in the dusk, making the height seem twice as great.

It rained in the night, a summer shower, and in the morning as we drove back to the main highway—Route 2— after Saint John, everything was rinsed clean and sparkling. A song sparrow on a fence post tossed its distinctive call to the blue-sky day, and swallows were darting like mad over a muddy pool on a side road. Then, rising from a hollow on that roller-coaster road, we saw them, a doe and her fawn, stepping daintily in the wet grass. We made scarce a sound with our going but the doe saw us and jerked her head high in alarm. The fawn, hopping on pipe-stem legs, chased a

butterfly a few steps, whirled about surprisingly and faced us as the doe retreated to cover. And both were gone before we had wit to think of the camera beside us on the car seat.

We drove through a long stretch of woods, miles and miles, and saw two or three mangled porcupines beside the pavement. Traffic was light and so it was that another porcupine, almost gray, started over the way at his slow rate. We had no trouble whatever in slowing and avoiding the animal and could not understand the type of driver who ruthlessly kills a rabbit or porcupine and leaves the mangled remains to greet other travellers.

Speed zones occurred now and then through scatterings of homes, a school, canteen, store or two and the usual filling station and then we reached Petitcodiac and parked on the main street. The paved way ran on the left and took you through at the rear of the town centre but we wanted to chat with someone and soon were in a store. The man we accosted simply stepped out on the sidewalk and hailed an elderly fellow who had some parcels under one arm.

"This man was born here," said the store fellow. "He'll tell you anything you want to know."

"Nobody can do that," retorted the oldster, but he had a friendly grin. "Nearly everybody tells you what you don't want to know."

We asked if Petitcodiac were an old town.

"Good gracious, no," he grinned. "We're really Humphrey's Corner, and we were really born some distance from here. You see, Petitcodiac is another New Brunswick town that moved up when the railway came through. Quite a place, too, in our prime. We've got quite a distinction, too, one of the few places in this province that is ninety-nine per cent English. We used to have a spool factory back in the good old days, and there was an organ factory in 1878. Lots of work then, and a dollar worth ten times what it is today. There was a tannery as well, and hitching posts one end this street to the other. People came here to trade and we had a typical old deacon who ran the Temperance House. Good meals, no menu—you took what you got—and three ticks, wood, feather, and straw. No nonsense with the deacon. He'd even smell your breath if you laughed too loud."

We supposed it was largely a Baptist place. "Right you are," came the response. "I recall that back when I was a youngster there would be as many as thirty baptisms over in a river runoff when the weather got warm. Our Baptist church was one hundred years old in '37. No, there isn't much to see now in the way of relics. Some folks just outside the town have some old creamers and bootjacks and candle dips. Quite a curiosity, the creamers as they were the first around here. They had the hole in the bottom to draw the milk. Right over there, across the railway, was an old Indian trail and when I was a boy you could follow it to the portage. No, there aren't any characters around now, not since old Jimmy died. He lived on a side road and cut firewood in winter but his wife was lonesome and fond of visiting. Often he'd go to the house at noon and she'd be gone somewhere and just a cold plate of meat and bread set for him. So when he hear of a bear being killed in its den early one winter he walked twelve miles to get the hind paws. Then he rigged them under a pair of his larrigans with the front to the rear and walked in from the bush and around his house and back again one night after dark. The next day when his wife was set to go on another visit she saw the bear tracks and nearly died of fright. She stayed in the house all winter, then found the paws in the horse barn and was so mad at Jimmy when she understood his trick that she was gone a whole month down in Salisbury."

He was a gentle old man and talked easily as he treasured his parcels, and it was a soft gentle morning but we had to keep going and said a reluctant good-bye.

Soon we were at Salisbury, no more than a hamlet, and

then we kept on and arrived at bustling, ambitious Moncton, once called The Bend, and making much of a rapid growth of population and business, and two unusual features, the Bore of the Petitcodiac and the "magnetic hill." Half the population is French but when you walk the streets it is hard to tell which is which, and the mayor, they told us, was a Jewish gentleman. There are no racial problems in Moncton. All are busy making the most of the present and they do not hide their ambition—to overtake Saint John as New Brunswick's largest city. And the mayor is a courageous man with more than average mental ability for he has come out bravely and stated what many have been thinking privately, namely that the Maritimes should go back to being one Province, with only one government to support, and, naturally, Moncton as the capital. The saving in government would be tremendous, and the three-in-one would have strong enough voice to catch the attention of Ottawa, a matter that became difficult a few years after 1867 and becomes more difficult with every passing year.

The Petitcodiac is a tidal river flowing into the head of Shepody Bay and at low tide has scarcely any water, nothing more than an indifferent stream rutting the broad mud flats. But the Fundy tides are the highest in the world and when the might of them comes surging up the Bay to the head the converging shores funnel tremendous pressure into the river mouth and the result is the "Tidal Bore" which is a solid-looking mass of water from three to six feet in height rushing in over the flats. You have to see it charge in to comprehend fully its force and suddenness, and Bore times are posted around the Bore Park for the convenience of visitors. And enterprising business men have erected a two-storied motel parallel to the best point from which to view the Bore.

Signs point toward the famous "Magnetic Hill" which is seven miles from Moncton so out we went for we had heard that a good eating-place was situated beside the marvel. The meal was excellent but the spectacle of cars rolling backward uphill was at odds with the law of gravity. We tried it twice. Drove to the foot of the hill, put the car in neutral, shut off the motor and simply coasted back uphill. It's the most amazing optical illusion. The conformation of the surroundings makes the slope appear to run in the opposite direction from what it actually does. We heard every sort or argument about it, heard a man from Michigan declaring there was magnet of some sort in the soil. But we had a look at a little brook beside the road, saw it, too, was running uphill, and decided we were all mesmerized.

We threaded our way through Moncton traffic again and soon were out on the highway and headed toward the Nova Scotian border. It is a good road and after we were over a series of slopes the marshes stretched before us, the dyked lands that had such appeal for the first Acadian settlers. There was a huge grim building on our left as we approached Dorchester—the penitentiary—then a sharp hill in the small town, a dip and we were away again and through a wooded stretch that ended in a vista of Sackville, a college town on the marsh. Then we were out again on a sweep of prairie-like marshes ribboned by the tide-ruled rivers that the Acadians dyked. Wild roses were blooming on the dyke banks and soon the eye could catch the low-flying mouse hawks that prowl the area.

A rising ground proved to be a slope that led across our way and signs turned us right a short distance and into a parking area beside Fort Cumberland Museum. A dozen or more cars were there already, representing seven different States, and in the museum we gazed at implements for the farm and utensils for the indoors that Acadians and Yorkshiremen had used. For we were now in the heart of the first Yorkshire settlements founded back in 1772 when the Maritimes were one Province—Nova Scotia—and life was good if somewhat precarious. We went outside and walked around the old sodden embankments of ancient Fort Beauséjour that the French fondly hoped would be the key of the defence against the English. Standing on the ancient earthworks, we could look across the Missiquash River and see the site of the English fort reared there as a counterpoise to the French stronghold. They were out of range of each other's guns but today's machine guns would have kept the garrisons of both under cover. We went down into an underground of massive stone and the air was cold as that of a cellar. In a similar casemate during the siege of Beauséjour some French officers and a British prisoner were taking cover when a British shell crashed through the roof and killed the occupants, and so terrified the garrison that a surrender was soon arranged. The victors took over and "Beauséjour" became "Fort Cumberland."

We started off again across the marshes and soon reached the river that is the dividing line between New Brunswick and Nova Scotia. Away on our right was a rising on the marsh and there a French nobleman had his stockaded head-quarters and was governor of Nova Scotia more than seventy years before Halifax was founded. He had a schooner and sailed around the Province trading with the Indians and collecting fines or permits from Boston rivals. Eldest in his family was a beautiful girl and he planned that she should be the bride of a French blueblood of old Quebec. He loved her dearly and named the boundary river in her honour— la Marguerite. It is so today on ancient French maps. Then the influence of June moonlight on the marshes caused Marguerite to sigh for romance and she could not wait the tardy coming of some aristocratic gallant she had never seen. Right at hand and available was a young man, or young enough, who paid her his respects and devotion, and what matter if he were a widower and the father of four children. He was only twenty-eight and Marguerite could not wait. So there was a first elopment in Nova Scotia and they were married by a distant priest and there was nothing the irate papa could do save change the name of the river. He renamed it the Missiquash, which was the ugliest word he could select.

Up from the boundary bridge the slope on both sides of the road is an immense lawn, and the highway divides to accommodate ingoing and outcoming traffic. A huge depression in the centre is a flower bowl and the rows were in full bloom. Cars were parked in a long line fronting an Information Bureau and more were parked on cross roads flanking the flower bowl. A stalwart Scottish piper in full Highland regalia was pacing the pavement and playing "The Cock o' the North." A dozen admiring children watched him with fascination and tourists with cameras were making full use of the opportunity. The piper stood six feet three or four inches and was built in proportion. His feminine audience fairly gasped admiration and he paraded again and again for those with movie cameras.

The view from the Information Bureau is impressive. The marshes extend for nine miles, their broadleaf grasses making a shimmering sea dotted with hay barns weathered to a dull grayness. There is always wind funneling up the Bay of Fundy to Cumberland Basin, waving the grass tops and tossing the gulls and crows that haunt the wide salt-rimmed flats when the tide is out.

The dominating ridge that holds the Information Bureau was the site of a prosperous Acadian village back in the seventeenth century. They had ventured up the Bay in their boats and found the marshes the haunts of wildfowl. The Micmac Indians came there in the spring and fall and killed fat ducks and geese with bow and arrow, but they offered no objection to the Acadians moving in and reclaiming the rich acres from the sea. Soon there was a tannery, a brickyard, chapel, log pier and many acres planted in apple trees. Twice New Englanders came and raided the village, killing cattle and burning buildings in retaliation for Indian atrocities in New England. Each time the Acadians returned from the forest where they had hidden and rebuilt their homes. Then came the struggle for possession between British and French forces, and the French at Quebec declared the Missiquash River to be the boundary between French and English territory. Soon they demanded that the people of Beaubassin, the village on the ridge, move across the tidal river. But they were loath to go as they had good farms and snug homes and life was pleasant. Then came the fiery Le Loutre, leader of the Indians in hatred for the British and they burned every home and barn and shed, thus forcing the inhabitants across the stream.

We took a road to the right on the ridge to view the inscription on a cairn beside the road:

Fort Lawrence. Erected in 1750 by Major Charles Lawrence, afterwards lieutenant-governor of Nova Scotia, for the defence of the Isthmus of Chignecto; garrisoned by British troops until after the capture of Fort Beauséjour in 1755, when it was abandoned.

A white-painted farmhouse in the yard used a portion of the old fort trench as its cellar, and the farm garden is formed on the old earthworks levelled by hard labour. Acadians were kept prisoner in this fort during the time of the Expulsion and one stormy night eighty-six of them escaped by digging a tunnel under the earth wall with a shovel carelessly left within the enclosure. If you look carefully over the fields of the locality you can still trace the old Acadian village road angling across the ridge. Many of the old cellars are defined by depressions and the local farmers are forever plowing up old implements and household utensils, ancient axes, pewter, even old toasting forks. The road slants to the marsh near a hemlock grove and there excavators dug no more than four feet to uncover brick lying by the old kiln.

Beyond a short distance more digging revealed layers of hemlock bark, site of the old Acadian tannery.

A car with Pennsylvania licences parked near us and a man with white hair used binoculars to scan the outline of Cumberland Basin. Presently he turned to us and asked about a curious rock formation to be seen on the marsh. The stone "formations" are countless barrels of cement left there sixty years ago by those who were constructing a dock for the famous "Ship Railway" that was to run across the Isthmus of Chignecto from Tidnish to Cumberland Basin. A great wide road bed leads the entire seventeen and one half miles but the enormous steel rails and ties have long since gone. Four thousand men toiled there to make the roadbed under the direction of engineers employed by the man who began the project, H. G. C. Ketchum. His intention was to save shipping taking cargoes from Saint John and New England to the St. Lawrence the five hundred miles around the eastern end of the province and Prince Edward Island. The cost was to be about four million dollars. Two parallel tracks were laid with rails that weighed one hundred and ten pounds to the yard. At Cumberland Basin an excavation forty feet deep, five hundred feet long and three hundred feet wide had walls of massive masonry to retain water regulated by a huge gate thirty feet high and sixty feet wide. Vessels would be admitted to float over a gridiron, a moveable part of the track, and this great cradle would be lifted to track level by hydraulic rams and presses. The cradle was two hundred and thirty feet long and forty feet wide, was in three sections and carried on one hundred and ninety-two wheels.

Away it would go across the Isthmus with the vessel and at the Tidnish end would be lowered into a similar basin and released to Northumberland Strait by an influx of water. Masons from Scotland built the masonry and the bridges along the way. The hoisting machinery was installed at the **Amherst end and all but three miles of track had been laid** when lobbying sea captains, fearing a loss of revenues when their sea mileages were so curtailed, succeeded in getting all governmental assistance withdrawn. The great project was never finished, Ketchum died suddenly and only the grotesque gray heaps on the marsh remain as a monument to a great dream.

We drove back to Highway 2 and within minutes had reached Amherst, a town once known as "Busy Amherst," built on the site of an ancient Indian village that was later an Acadian settlement. An old factory a distance on the marsh has an uneven outline, this for the reason that its foundations were not secure. Diggers who went down seeking solid ground had to go nearly thirty feet through the silt of centuries, for the marshes cover what was once a vast forest. As some time an unheaval sent the sea rushing over it and the diggers found the stumps of great trees well preserved in the silt.

The first site of Amherst was some three miles to the westward where the first Anglican church was built and the militia had a training ground. There was also a large inn boasting a "four-seater" outhouse. From the inn it was a short distance to a ferry taking passengers across the head of Cumberland Basin to Minudie. Amos "King" Seaman, a lad who learned to read and write after he was married and became a millionaire through the operation of grindstone quarries and trading with the West Indies, built a grand mansion on the Minudie side where he owned thousands of acres farmed by tenants, had a great wharf, a store and the first steam saw-and-grist mill in Nova Scotia. The old home still stands, a gaunt spectre, its roof intact but its spacious rooms opened to the elements as the windows are gone. Those who drive around a few miles now to visit the spot are intrigued by the unusual form of shad fishing. Tall weirs are built far out on the flats at low tide and strung with nets. Fat shad swim at high level, are caught in the nets, and remain there as the tide ebbs. Then the farmers go out with horses and wagon and ladder and take the fish down from far overhead.

Romance has spread its blessing over the Maritimes with a free hand, and its touch is found in the most unexpected places. Back in the days when the British had a garrison at Fort Lawrence one of the soldiers became weary of the eternal round of guard duty and decided to desert. He stole away one evening and found a boat on the basin shore, embarked and began rowing toward Shepody Bay on the New Brunswick side. Soon he saw a dark object ahead on the water and was astounded to find it was an Acadian girl in a dugout canoe drifting out on the tide without oar or paddle. She had some grasp of English and he could understand some French so soon she was in the boat with him and he had her story. Her father had arranged that she marry a man twenty years her senior and she had simply stolen away from home and embarked in the dugout, not caring where it took her. The soldier rowed strongly and, with the help of the tide, reached the shore of Shepody Bay. They landed there and started to walk along the coast toward Saint John. But prowling Indians had seen them and they were captured and walked all the way to Quebec where the redskins received a reward for their work. The soldier and Acadian girl spent the winter in Quebec as prisoners but in the spring were taken to Boston to be exchanged for French prisoners. Released there, they were married, and made their way back to a small settlement on the New Brunswick coast, evaded the Expulsion and left numerous descendants in the district.

Highway 2 winds over Amherst ridge and reaches the marsh again at Nappan. Some distance to the right is a modern salt plant that pumps up gallons of brine per minute and affords employment for many residents of the area. Veteran residents of the marsh regions still talk about the great Saxby Tide of October 5, 1869, named after the officer

who predicted it. A hot and still afternoon ended in a great
wind that swept behind the incoming tide and piled in waters
at a record depth, flooding the marshes and swirling the full
hay barns and hay stacks into upland reaches. Cattle and
sheep and horses were drowned. Five men were out on the
marsh. Two drowned but the other three clung to the timbers
of wrecked barns until daylight and were saved. The tide
swept into one house on low ground and washed out furniture and belongings including a trunk that held the family
savings. A farmer-carpenter in the Nappan district made coffins
for the neighbours greatly to the annoyance of his superstitious
wife. He had just completed one and it was in the kitchen
loft when the tide came. The man was away from home but
his wife was there and retreated upstairs as the water came
in. Soon it appeared she must be drowned like a rat in a
trap but she thought of the coffin, embarked in it from an
upstairs window and, using a bed slat as paddle, reached the
nearby upland.

Highway 2 leaves the marshes at Nappan and climbs the
Fenwick hills. At the crest the motorist can look back over
a vast panorama of marsh and upland. The Fenwick hills are
wooded with sugar maples and roller coaster grades soon lead
to the town of Springhill where several terrible mining disasters have taken the lives of many citizens. The first great
explosion took place in 1891, when one hundred and twenty-
five men lost their lives. The last was in 1958 and now the
shafts have been closed and a drive is on to secure other
industries. A fire swept the town in 1957 and almost destroyed
its main street but its citizens are rebuilding.

The road turns toward the sea from Springhill, passing
through the hilly area of Leamington and East Southampton
where fine groves of sugar maples produced the finest maple
products known, extremely light in colour, and delicious to
the taste. These products have easily won prizes over samples
from Vermont, Quebec and Ontario. At Southampton the

road swings left and heads through West Brook to Parrsboro. Southampton was settled almost entirely by Yorkshiremen who came to Nova Scotia by the shipload in the 1770s. Their first road through the settlement can still be traced, and one family is still on land given in a first grant to the original settlers. The Yorkshiremen were noted for their wood carving and one eccentric oldster built a coach on four stumps in a clearing. The coach was complete in every detail, was designed to carry mail and carried the king's crest, beautifully carved, on both doors. It remained in the glade for more than twenty years before yielding to the elements.

Through the West Brook the highway is almost straight for seven miles, the longest straight section in Nova Scotia. It passes through West Brook corner where a Baptist church on one corner and a Methodist on the other gaze at each other with grim indifference. Parrsboro is a quiet little town and its citizens are proud of it. They point with pride to the beach that can be reached by a route past a waterway with ancient pilings protruding like the teeth of an old hag that had chewed on the blackened timbers. Gulls settle occasionally on the derelict posts and complain in querulous tones about the lack of fish offal. We stopped for the night at Riverview Cabins and found it a restful spot with a small lake at the rear where a bride and groom rowed in a boat and fished. There were ducks by the water and robins were singing in the trees that shelter the cabins from traffic and the main road. Mrs. Antrim, the proprietor, took us in her car around a back road past an amazing golf course with amazing views and into a settlement deserted with the exception of two farms.

The usual oldster was easy to find with Mrs. Antrim as a guide. He talked old times in Parrsboro when the coal train from Springhill and a score of vessels would be loading with lumber at the various wharves. Parrsboro had been a boom town then, had even attracted a circus to the place and two small boys ran away with it, hoping to get steady work carrying water to the elephants.

"You ever hear of our sea-horse?" asked the oldtimer.

We admitted we had not.

"There ain't anything to match it in Nova Scotia," he announced, shaking his head, and shrugging. "I guess we don't count much in the papers away down here. Well, years ago, afore cars, horses were in good demand and often men from here would go across the Bay to buy from farmers in the Valley. Tom Smith did just that. He bought a fine mare and fetched her over and her foal was one of the finest ever seen on this shore. Tom had many offers for the horse but always refused and for six or seven years he took the lead on any roads around here. Then over came the man from Canning who had sold Tom the mare. He had a look at the black horse and suddenly wished he had never sold its mother. Something must have stirred him tremendous because he up and offers Tom more'n twice the going price for horses. Tom was a man who watched the dollars and he just couldn't resist. He took the money and the man from Canning took the boat back and Tom drove around by Truro and the Black Rock ferry and delivered the animal. He got an extry ten dollars for the trip. He was no more'n back home when he happened to look toward the pasture and there was the black horse. Tom couldn't believe his eyes but he knew the horse. He went to the beach and as the tide went out saw the hoof marks where the black had come ashore. The tide goes out a long way and that horse had known enought to wait for it, but made a mighty long swim just the same. Next day Tom took the money and went back to Canning. He told the man be couldn't sell a horse that wanted to be with him that much, and the stranger agreed."

Then we drove in the opposite direction to the original site of the town at Partridge Island and saw there historic Ottawa House, once the summer home of Sir Charles Tupper, famous Canadian statesman who was one of the Fathers of Confederation. Back of the place was an old stone school that had first been a powder magazine for a blockhouse which stood on the hill. We climbed the steep elevation and found the big stone that held the blockhouse timbers, stood there in the twilight and visualized the privateer from Maine sailing in to attack. He met with a hot reception, was killed along with two of his best men and the ship was captured. Amethysts, agates and attractive trap minerals are found along the shore. Footprints of prehistoric animals were discovered, so well preserved they were photographed and plaster casts made for the National Museum at Ottawa.

# 2

## Basket Shops, Sir John Beading, Boomer-Horn, and Clam-Shell

WE WOKE TO A LOVELY MORNING, and breakfast, and were soon following a winding highway into Five Islands—so named because there are five abrupt risings from the sea, said to be clods hurled by the Micmac man-god, Glooscap, as he tore out a beaver dam and created Minas Channel. The island most noticed had an opening through it, and there are many legends about pirates burying their loot in the area. Many parties dug there by moonlight in times gone by and fearful were their tales of the devil appearing and filling their nostrils with the smell of sulphur.

Economy Mountain loomed across our way and looked a rugged drive but there is no trouble to go up on high gear. Stop at the top if you want the finest drinking water you ever tasted, and a view of the whole Minas Basin. It was a distance beyond the foot of the hill that a whale of enormous size got stranded as the tide went out, and died. Four local farmers had seen it and they visualized easy money as they got eight teams of horses, long ropes, and waited for high tide. They then hauled the huge carcass in and erected a wall of old canvas sails around it. Word of the whale had spread like wildfire and people came from far and near to view the remains, paying twenty-five cents per head for the privilege.

The men made over fifty dollars the very first day then had the added advertising of those who had been reporting about the monster. Its size was not lessened by repeating the story and over in inland Oxford an oldtimer in 1930 wrote that he had been one who visited the whale and it was large as the new skating rink, only longer. Prosperity smiled on the four partners for a few days and then the sky turned brassy and the thermometer began climbing. It was said that for three days the temperature was ninety degrees, and the whale began to send out a stench so powerful that people driving past said they were made sick by the fumes. So the constable arrived at the scene with a paper telling the partners they must remove the nuisance and at once.

No one could move such a hill of rot, and the next day each farmer was fined ten dollars. People had to move from the nearest homes. Seven acres of fine hay was not cut that year and cattle would not stay in the shore pastures.

Bass River is a cosy little village and the main feature is a chair factory.

A broth of an Irish boy, James Fulton, qualified himself as a land surveyor and came to Nova Scotia from New England in 1765 to help survey the Province. The chief part of his pay was to be a grant of land in an area of his own choosing, and he decided on the land surrounding Bass River, cleared a farm, built a fine home, married a Scottish girl, and penned twelve verses to formulate his philosophy of life. The lines, in a parchment folder, can be read today, and the last verse reads:

Oh, Man, now see thou are but dust;
They Gold and Silver are but rust;
They time has come, they glass is spent;
No worldly care can death prevent.

Fifteen children called Fulton their father and thirteen of them lived to ripe old age and produced one hundred and seven boys and girls. Fulton died in 1826 but none save a

Fulton has occupied the old homestead, and there are but few residents of Bass River who do not have Fulton blood in their veins for four brothers of James came to live in the area and all raised large families. One brother, Samuel, was a giant possessed with a giant's strength. A bear invaded the sheep pen and Samuel rushed out and picked up a pole, beat the invader over the head and sent it bounding back to the forest. Another bear, that weighed four hundred on the mill scales, faced Samuel in the woods where he was cutting firewood. He grabbed a three-foot length and with one blow caved in the bear's skull.

In 1860 two Fulton men built a sawmill near the mouth of Bass River and soon after installed a lathe. A chair factory was sold by the sheriff in another part of the Province, bought by the Fultons and moved to Bass River. The industry has been operating ever since though fire has three times destroyed the main building. There have been nine managers in the factory, all descendants of the original Fulton, and many of the hands have over fifty years service in the factory. Bass River residents have chairs that were the first made in the plant and are as good as ever.

Soon we were in Great Village, pretty beyond description with lofty elms guarding the approach. We stopped at the filling station for gas and a man in shirt sleeves came along, eyed us up and down and mustered courage to ask if we would give him a lift far as Glenholme a few miles along. We said we'd be glad to and he smiled his thanks as he climbed in.

"My wife's sister lives there and she's always discovering something to phone us about. This time it's some new cookie tins that make animals. The church ladies are comin' over tonight so nothing must stop me goin' down to borrow them blamed tins. And I'll have to take 'em back tomorrow. If ever I get married again I'll move off afore I settle down, clean out of reach of any of my wife's relations."

He was quite peeved, no doubt of that, but accepted a candy bar and thanked us politely. "Don't go thinkin' I'm a crank," he pleaded. " 'Cause I'm not. But they're on the phone half the time on account an old maid sister of the wife lives with us month about. She eats more'n I do and don't help much, but Daisy likes to have her."

"Sisterly love," we commented.

"Not too much," he replied. "It's just that they like talkin' and not too many would listen to them on account half the time they're talkin' about the men they might have married."

We let him out at Glenholme, drove on and stopped at Masstown, a great strawberry centre. We had a box of fruit to eat and the good lady at the canteen told us that once a large Acadian village occupied the site, that a large place of worship, the Church of St. Peter and St. Paul, had stood near the water's edge so that distant settlers could reach it by boat. She said it was still possible to trace the church site and so we turned from the pavement and explored some dirt roads but luck was not with us. We stopped at four farms and in each case the farmer was newly over from Holland and knew nothing about history.

The area from Masstown into Truro was settled by the Irish after the Expulsion. The majority came from Ireland but others came from New Hampshire and during the first years the settlers lived together in log blockhouses for safety. Legend has it that one of the young men who had a promised girl back in New Hampshire caused his mother great anxiety when he sent her a letter in the late fall telling about the acres he had cleared, the house he had built, and the fine crop of potatoes he had gathered. He added that though he had tried his best he found it very difficult to keep Nellie out of his house so had let her have her way and had taken her in for the winter. He would, of course, he wrote, get clear of her before his bride-to-be came in the spring.

The agitated mother wrote to friends in Truro and begged them to go to her son and show him the error of his ways and to take any needed methods to get rid of Nellie. The friends came, uneasy over their mission, and were vastly relieved to find that Nellie was only a small pig that squealed all night if left in the pen but would sleep quietly in the kitchen.

Truro is the hub of Nova Scotia, with fine residential streets, shady elms, busy factories, enterprising citizens. The town had a Normal School by 1855. The first oatmeal ground in Nova Scotia came from the mill of Thomas Dickenson of Truro, and the first model farm in Canada was established at Truro in 1857. First wagons were made in Truro and there is record of one fine vehicle constructed in 1814 that was strong enough to withstand the roads of that time, and heavy enough to need five horses to haul it to Halifax. Victoria Park is the show place of the town, a natural playground of one thousand acres, with a wishing well, alluring footpaths, arbors, board walks, footbridges and picnic glens. We explored at leisure and then drove back to the outskirts to one of the finest eating places in Nova Scotia—Paliser's Restaurant—in a beautiful setting alongside the river.

A short distance beyond Truro is Millbrook where "basket shops" operated by Micmac Indians display their wares. Baskets of every type from tiny holders to hampers and strong fishing creels can be had. They also sell toy birch canoes with whittled paddles, bows and arrows and other carved items. There are filling stations along the way and small villages, and then we entered Stewiacke where a new bridge was being built that would take the highway past the town instead of through it. There were two large general stores and we talked with a man who had a little wedge of a beard that narrowed his face, and asked if there were anything unusual about the neighbourhood.

"Not now," he said, "but sixty years ago there were people

who made any place different. Every settlement had a few
of them. I remember when I was a boy going with father to
call on a couple that had come from the Old Country. They
had bought a small place with a good-enough house and
denned in it for the winter. They never went around any,
only every two weeks or so they'd come to the store with a
hand sled and stock up provisions. They always paid cash,
too, which was something in those days. My father hated
to go to the house but he was in charge of the roads in our
district and had to see they were broken in winter. He'd sent
word to this man three-four times to fetch his shovel and
join the others after a big snowstorm, but the man never came.
They lived in a small house and never used the front door.
We knocked at the back and the woman looked out at us,
smiled, friendly as a slice of pie, and asked us in. She had her
hair up different from anything I'd seen, with little curls
hanging in front of each ear, and she was wearing a necklace
of blue stones that glittered.

"She pulled out two chairs for us, and her man was sitting
in a third, scarecrow thin with the winter between his ribs,
and veins on the back of his hands like whipcords. He nodded
greetings and acted as though we had interrupted his thinking.
The woman had a rocker beside him and she sat in it looking
amiable, just warm and near him, like the stove.

"Father got to talking right at once and said he was sorry
he had come, pointing out that his job was to get all able-
bodied men working on the roads, but anybody with half an
eye could see that Mister—er—Mister . . .

" 'Beading,' broke in the woman. 'John Beading. He
would never work on your roads no matter what his health
might be.'

"She spoke as if she were impatient with people who could
not understand that she and her husband were above average,
and you could tell she wouldn't take advice from the Twelve
Apostles let alone father. Her petticoats hush-hushed as she

went into another room and came back with a glass. It held something to drink and as she passed near me her breath had an unpleasant, sour, winish smell. Father never drank anything other than water or tea, and said so, while the man patted his chin to smother a yawn, and made no remark. It didn't take long for father to say he must be going as the man would not talk at all but sat as if he were Pontius Pilate on a throne.

"The woman followed us outside, rubbing her hands nervously, and hoped aloud we were not offended by our reception. 'Don't tell anyone, please,' she said, 'but you were calling on Sir John Beading.'

" 'Sir?' gulped father.

"The woman drew a breath that went out in a milk-blue cloud, and nodded.

"He's the fifth with the title." She rattled on in a low tone, so the man inside could not hear, and said they wanted privacy above all else, that Sir John was slowly recovering from a wretched illness, that they liked Canada and leaving England was like getting over a cold.

"Father was very impressed, and ordered me not to repeat a word of what I'd heard. It didn't make too much difference, however, because soon every person in the place knew we were entertaining real aristocrats, and there was enough talk about them at quilting parties and the like to tire a horse. Come spring, they up and left, owing six months rent for the house. The man who owned the place couldn't trace them in Halifax but that summer they were arrested in Boston and we read all about them. They were counterfeiters, had made a bundle of money that winter, and were no more royalty than my old cow. Mother used to rib father about it any time he tried to tease her, and he was absent-minded half that summer after he heard there'd been a five-hundred-dollar award for information about the couple."

We went on to Shubenacadie and just before reaching the

village saw a sign pointing left and followed some other cars over a hill to a regular "zoo" in the woods. There were deer to look at, rabbits and pheasants and foxes and raccoons, a bear, a wildcat, a squirrel doing tricks in a cage, a beaver pond, many cages and exhibits. The children were having a wonderful time feeding the raccoons and petting a doe that came to the fence.

Back in the village of Shubenacadie we were told about the local museum in the form of a combined garage and workshop at the back of the home of W. G. Nelson. One of the items that will catch the eye of any visitor is his one-cylinder Pope Tribune car, which dates back to the beginning of the century and is still in good working order. It is the first car that came to Shubenacadie, and before that Mr. Nelson had the first motorcycle ever seen in the district. He also owned the first moving picture projector in the place, still has it and can, if he wishes, show films that are now collector's items. Another precious relic is the first gramophone heard in the area. Away back, he had first cameras, has one of the old ones that used four lenses to take four daguerrotypes at once. Mr. Nelson advanced to tintypes, then to plates, finally to films in the picture-taking realm. He has a small steam tug brought from England, a clock with wooden works that is over 150 years old, a huge brass telescope made in 1828. A most interesting relic is a hat box containing a specimen of the plumed headgear worn by military officers in the old days. This was discovered buried in the earth when excavating was going on for a drain. The container bears the crest of the Saint John Fusiliers, and the name engraved on the metal plate is "Major Jas. Devlin." At one time Mr. Nelson used to place the one-cylinder car on the lawn as an exhibit but so many cars stopped as people wanted to examine the relic, that traffic jams occurred, so the car was kept indoors.

Shubenacadie, we learned, is the headquarters of the Micmac Indians, and we saw a large residential school there, and were told that nearby is the site of the largest Indian village in the Province. We did not take time to go over and see the place as one of the men at the zoo told us we could turn right on a new paved highway and go through Rawdon and on to Brooklyn and Windsor, cutting a lot of miles from the old route around. So we turned and drove on Highway 14 and found new smooth pavement that was sheer delight, scattered settlements and very little traffic. We saw old gray horses in the same pastures with cows but never mixing with them. Wire fences had replaced old zigzag pole structures, and gates swung where once bars had to be taken down and put up after every coming or going. It was evident that farmers had been cutting Christmas trees in pastures that were struggling back to forest, and in places alders have encroached on farm brooks until it is impossible for a stranger to tell where first clearings began.

Many of these country places look the same. There is the school with its name proudly lettered above the door, the adjoining field with base paths trodden plain by scampering feet, the farmhouse with a metal plate saying "post office"; the community hall generally looking the worse for wear, veterans of pie socials, political meetings, farm forums and elections. All these identify the settlement, hinting at a balance in society, a tempered ambition, a concord of work, of religion, of public aim and private concern, the characteristic stamp of small but persistent endeavour peculiar to off-trail territory.

At Rawdon we stopped by the roadside where a lean man was repairing the bridge to his driveway, and engaged him in conversation. He had worked in the woods as a young man, he said, then had worked with an uncle on a farm.

"An old skinflint he was, too, if he was my kin. He'd go to bed at dark to save lamp oil, and be shoutin' you up at daylight. He give me a heifer calf for three months work, and I sold the animal for ten dollars. A neighbour had give me a set of ox horns and I worked at them in the evenings and the next summer sold a boomer-horn to a tourist. A boomer-horn! Mean to say you never saw one? Why down around this way they used to be common at one time. A woman could call the men from the hayfield with one, and no two sounded the same. You had to pare the horn thin on the underside and fit the wood in just right. Well, I left that uncle when he tried to make me split half the horn money with him and went to live with another relative near Windsor. He raised turkeys and they took a sight of tendin' in the spring if it were wet weather. He got good money for his on account they were white birds, and he always told customers their meat was cleaner. There was a bank manager in town used to buy four-five from him every fall and pay a tremendous price for 'em. He said he never tasted such turkeys anywhere else. Them turkeys were no different from others far as I could see, but the trick was to put a swig of good rum in their feed when you're goin' to kill 'em. I've heard turkeys can smell blood and they get so worked up their meat tastes strong. But when they get a jag of rum they totter around and grin and don't give a dang about anything. Their head is off afore they know it and their meat is sweet as sugar. We never let anybody else in on that secret."

Brooklyn was a sleepy little place and then we were back on the main highway, now Route 1 from Halifax to Yarmouth. An American car stopped as we waited to emerge from Highway 14, and asked the way to Grand Pré. "We've just been at Mount Uniacke," he said. "You can't afford to miss that place."

So we drove back a distance toward Halifax and turned in a driveway where we saw the sign. We arrived at a fine parking ground and were told we had entered by the old stage road, that mile stones were still to be found under the trees. Great oaks were everywhere around the fine old mansion as a cask of Irish acorns had been brought from across the sea and planted with a lavish hand. The house is majestic in appearance, at the top of a slope leading from a fine lake. Across the front is a very wide veranda, its roof supported by four great pillars that rise two stories in height. The Uniacke Ar.ns are on the wide door, and a full head in brass makes an unusual door-knocker. The main hall is impressive and twelve Adams chairs there are said to have been used by the twelve Uniacke children during morning prayers. A grand-father clock ticks off the hours solemnly, onyx-and-brass oil lamps hang from the ceiling. Every room is richly furnished, upstairs and down. There are seven great bedrooms, a huge kitchen in the basement with a fireplace large enough to hold a dozen kettles. Food went up to the dining-room above via a mahogany dumb waiter. The closet doors have cat holes in them, as Uniacke hated mice and always let the cats have the run of the house.

Windsor had first lights glimmering as we had spent a long time at the Uniacke House. It is an old town and surrounds what some call the "fort hill." The French settled there in 1703 and called the place Piziquid. Then the British came and built Fort Edward. Hills dominate, two hills that look out on the reddish waters of the tide-ruled Avon River when the tide is in and upon the seamed mud flats when the tide has ebbed. Both hills are attractive and one is set with fine old trees. One hill has known blood and sweat and grim discipline; the other is a hill of laughter and echoes of the social life of Windsor a century ago. An inscription on a cut stone monument tells you that Windsor had the first agricultural fair in all Canada, held on Fort Edward Hill, 21st May, 1765. On the top of a hill is an old blockhouse, the last survivor of its kind in Nova Scotia, and one can trace the moat of old Fort Edward now no more than a shallow depression. The Windsor Golf Course takes over one of the old bastions of the stronghold and the view is magnificent.

Another hill of Windsor leads to Clifton, the home of Thomas Chandler Haliburton. A winding driveway leads up under a canopy of greenery and the flowers are always beautiful. The house is just as it was when the famous author of *Sam Slick, the Clockmaker*, paced the library and dictated his work to three secretaries. His desk is there, the furniture, with old fourposters and "sleigh beds" upstairs and the great kitchen downstairs. One can spend hours examining that aristocratic old home and then wander around the grounds and begin to understand Haliburton's love of ease and elegance in living. Over on another slope King's College was founded, the oldest University in the King's overseas Dominions, and there many a famous Nova Scotian was grounded in the three R's and all that followed after.

Back in the sedate days Windsor had one of the first "Improvement Societies" in Nova Scotia, and its members had to obey many rules respecting the clearing of weeds from lanes and driveways, respecting the observance of the Sabbath, and the attendance at divine service. Tough it was that the husband of the first president, Abraham Longmire, used profane language when he scalded his leg as he was butchering pigs and was required to pay a fine of three shillings. He paid the money and took himself to the tavern to brood on such measures and there had a dram too many so that he strayed into the cemetery and fell asleep there. He was found and fined another three shillings for such actions, whereupon he simply shook the dust from his feet and left the town and Mrs. Longmire for the rest of his life.

On main street we saw an old buggy with an upholstered seat turning green with age. A patient horse in the shafts gazing steadily at its reflection in a store window and switching a long tail at bothersome flies, looked as old as the vehicle, and when a man came along with some parcels which he dumped under the buggy seat, we hailed him with interest. He had a fringe of snow-white hair on his head and the kind face of the very old, yet moved easily and with vigour.

"Passed my eighty-fifth in May," he told us, smiling. "And

old Joe here," he glanced at the horse, "is twenty-two. He's slowing up, and it's likely I will, too, when I get old. Yes, born and raised here in this county, I was, and in all my life I've never been farther than Saint John. I was there to a circus away back forty-fifty years ago. Outside of that I've stayed close to home, 'cept visiting cousins I had up in Pembroke. Jim was about my age and we did a lot of bear hunting together. In them days there were bears all over this county. At Jim's home they had a pig-killing one fall and in the night Jim's father heard something in the woodshed. He went to see and it was a bear that had pushed on the door until the latch broke, and the brute was tearing away at a carcass hung in the shed. Jim's father got the gun from hooks in the kitchen, cocked the gun and fired without thinking. It was loaded with shot for partridge but he was so close to the bear that the charge blew a hole in the bear's neck you could put the gun through, and that was that. They had a bad mess to clean up in the woodshed, though, and after that Jim vowed he'd keep killing bears long as he could walk. With me it was different. I was getting the cows from a back pasture when a cub appeared and began playing around a bunch of sheep laurel. I stood and watched when all of a sudden an old she-bear came out of the woods after me as if I'd done her wrong. I just had time to get up a young maple and the tree was so slim that my weight bent the top over and that bear reared on her hind legs and almost got me. I yelled my loudest and father heard and come running with the axe. The bear and cub took into the woods, and I took to hunting bears and shot my last one about twelve years ago."

The old man paused and we were afraid he would get into his buggy and go. So we hastily asked if he would like an icecream or something like that.

"Sure would," he grinned. "Banana split, that's what I like, only I can't afford it."

We quickly escorted him into a nearby icecream parlour and ordered a banana split of the very best they could produce.

"A bear killed three sheep for us one fall," he began talking, "and the last one was left by the fence, hardly damaged. Father thought the bear had been scared off and would be back that night. So he loaded the rifle and wired it to the fence with the muzzle aimed along to the neck of the ewe. Then he tied a cord to the carcass and run it around the fence post and back to the trigger of the rifle. Mother kept telling him it was a foolish idea and to go and borrow a bear trap but he didn't. That night we heard the rifle. The report echoed and father lit the lantern and I went with him. There was mister bear dead as he could be. The bullet had gone in back of a shoulder and lodged in the heart. We had that skin for twenty years after, and always liked showing people the bullet hole. Mother was in our back pasture picking blueberries that fall. They were very thick and she was filling a pail when she glanced over the old log beside her and there was a bear stripping the berries off faster'n she could. She got away from there in a hurry and after that never said anything against my going bear hunting. There was a very early snowfall one year, on October thirtieth. I was out and saw bear tracks by our barn. There was only half an inch of snow and it was melted by noon but I tracked that bear an hour and found it under a windfall, asleep. I went up within six feet before I fired, and it hardly stirred. That fellow was bedded there for the winter. Father helped me skin it and I left the head on and the next night being Hallow'een, I rigged the skin and head in a bush by our gate and when some young fry come around to upset our carts and grindstone one of them saw the "bear." They come into our house like a cyclone and mother dressed them properly as she'd just scrubbed the floor that day, and she didn't know what I had done with the bearskin."

We asked him if he enjoyed life now, with cars and television and all the modern gadgets.

"They don't do any hurt," he said," and a body gets used to everything. But I know we had better times back when I was a young fellow. We had barn raisings and chopping frolics and quiltings and singing classes. Us young fellows would go to singing classes no matter if we croaked like frogs. The girls were always there and we'd walk them home, likely get invited to a candy pull or the like. But I've nothing against the folks today. They have their fun, and I've had mine, but not all of it—yet. We've always had plenty of flowers around the house outside. Half the lot are ones Mother planted. I have an old rocking-chair I take out there and I sit by the bee balm and hummingbirds come and almost light on my head. I reckon they think I'm an old stump. And there's been a family of chipmunks in a stone pile back of the apple trees ever since I can remember. The lad that has his family there now will come and take crumbs out of my fingers. I like to hear them chatter. And we've had robins nesting in our apple trees for fifty years. The trees don't have much fruit now but we never cut one down. Farming isn't what it was, either. They can't do anything without a tractor. In my day we used steers. We'd use them three years and then sell them for prime beef. I used to start training steer calves in the barn floor on rainy Saturdays. 'Teach 'em young and half the battle's won,' grandfather used to say. I had small yokes I'd put on them in the winter and when they were big enough they never minded the real thing. I was always proud when I had them trained so I could sit on the sled and direct them by voice. Yep, it's different now. All speed ahead. Tractors and the like. Grandfather used to say driving steers was good training for that boy, too, and I reckon it was. We never got speed crazy."

"I'll bet," the old man said, "there's one story of this county you haven't got."

We agreed there were probably several.

"Up on Noel Shore," said the old man, "there's a story that can't be matched in Canada. You ever hear of Willard and Harry Miller? Well, not many have, all the more pity. Their father's people came from Holland but the mother was Scottish and a sister of the President of Acadia University. The father bought land but was a master ship builder, designing each ship and making all his own models. He built and launched ships up and down the Bay—seventeen for one firm alone, and worked in shipyards of the U.S.A. There were eight in the family but the only two crazy about the sea were the brothers, Willard and Harry, and they climbed the rigging of schooners every chance they got. Willard reached sixteen and ran away from home to ship as an able seaman, and Harry did the same when he reached that age. In 1897 they met in Boston, decided they'd had enough of sailing ships and joined the American Navy. When the Spanish War came along Willard was in his twenty-first year and Harry was two years younger. It was feared by the American forces down at the West Indies that the Spaniards were using the Atlantic cable at Cienfugos, Cuba, to get word across the sea, so an expedition was organized to cut the cable. Only volunteers would be used and each man must work quickly, taking the risk of enemy fire. Away the little band went on a chosen night and though the shells and bullets came like a storm the small party was a small target, and got to the objective and cut the cable. Some were killed and some were wounded but neither of the Millers got a scratch and the Americans were so pleased with the result of the raid that they presented both brothers with the Congressional Medal of Honour. It's a medal on a par with the Victoria Cross, and no other brothers have ever won it, especially for the same nation. Yes, siree, that little Noel Shore produced two real heroes of top rank."

We watched him climb into the buggy and cluck to old

Joe, and wished we could be like him when we were eighty-five.

A schoolmaster was there with half a dozen boys and by the blockhouse we paused to listen to his talk: "This plaque attached to the blockhouse reads—

Flora Macdonald. A name that will be mentioned in history, and if courage and fidelity be virtues, mentioned with honour. The preserver of Bonnie Prince Charlie spent the winter of 1779 here with her husband Captain Alan Macdonald of the Royal Highland Emigrants, when returning to her old home in Skye, after exile from her new home in North Carolina. Her loyalty and devotion in the midst of troubled days have long been told in Scottish song and story.

"Now, boys, imagine that you are here in the long ago, that you see Flora Macdonald walking by the fort, that you hear her rich Scottish accent as she talks with one of the sentries on duty. We must learn to appreciate our history more. Flora Macdonald spent five years in North Carolina and when she was leaving was in such circumstances she had to sell her silver to get money enough to pay for her passage home. Some of that silver is exhibited at Red Springs, North Carolina, at the Flora Macdonald College for Girls. There is a letter she wrote in 1772 saying that they were losing everything in Skye and must leave. It reads: 'we lost within these three years, three hundred and twenty-seven heads of cattle and horses, so that we have hardly what will pay our creditors.' In August, 1774, Flora, and her husband, with her two sons, daughter and son-in-law, with eight servants, sailed for North Carolina. They were well received and the house where they stayed a short time is called the 'Flora MacDonald House.' They got land cheaply, cleared eighty acres, built a house and barns, and then came trouble—the American Revolution. Flora's husband was offered a captain's commission and became a recruiting officer in the Loyalist service. The two sons followed his example, and a great force of Highlanders paraded and were addressed in Gaelic by Flora before marching to battle at Moore's Creek. The enemy trapped them cleverly as there was but one narrow bridge to use in crossing over and in the night most of the planks were removed and the stringers greased. As the Highlanders charged over they slipped and fell, many going into the stream, while the rebels poured a deadly fire on them. The rebels had cannon as well. Soon the whole attacking force was demoralized by the turn of events and before night came over eight hundred had been taken prisoners, the MacDonalds among them. Finally they were released and Flora joined her husband and they came to Nova Scotia for a year before going home. They had encountered adversity throughout but their courage was still high, and it is said Flora made no complaint as she waited for the snow to go in this New Scotland."

It was a talk given in the careful schoolroom manner but the faces of the listening lads told us they were absorbing every detail, and we thought it a pity that the talk could not be recorded and made available there by the blockhouse for any group of visitors who wanted to hear the story.

Route 1 wound over slopes and past orchards and over Mount Denson and then we crossed a bridge and climbed into the town of Hantsport. A fine memorial at the entrance keeps attracting many visitors for it is a memorial to William Hall, V.C. Hall was born not far from Hantsport in April, 1827, the son of ex-slaves who had escaped to Nova Scotia. He served as a Royal Marine through the Crimean War, then went on board the *Shannon* conveying troops to Hong Kong. From there he went in a force to relieve Lucknow, and his gallantry in serving a gun when the rest of the crew were dead or wounded won him special recognition and the Victoria Cross. Hantsport proved a quiet little town of friendly people and many flowers and robin song in the early evening made it seem an enchanted place. We drove on over winding roads and across a bridge. Beyond, the orchards closed in on us and we were in historic land, that was regained from the sea by the Acadians, a land of dykes and marshes, a land crisscrossed with ancient Indian trails and marsh foot-ways and hunter's paths and New England Planter's cart roads. First stars were beginning to shine above the great bluff that is Blomidon as we came to a delightful motel in Grand Pré and arranged to stay the night.

We had dinner in the tiny restaurant that was neat and clean, and found the food satisfactory. At the next table a weather-worn farmer and his wife talked about an evening meeting in some church, and we remembered seeing many little country churches with ancient horse sheds still at the rear, with wide plank platforms at the front on which folk gathered to chat after the service, with heavily latched doors that always swung inward with creaking protests. These aged unpreten-tious buildings hold many memories of midweek meetings and fervent prayer, hold echoes of sonorous preaching, of untrained choirs. The organ is always a wheezy veteran, a survivor of half a century of weekly services, weddings, revivals and funerals, its pedals worn to the bone by impatient feet. And always, close at hand, we had seen the local grave-yards with old stones gone gray and dark with years, their legends giving much of the history of the community. After we had eaten we went up to our quarters and saw a robin settling for the night in its nest scant feet from our door, in an old gnarled apple tree.

After breakfast next morning we drove a few hundred yards from Highway 1 to the entrance of Grand Pré National Park. In the beginning the land comprising the Park was acquired by the Canadian Pacific Railways and the place made appealing to those who travelled by train. Every summer saw hundreds of visitors buy rail tickets to the Park but with the coming of cars this travel fell off until no one came to Grand Pré by train and the Railway wanted to unload the burden. It was taken over by the Federal Government as a National Historic Park and now is being made a regular show place. The site is what was once the centre of the Acadian village of Grand Pré, the village well is there, and some of the ancient willows planted so long ago. A replica of the first Acadian church is now a museum of Acadian relics and nearby the statue of Evangeline, in bronze, gazes sadly over the fields of her beloved village. Here are the wide marshlands that made up the "great meadows" and attracted two Acadian families away back in 1680. They prospered, and so others came and finally the village spilled over its boundaries and others were formed. The cattle were fat and the poultry plenty. Crops were abundant. Families multiplied until there were more Acadians at Grand Pré than British at Port Royal. By 1720 the cleared lands of Grand Pré stretched for four leagues producing endless bushels of good wheat and peas and flax and barley. There were fine orchards on the uplands, great herds of fat cattle and plenty of sheep, and supplies were sold to French garrisons. Very little was for sale to any British buyer and emissaries of French Quebec did their best to stir the Acadians against the English.

The Governor of Massachusetts had long been watching the doings at Grand Pré and had come to feel it might be used as a rallying point for an attack on Acadia. So he sent Colonel Arthur Noble there with 470 New England soldiers to establish a blockhouse. The winter came early, however, and the ship with the building supplies was frozen in the ice. The blockhouse could not be built and the men were quartered the long length of the Acadian village as deep snow came early and the weather became bitterly cold. Several of the young Acadians slipped away in the darkness one night and traveled overland to Chignecto where French troops were in quarters for the winter. They explained the excellent chance there was for a surprise on the scattered

English garrison and soon a French force was headed for Grand Pré. It was joined by some Indians and arrived in dead of night, February 9, 1747. There were no sentries on duty and the French soldiers and Indians silently entered the houses and killed the sleeping English in their beds until alarm was given and the English in the farther houses stumbled out, scantily clad, bewildered, to give battle. Every advantage rested with the attackers but the Indians fled when the first English shot was fired and the French found it very different to face men who were awake and ready for them. Soon their attack came to a halt and a truce was called. The survivors of the massacre were allowed to march back to Port Royal, and from that day on the Massachusetts governor knew there could be no peace with such treacherous Acadians in the land.

There were various happenings after a New England force came to Nova Scotia and captured the French stronghold of Beauséjour. On the 5th of September, 1775, Colonel Winslow of New England gathered the men of Grand Pré in the Church of St. Charles and told them his orders. They and their families were to be deported and their lands confiscated. The men were held and were told the day of embarkation. The women were told to pack up their belongings and make ready to move but gave little heed. Over the years the Acadians had defied British authority time and again, had stubbornly refused to take the oath of allegiance. So chests were filled with linen and treasures and hidden in the woods. Money was hidden in wells and other places. Then came the day and the ships were loaded and on October 29th a fleet of twelve ships carried away 2,921 Acadians to strange lands and people. It was a sad ending to the village, the fruit of years of hatred spread by Quebec.

Longfellow was never in Nova Scotia. Seventy years after the Expulsion he heard the story of it from a man who heard it from a friend who had lived in the Province. The fact that "Evangeline" was pure imagination on the poet's part did not hinder in rousing the sentiment of millions of people. No publicity that Nova Scotia has devised has a fraction of the power of the story of the Acadian girl and her lover.

Wolfville was our next stop and we found it a most attractive little college town tucked away among orchards and shade trees. Acadia University there has a campus second to none, and all the main street is lined with beautiful homes. The Patriquin House is a grand old home on main street that has been preserved as it was in the other days as a delight for those who are historically minded. There is no admission fee. A side street leads uphill to what is known as "The Stile," and there thousands of students and others have loitered to enjoy the moonlight or have gone there afternoons when the air is clear and the little Gaspereau Valley with its checkerboard fields and lanes and orchards looks like a lovely painting spread for your benefit.

We walked under the trees of the campus and met a grizzled gardener who was trimming the lawns. He shrugged as we complimented him on the beauty of the great elms and sheltered lawns. "It's purty, all right," he admitted. "Here's where most of them get their three R's."

"Oh, no," we said. "They get those in the class rooms."

"Not my three R's," he returned. "I mean romance, remorse and rheumatism."

We drove on through New Minas, with canteens, modern stores and motels, to Kentville, a bustling little town with a good hotel, a champion baseball team, a Government Experimental Station and controlling interest in Nova Scotia's greatest summer attraction—the Apple Blossom Festival. This usually is staged the last of May and first days of June, lasting from Friday to Monday, with parades, the crowning of the Queen of the Festival, and a grand meeting on Sunday at Grand Pré Park. Hundreds of cars are parked in fields and experience has enabled the Kentville management to look after traffic with competence. The apple orchards are miles of beautiful bloom and the aroma of blossoms fills the air. Miles of colour film are exposed and anyone who visits the Festival once is sure to go again.

Not far from Kentville we came to something novel— Palmeter's Country Home. A dozen cars with American number plates were parked at the rear of a huge farmhouse. To the right was a huge barn. To the left a pond with rowboat and miniature log cabin. We went up on the veranda and faced a wonderful display of glass and china, more than the average store would carry. Inside, the display halts visitors to open-mouthed admiration for it is the finest and largest store of bone china in America and, as stated in *Harper's Bazaar*: "A store that bends over backwards to sell you the best bone china in the world." Afternoon tea is served. There is every sort of Nova Scotian handcraft on sale, and the barn is another big store offering cheaper varieties in glass and china.

The drive along Highway 1 through the Annapolis Valley is a continuous delight of fine farms and orchards and roads lined with graceful elms. It was to this belt of country the New England Planters came in 1761-1762. The general idea prevalent is that they came greedily to occupy the lands left by the Acadians but the truth is that they wanted religious liberty more than anything else. New England settlements had flourished in something close to seclusion for nearly a century and a half, and had been dominated by bigoted leaders who were responsible for the witch hunts at Salem and other tragedies. Expansion had begun to back areas and a general movement to escape the strait-jacket rulings of the fanatics was under way when the proclamation called "The Charter of Nova Scotia" promised religious freedom to all Protestants, and representative government. No other inducement was needed. Twenty-two shiploads came at one time to one place. Within two years all the Valley had been settled.

A short distance off the Highway is Berwick, a pretty village where each summer week-end religious services are held at the Camp Meeting Grounds. The traffic is light in Berwick and children play everywhere. We looked along the street for some feature and were told to go up a flight of stairs over a shop and visit Miss Grace Chute who has become world famous for her dolls. Miss Chute began designing dolls quite some time ago and arranged a collection of historic figures for display by the Government of Nova Sotia. The collection has been shown in many parts of the country. Choosing miniature dolls of the best quality, fine handiwork has brought to life tales that have become a part of the history of the Province. There is a tiny fisherman representing his fellows who have carried on their occupation for centuries along the rugged coast, a Scottish lassie reminding all that Nova Scotia is New Scotland. One doll that every visitor notices is Ulrica, the Dutch girl. It was she who followed a blazed trail through the forest from Lunenburg to Grand Pré to secure for herself one of the many cattle let loose at the time of the Acadian Expulsion. She had a lover in the old land and was hoping to raise funds enough to pay for his passage over. She found one cow and after some trouble was able to get a rope around the cow's neck and start the return trip. She was desperately tired, however, after her long venture through the forest and decided to rest in the safety of a cellar. She tethered the cow and was in her haven when she found a brick loose in the partially toppled chimney. Investigating, she was able to remove the brick and out tumbled a pile of gold coins. She tied them in her apron and made the journey back through the forest with light heart and feet, for she had much more than enough to pay for her lover's passage, and a fine cow as well. There are all kinds of dolls for sale at Miss Chute's shop, and visitors never go away without making a purchase.

The winding village of Aylesford leads to what was one time the summer home of Bishop Inglis, who defied Washington and his armed men by reading prayers for the King and Royal Family in Trinity Church, New York, when the General attended the service. He was banished from New York for his boldness and came to Nova Scotia where he soon became the first Bishop of the Province. In 1797 the Duke of Kent had a chair made for him, and the chair now rests in an Aylesford home that was once an inn.

Lower Aylesford was renamed Auburn some years ago and there we visited famous St. Mary's Church, built in 1790, its walls covered with metal-hard plaster made from powdered mussel shells left in great heaps on the shore at Morden where Acadian refugees practically lived on the shell fish through one long hard winter. The wood frames and windows of the church were brought from Halifax on horses and the handmade nails and spikes were carried by soldiers who were marched from the capital, Halifax, each man carrying a fifteen-pound packet of the nails. There are three large gilt balls on the spire and one was blown from its place during a gale some years ago. When picked up it was found to contain a record of all details relating to the construction of the church, even to the names of those employed in every phase of the building. The account was copied and the gilt ball restored to place. It is a quaint old place with the Ten Commandments and the Creed inscribed on the wall. The little gallery has a very narrow stair and was used formerly by the younger ones of the congregation.

We stopped next at Kingston, with lovely tree-shaded drives, a thriving village with Greenwood Air Station as its backbone. Greenwood has become a little town with its own shops and theatre, etc., and is a decided asset to the Valley. We stopped near a garage where an oldster in tired overalls seemed to be waiting for a bus, and asked him whether Greenwood had not been a great help to the neighbourhood.

"Sure has," he returned, with the eagerness of one wanting a chat. "In more ways than one. Them air fellows spend their pay around here, and many have their wives and families living here. Some of our chaps have jobs in Greenwood at one thing or another. It's a big help all right. This garage gets twice the work they used to have and they keep going all winter. I never thought I'd see so much change as there's been the past ten years around here."

Soon he was talking about Greenwood being free of fog and air passengers coming from Halifax on days a flight would not leave the capital. This led him to the subject of weather.

"I never heed them chaps on the radio," he said. "You can't tell weather sitting in an office, and that's why they're wrong half the time. Now you listen to a bluejay screech in the spring and you'll know when it's going to rain. If there comes wet weather, watch the hens and you'll soon know whether it's a shower or setting in for a steady. Long in July and August just watch the barn swallows and you'll know when there's going to be a change. In the fall you watch how a chipmunk holds its tail. If it slopes to the rear that means an easy time. If the tail is straight up that means average cold and snow, and if the tail slants the way the chipmunk's running you look out for a long hard winter." He said winters didn't bother him now as he always had a well-filled woodshed. "If'n you have your wood in, and a good well, and lots of taters in the cellar, a winter can't bother you much. We've a parlour stove that I set by a good deal and I always have a big pile of knotty chunks for it. They'll burn slow on a zero night and leave a good bed of coals. Just open the draft in the morning and put on more wood and you're warm in no time. 'Lectricity's fine but not reliable.

I keep a gallon of kerosene handy and my lamps and I never sweat over any power failures."

Then he told us about his son who had married a girl who liked a good time. With the opening of Greenwood there was a livening of social life in the area, and the girl, Gracie, got to playing bridge. Time and again the son, Jim, would come home to find a note telling him his supper was in the frig, that Grace would be playing bridge through the evening. Jim was not the complaining type but he became quiet and thoughtful and at last Grace began to wonder if she were overdoing the gay life. She talked it over with a close friend and decided a way to cheer him. She would write a letter to her sister in the next town, purposely forget to put on the address and purposely not seal it. The letter would be handed back and Jim would get it and, like as not, have a look at the contents before sealing it. In the letter she would say how much she loved Jim, and wished she could give him more attention, but she was becoming more popular and now had a good chance to become president of her club. Jim got the letter as she expected, glanced at the contents as she expected he would, then sat some time in deep thought. Finally he added a few lines on the last page. "Grace forgot to seal this and I had a look at what she says," he wrote, "but don't you worry. I'm quite happy the way things are going and don't mind her being away playing bridge. There's a new girl where I work and we often have our lunch together, just friendly you know, but it's nice. Don't let on to her about it but just write her you're sure I don't mind her ways." There was a new girl where Jim worked, and Grace saw her soon after, saw that she was a pretty blonde of the friendly sort. Jim hasn't come home to a note since. There is always a hot dinner waiting him, and Grace plays her bridge in the afternoons. Of course the blonde has never been mentioned.

The old man cackled as he told us the story, then gently

hinted that Jim might have inherited some of his father's good judgment.

We drove on to Middleton, a busy centre with fine gardens and famous for having two good salmon pools within the town limits. The town's champion angler is Gordon Marshall who works in a grocery story, keeps his tackle in the back shop during the spring and at closing time will slip over to Cemetery Pool and be hooked into a fighting salmon within a few minutes. The next town was Lawrencetown and a sign at the entrance said "Lovely elms. Dangerous Curves."

It was very still along the main street. There was not a puff of wind and the sun was hot. A black dog lay in the shade of some shrubs with his pink tongue hanging as he panted. Two little girls in brief play suits pushed a doll cart on a lawn and argued fretfully. We drove along very slowly and saw a man walking in the direction we were going. His shirt was open at the neck and his Adam's apple bobbed as he said he'd appreciate a lift if we were going as far as Paradise. The road map said it was the next town and we assured him we would go that far.

He wheezed a bit and he was very warm, he said. "All my family's been bothered with asthma," he complained. "I guess we inherit the curse. And the only one ever cured was my uncle. He took several papers including the *Montreal Star*, and the *Family Herald*, and whenever he saw a cure for asthma advertised he'd send for a bottle. He'd take a few doses and when there was no immediate relief he'd stack the bottle on a high shelf out in his hen pen. He kept a lot of hens and he had an old easy chair in a corner of the pen where he'd sit and watch to see if any hens were eating their eggs. One day a cousin of mine, his nephew, came on a vacation from the city. He was in the hen house and saw the long row of bottles on the shelf. Must have been fifty or so, going back over twenty years. He came the next day with a bottle of rum, the best going, and filled over half them bottles

to within half an inch of the top, the others not quite so full.
One day that fall uncle had asthma bad and happened to
glance at the bottles, wondering if any would help. He was
amazed to see he'd taken so little of some of the cures and tried
one. He paid no attention to the directions on the bottle but
kept taking sips all that afternoon and evening. Next day
he finished the bottle and felt better. So he started at another.
It ended with him emptying practically all them bottles, and
being cured! Yes, I don't care what you think, he was cured.
Never had another wheeze. He claimed it was through his
taking so many different cures so fast. But I've tried a dozen
at once, fixed up with rum, and it only made me worse. Here's
Paradise, my friend, and I'd like out right here. I got word
last night that folks from the States is visiting a cousin of
mine here and they tell asthma isn't a real disease at all.
Just something in your mind, like one of them allergies. So
I'm going to have a talk with them. Hope you never get
it. So long."

We drove along and reached Bridgetown, turned left by
the town clock and found a parking place on the right of
the short main street. We wandered into a shop that sold
books and looked around, accosted half a dozen people there
and outside on the sidewalk, but had little luck in getting
information. Then a man with few teeth who was eating
icecream from a cone listened to our chat and said we should
get a book on the district. "It's called *The Mountain and the
Valley,*" he said. "And she's a humdinger. All the truth but
blunt put. The ladies around here made a fuss and wouldn't
let them sell it in the store, but people only read it more on
that account. You'll not likely see a copy if you get into
houses hereabouts, but I'll bet there's one book in every
house. And don't you let yourself be fooled by ladies making
protests. Them very ones will read that book if they have
to wait till they go visitin' some place. One day my wife
had the mission society or some church bunch at an afternoon

meeting at the house. I'd taken the furnace pipe down for the summer and put a piece of oilcloth over the hole. After they were in a time I had to go into the cellar from the kitchen way and their voices come down through that pipe hole plain as anything. One of them had just got married a second time and was givin' an account of her honeymoon. After that when my wife acts prim I don't say anything but they don't fool me. No, sir, they talk smooth as cream in public and look like saints in church but they ain't one mite better'n the men."

He told us where the author of *The Mountain and the Valley* lived but we drove on through Tupperville and Round Hill and into Annapolis Royal. We had lunch there at the Queen Hotel, open all the year around and with a friendly atmosphere that makes you want to go there again and again. It has a great story, the Queen Hotel, for it was built by an Englishman, we were told, who wanted to outdo the hotel across the way, owned by a sister of his wife. He was going to inherit a large sum of money, he explained, and had proof enough to obtain funds and begin building. It was a very fine mansion for those days and situated in a beautiful setting. But when completed news came that the English relative had died and left his fortune to another. For some time the great house stayed open to the public who were curious, and then it was a school. It passed through various hands. The daughter of a charwoman in the town became famous for her swimming feats and a Boston sea captain saw her, induced her to return to Boston with him and there had her hired to perform. She easily out-did any competitor and began making large sums of money. Her kind friend and manager died suddenly and she placed her affairs in the hands of a lawyer and made a trip back to the scene of her childhood. The big house was empty and she decided she would make her name in the town. She bought the building, ordered all the dishes and

furnishings needed, hired a staff, invited all the social élite
for a grand opening night and engaged the local orchestra
to play on the occasion. She had kept in good by buying
hymn books for the church she would like to attend and all
seemed happy as a marriage bell. Then, on the eve of the
dinner, word came that her lawyer had drawn all her funds
and fled the country. She was ruined. She could not pay for
the things she had ordered or the servants. So as the party
gathered she quietly slipped away by train and was across to
Boston by boat before she could be located. Later, she renewed
her swimming exhibitions, married a suitable sugar daddy and
lived to a ripe old age in California. But in the old memories
of Annapolis Royal there lives the story of the big night when
the hotel opened for business with all the pomp the area
could muster—and there was no hostess.

We went to old Fort Anne and roamed around the grounds,
explored the Museum that used to be the Officers' Quarters.
We were shown papers telling about the great celebration in
1955 when the old fort and town were 350 years old. There
had been ships sailing up the Basin and from these a great
force of men in uniforms of the seventeenth century swarmed
up the ramparts, with Indians helping them, and were met by
the fire of the small but courageous fort garrison. It had
been a beautiful day and movie cameras ground out miles
of film as the attack went on and on and men fell on the
green and wounded were carried off in stretchers. We hoped
that some day we might see the movie that was made.

Annapolis Royal today is a dreamy old town in modern
surroundings where the ghosts of the past glide around carefully and benevolently in their haunting. The population is
only eight hundred but the town is a trading centre for an
area holding six thousand. It is a quiet old place with
beautiful gardens and trees, where fine peaches and pears
and plums are grown in backyards that are not even imagined
by those passing along the street; where calling cards are still

left on shining brass hall trays, where some of the tourist homes keep the old-fashioned bedroom bureau washbowls on display and real warmth-giving fireplaces are flanked by ancient brass and dull copper utensils. It is a town where people are proud of their heritage, where old houses have been used by four and five generations.

We visited the old Banks House, said to be 250 years old, with low ceilings, wide floor boards, old "Holy Lord" hinges on the doors, and saw the upper room where an old time mistress of sadistic nature used to tie her slaves to an iron upright and beat them. There is a ghost at the Banks House but it is a quiet old lady who never makes any sound and keeps to the corners if she does happen to enter a room while you are there. The builders of the house had some idea of insulation as a second roof was built a few inches above the first one, keeping the house warm in winter and cool in summer. Fort Anne is in an Historic Park and most interesting. There is plenty of room for parking on the old parade ground in front of what used to be the officers' barracks and is now a museum with a Port Royal Room, and Acadian Room, a Garrison Room, a Queen Anne Room, and a Haliburton Hallway. The Acadian Room has all the furnishings of an early Acadian home. Outside, we roamed around the extensive earthworks, saw the old powder magazine, the site of the blockhouse, and the great view from the sentry posts. The old stronghold was captured and recaptured seven times before the flag of Britain went aloft to stay, and thousands of visitors go there every summer and dream in the historic atmosphere.

There is the old cemetery with many quaint inscriptions. One stone records the death of a child a year before it was born. The old town hall has the mounted heads of almost every animal in America, and there are countless old houses with all sorts of legends about them. In what used to be an old hotel one can read an inscription on the ancient window pane:

"Here I am after a hard day's ride. An empty stomach and a sore backside. Take my advice your stomach fill. Plaster your . . . and pay your bill."

Some of the boys who played around old Annapolis Royal became famous persons. One became General Sir William Fenwick Williams, a military figure in Turkey, Governor of Gibraltar, Commander-in-Chief of the British forces in Canada. Another boy became Sir William Winniett, Governor of the Cape Coast District. Two other boys, Nathan Cosby and William Wolseley, became Admirals in the British Navy.

Just seven miles on fine pavement takes one across the river to old Port Royal, first permanent settlement north of the Gulf of Mexico. Away back in 1605 the Micmac Indians were intrigued by the huge building of the white men and glad to hang around at evening time and have a slice of the bread the white men ate. Here Champlain and his good men planted first crops in Canada, built the first water mill in Canada, and organized the first fraternal club in North America—the Order of the Good Time. Each member had, in turn, to take office and that meant providing the membership with all the meat and fish and fowl necessary for a proper dinner. The Indians helped get moose and ruffed grouse and caribou and porcupine, and trout and salmon. There was always a good supply and America's first poet and playwright, Lescarbot, wrote back to Paris that he and the others were enjoying as good a fare as any in the French capital.

English raiders came and burned them out but the present establishment is a perfect replica of the original, situated on exactly the same spot, a group of buildings arranged around a courtyard in the manner of sixteenth century farms in northern France, and is fortified at the two southerly corners by a cannon platform and a stockade. The entrance building is framed with hewn oak and has walls of contemporary French construction, known as "en colombage," and is roofed with oak shingles of the same size as those used on small buildings of the period in Picardy. The studded oak doors are handmade and hung and fitted with wrought ironware of period design. The peep-hole in the outer door is known as a "Judas." The small building next the entrance has a fireplace of local stone and leaded glass windows of contemporary French pattern. The roof is covered with hand-split pine shingles and the building was used by Champlain as a storehouse for rigging of their pinnaces. A blacksmith shop is next with a forge of handmade bricks and local stone, and the casement windows are filled in with oiled parchment, treated as a substitute for scraped and oiled buckskin.

There is a kitchen, a bake shop, the community room, artisans' quarters, the artisans' dormitory, the chapel, the priests' dwelling, the gentlemen's dwellings, the governor's house, the storehouse, the cellar, the trading room and the well. When the reconstruction took place the original well was identified and its walls rebuilt with field stone. There is no other spot like it in North America and summer long visitors roam about the buildings, dreaming of the long ago, and taking pictures.

We drove back slowly toward Annapolis and Highway 1 and saw an old man sitting by a garden featuring peas and string beans. He looked lonely so we stopped and went to ask some simple question about the country. He started from his reveries and began talking.

"No, you won't see many oxen teams nowadays, but in my time—I'm eighty-six—they were on every farm. The first thing I remember about our place, which was forty miles from here, was the great heavy two-wheeled dump cart father used to draw out the manure in the spring, and to haul in the potatoes and turnips in the fall. Our oxen had brass tips on their horns, were big bony animals and very slow-moving. They were powerful, though, and never got excited like horses if the cart got stuck. We used neck yokes but some of neighbours had head yokes and there didn't seem to be much difference when it came to hauling a sled or cart. Father used to whittle small yokes suitable for calves and I would put them on and sometimes hitch a yearling to my sled. By the time the lad was two years old he was fully trained. Of course two were yoked together and I always tied their tails together as well so they couldn't swing around. Once father had a big pair of black and white steers who were a bit on the lazy side and if the load were real heavy they would often lie down and the only way to get them going again was to light a birchbark roll and singe them a bit. A neighbour worked with us one fall and saw father handle the bark to get the steers going and thought it a pretty smart trick. One of his cattle got hurt and he came and borrowed our steers to haul in some hay he had stacked three miles away. It had snowed the day before and the road was not well-broken so after two miles of wading the oxen became tired and lay down. The man let them rest a time and then tried to get them up but they would not budge. He pulled a bunch of hay from the load, touched a match to it and put the blaze under one of the oxen. He jumped up quickly and the other jumped with him. They had much experience with the fire treatment. But they only jolted the load ahead enough to be over the blaze and there they stood and the hay caught fire. The man ran up the sled tongue to pull out the lynch pin which held the chain from the yoke but before he got it out the oxen, sensing the fire, started to run. So a nearby farmer beheld the spectacle of oxen plunging in a run, their load a great blaze, their driver up on the pole trying to pull out the lynch pin and shrilling wild commands and condemnation. The rumps of the steers were well singed before he released the chain, he was singed somewhat himself, lost all his load and binding ropes and the hay frame. I never heard such language as when he came down the slope to our place with the ruin of his sled and the singed cattle. Mother who had come out, rushed back in the house with her hands over her ears."

The old man chuckled quietly for some time, then looked up in droll fashion. "Do you know, friend, that the oxen were cured. After that they never tried to lay down and they'd jump a foot if a man scratched a match to light his pipe."

We left him still chuckling and scratching his head and drove along through to Clementsport, where we drove up a roof-steep hill to the old Loyalist Church of St. Edward, built by Dutch, Hessian and other German Loyalists in the 1780s. After it was transferred to the Church of England a hymn was sung in the Dutch language every Sabbath before the beginning of the ordinary service until there were only two old veterans left to sing and their voices feeble. The timbers of the church are massive and the width of the boards is a surprise to every visitor. The lime for the plaster was made by burning clam shells and is so hard it cannot be pierced by an ordinary nail. All the nails and spikes used were handmade. The builders were familiar with boat building and when we climbed into the loft it was like looking up into an overturned schooner. Citizens of the area have donated so many old relics that the building is almost a museum. In recent years cabinets have been installed to hold these treasures and the three carloads of Americans who came in while we were there were intrigued with everything they saw.

When we went out and carefully rounded the turn down hill to the bridge an old chap with a truck was across our way. The engine had stalled but we told him not to hurry and after many attempts he got the motor chugging again, then pulled to one side. We parked behind him and he told his machine was fourteen years old and nearly good as new except when it got "tantrums." "Just like an old female, that engine," he complained. "And sometimes I give her a good kick and she starts off."

There was a chatting group in front of the little store by the bridge and others joined it. We asked if anything unusual had happened.

"Well, yes and no," said the man. "One of our men has run off with his neighbour's wife. Usual, maybe, but they've been making soft eyes at each other a good year or so. No, they won't get them back. They're over in the States. He's a good mechanic and he'll find work. Worst of it is, he was treasurer of our Lodge and he took the funds with him."

"Too bad," we offered.

"Too bad all the way round," he affirmed. 'I don't know how we'll get on without him. He was the best Sunday School superintendent we ever had, and it'll be a job to replace him. Yep, it's too blame bad."

We drove past the great naval base at Deep Brook, saw men drilling and some sitting in the sun to shine their shoes. Then we were at Smith's Cove where there were many signs pointing to motels and hotels, and tourists were strolling here and there and one carload were in bathing suits. Soon after we reached Joggin Bridge and stopped at a small store where two oldtimers were passing the time of day. We asked them if there were anything unusual in the area.

"No, mister," wagged one old fellow. "Just unemployment and high taxes. But come around election year and you'll really have something to write about. You'll learn this is a land flowing with milk and honey."

"But has nothing ever happened that was unusual?" we persisted.

"Tim Smith got married at sixty-two," grinned another old lad partly toothless. "Through letter writin,' they say. Made a good match, too, cause she's three-four years older'n him and gettin' the old age pension already."

"Back thirty years ago," said the third man, "a man up the road had a fat old mare that fell into a well. They tried every which way to get ropes around her and hoist her but it couldn't be done. Then somebody noticed she was sort of stayin' afloat, for the well was deep, and as neighbours were gatherin' they started a bucket brigade from a brook close by. Pretty soon others arrived and more buckets. They kept pourin' water into that well in near a steady stream and you'd hardly believe the way it filled and floated that old mare right up to the top. They slung a rope back of her and hoisted her out on the ground. If I hadn't been there to see it I wouldn't have believed it."

His story was confirmed by his cronies and we were leaving when the first speaker mentioned Joe's Nancy. "She doesn't live a hundred miles from here," he said, "and you don't need to know where. She kept gettin' fatter and fatter on account she called around a lot as she was agent then for Spirella corsets, and everybody'd make her a cup of tea and have some cakes. At last she got so no corsets could hold her in and Joe took her to a doctor in Digby who knowed her well. He didn't take long examining her and shook his head. 'Only way to do with her, Joe,' he said, 'is put her on a diet.'

" 'Gosh!' said Nancy. 'I've heard they're hard on a person.'

" 'Could be,' nodded the doctor. 'But if you want to keep mobile you keep to three meals a day, and no more.' "

"She went out madder'n a wet hen but Joe spread the word around and nobody offered her as much as a glass of water after that," added the second man.

"Mister," said the third oldster. "You drive up that dirt road a short bit and turn left into the first driveway. You'll see something out of ordinary."

We thanked him, followed his directions and turned into the yard of a great house with a huge veranda across the entire front. A lady was picking plums from a tree and a man well on in years smiled greetings. Soon we were inside and inspecting a most remarkable dwelling.

# 3

## Attic Smoke-House, Digby Chicken, Cow Creamers, and Sea Serpent

IN 1784 A UNITED EMPIRE LOYALIST family by the name of Oakes came to Digby county and took up a government grant. Their son, Henry, looked around and bought two thousand acres in this Acadia Valley that abuts Joggin Bridge. He got the land cheaply and selected a lovely site for his house where a wooded hill sloped gently forward toward the small river. Across the stream another hill rises abruptly and affords shelter from a storm. The woods were cut down and orchards and garden planted. Workmen came and lived in temporay quarters as the house timbers were fashioned. A small forge was set up and all the nails were made, and spikes. The original timbers in the house still show the marks of the adze, and the doors are equipped with bevelled hinges making sure they close unless held open. The old Holy Lord hinges are used in closets, and some of the doors have a carved cross on the upper part. The mantels for eight fireplaces were especially cut and carved by hand. Clay from a nearby bank was baked in a kiln and 49,100 bricks made for the chimneys and fireplaces. The roofing is composed of feather-edged boards covered with birchbark, having an outside cover of shaved pine shingles. The base-

**73**

ment has a brick-floored dairy room with plastered walls. The attic was finished like a living-room and a feature there is a smokehouse built as an integral part of one of the chimneys and connected with the flue from the kitchen fireplace. Removal of bricks in the top and bottom of the chimney wall permitted the smoke of hickory wood to circulate in the compartment and cure hams. Another feature of the house is a secret closet. We were told there was one and took our time and made careful inspection but saw no possible place for it. Then our host removed a tread from the attic stairs and hoisted a wide panel through the space. We went down to a bedroom below and entered its large closet—to find an opening into a second closet large enough to hold three persons.

This amazing old place is not two minutes from Highway 1 and yet summer visitors never glimpse it unless told beforehand. Mr. Oakes made a road through his own property to Digby, imported a fine coach and coachmen, even a coach dog, and when he arrived in the town once or twice a week always created a stir. That road has now become a part of the provincial highway system. At the top of the hill he built a church and once a year service is held in the ancient structure. One large room upstairs in his house was used as a schoolroom, and a teacher was hired to instruct the children of the household and those of near friends. Stately Lombardy poplars were planted to flank the house at a distance of twenty paces and there they remain today, fine old guardians, their leaves forever atremble though no breeze may be stirring. Six generations have occupied the property and the old man was worried over the fact that his son lives in New Orleans and will not return to Canada.

We drove to Digby and on the way were stopped by seeing some people inspecting an ordinary spot by the wayside. Being curious, but careful, we stood near and finally

realized they were discussing some historical feature that
should be marked. Finally we summoned courage enough to
address a thin-faced man who wore no hat and looked
impatient.

"It's the Edison house we're talking about," he said. "John
Edison came from New Jersey with the Loyalists back when
Digby was founded, became a director of the town marsh and
an assessor. In 1804 Samuel Edison was born right in this
area where we stand. He went to Ohio and his son was
Thomas Alva Edison. You could just about call him a half
Nova Scotian, and now they're talking of putting up a
marker to tell people this was the Edison homestead. And
they were great folks for getting into trouble, the Edisons.
When the American Revolution began he was found guilty
of helping British troops and was sentenced to be hanged.
But someone put in a good word for old John Edison and the
sentence was changed to banishment from the United States.
That's how they landed here. In 1811 the family went to
Ontario and Thomas Alva's father became active with the
forces of William Lyon Mackenzie in 1838 and the Edisons
had to scamper over the border into Ohio. Yes, sir, quite a
family—the Edisons."

We murmured we were glad to see people taking an
interest in things historical and ventured the opinion that
Digby had much to be proud of.

"Sure," agreed our friend, becoming less impatient looking.
"We've got the Admiral Digby Horticultural Society beauti-
fying the ground around the site of the original well belonging
to Admiral Digby, and looking after the 'Welcome to Nova
Scotia' sign near the head of the pier, and now they're looking
after the old Loyalist cemetery that dates from 1783. They
tell me that one old chap buried there started the story about
Digby 'chickens.' You know away back at the start of Digby
the firstcomers arrived late in the fall and freeze-up came
before they could clear ground and put up cabins. So many

had to stay on board the ships which were frozen in the harbour. When Christmas came there were no chickens or turkeys in the new settlement. In fact there was no meat at all, and the people were practically living on salt and smoked herring. They took it in their stride however, and laughingly called their Christmas dinners 'Digby chickens.' Since that a smoked herring is known in Nova Scotia as a 'Digby chicken' and it has helped keep Digby on the map. I'll bet more know about the chicken than about our scallops, and that we have the largest scallop fleet in the world."

He was beginning to sound like a Board of Trade speaker so we thanked him for his courtesy and drove into the town. There was parking space by the Travel Bureau and we were interested to see the number of old cannon that were ranged along the embankment, pointing seaward. It is a quiet little town with some fine little shops selling to the tourist trade. We went through the town and around to their main boast, "The Digby Pines," truly a fine summer hotel in a beautiful setting. Then we headed out along Highway 1 again and rolled along through pleasant countryside of villages and filling stations until we saw two cars with New York license plates come slowly to a halt. The driver of one car waved us down and wanted to know where he could find the "Judge Savary House."

A voice called from back of a hedge before we could shout an answer, and said he was parked in front of it. So we got out, too, and went into a sunny lawn back of the hedge and saw a large plaque on the left of the front door. It read:

Alfred William Savary; Lawyer and Legislator; Inspector of Schools, Digby County 1869-72; Member of Parliament for Digby 1867-74; County Court Judge for Annapolis, Digby, Yarmouth 1876-1907. Author of *History of the County of Annapolis*, and other volumes. Born in this house, 10th October 1831. Died in Annapolis Royal, N.S., 30th March 1920.

We were taken in and shown his study and many volumes of his library. It was easy to see what a fine old residence it had been back in the 1820s when it was erected.

As we came out a man passing listened to our talk and began telling us about Captain John. K. Smith, who lived in the village—Plympton—and had some very interesting relics in his home. He is descended from a long line of seafaring men and one proud exhibit is a small cannon about a foot long that could be bolted on a ship's rail. On the barrel are two ornamental dolphins and the French coat of arms. A bronze shot mould was dug up with the cannon when it was unearthed during the excavating of a cellar. There is a brass scale card and rule device that was found in the cellar of an old house. There are many objects of interest and the captain's tales of the sea add much to the entertainment of any visitor.

The next place we stopped was Weymouth, sprawled on the hills and around a bridge in the hollow, wanting to be more than a village, and yet not a town. A small traffic jam before the bridge gave us an idea to pull to one side and start talking with some people who looked oldfashioned for the two ladies had very long dresses and their hair was pinned in tight knobs at the back. They answered questions readily about the locality and the man, who wore a dapper white moustache, informed me that no less than three writers of some repute in the newspaper world had gone from an area of less than twenty miles in the Weymouth district.

"And one was our cousin," said the eldest-looking lady. "She could write nice poetry and if there had been editors with a grain of sense they would have published her work. Do you remember that in 1939 war had begun and half the people in the Empire were scared sick. And that Christmas the king gave his message and finished with 'And I said to the man who stood at the gate of the year, Give me light that I may tread softly into the unknown. And he replied, 'Go out into the darkness and put your hand into the hand of God. That shall be to you better than a light, and safer than a known way.'

"There was such a stir after," the woman continued, "that all the bigwigs over there started looking for the author, and it was two days before a London newspaper found that a retired school teached, Minnie L. Haskins, was the author of the lines. She died in obscurity but her writing inspired a king and his people, and I feel that my cousin might have done as much."

Before we could make any answer the lady posed with her gaze afar and began reciting a poem about a lad who dreamed about pirates and was always looking from beach-stone cones to see if a flag had the skull and crossbones. There we stood in the sunshine, with traffic grinding by to the bridge, and heard about ten verses filled with brine and homing tides. She finished with a gesture and we assured her that such poetry should find a market.

"No," she snapped. "They'd sooner publish such stuff as:

Down here in Nova Scotia there are names to stir the soul; there's a place called Ecum Secum, there's a Kitiwiti Shoal, there's a homey Chimney Corner and a pastoral Cow Bay, and there's old West Newdy Quoddy that you ought to see some day; and if we were minus Minas would we mind it very much, as long as we had Paradise, Elsyian Fields and such? We amble up to Aspy Bay by way of Chezzetcook, and then come back by Stewiacke and finish at Banook. Or we can romp on Rogge's Roost, and maybe scale Skir Dhu, then if you wish there's Ingonish, seductive Sissiboo; or start the day on Breakfast Isle, have lunch at Sandwich Point; at sundown dine on Lobster Claw or gnaw a Grampus joint. For warlike lads we've Conquerall, for Scots, Economy. The kennel club loves Pugwash, musicians Harmony; Skull Bob's Lake for scary souls, Maligant Cove for crooks, Oysters Pond for connoisseurs, Frying Pan's for cooks. But you can have each place I've named, to scupper, bust or rob it, just leave to me the sweetest yet—our Upper Musquodoboit.

When the man smiled the trim moustache never moved and we were fascinated by the performance but the lady who recited was hard to control and so we left them without discovering the name or the manuscript of the Nova Scotia Haskins.

It was delightful to drive through "the longest main street in America," as it is called, thirty miles of Acadian seaside villages. The homes are well kept and the houses painted. The churches are huge and on Sundays every person in the place goes to Mass on foot or by truck or car. They hold great fairs in the autumn, our informant at Belliveau Cove said, and American visitors give them much encouragement as they play the fair games and buy tickets on everything raffled. We were shown a house that is the oldest on the shore, with huge beams as sound as when they were hewn, and the building is set so the utmost sunlight enters by the windows. This was calculated by the builders as a means of saving candles, and the lady in charge said the first tree cut down at the Cove was felled by a Mrs. Belliveau. A stone memorial marks the site of a first log chapel erected in 1769. One village is called "Grosses Coques" which means "large clams" and we were told that these shell fish were so plentiful in the old days that the entire village lived on them during a winter when food was scarce. There was an inn beside the Metaghan River and a man there said the proprietor had got his start by catching rattlesnakes in Florida, shooting them in the moonlight or snagging them with a forked stick and carrying them home in sacks. He reckoned he had taken more than three thousand rattlers from the swamps and had never been bitten. And he had brought home with him the skin of a seven-footer that had been strong enough to floor him twice before he could handle it. We declined an invitation to inspect the skin and hurried along for it was getting late. There was quite heavy traffic in Port Maitland though it was the supper hour and we were glad to reach Hebron and turn in at the Green Tree Inn for the night.

We were shown to a room that was different and restful, with books and magazines in plenty, restful chairs and convenient lights. We had dinner in what was the stable in the old days and is now a wonderland of beauty. The food was exceptionally good, and when our kind host saw us gazing in wonder at shelves of rare cow creamers he invited us to his sitting-room and there we learned much about The Green Tree Inn and the cow creamers. In the long ago the Inn was a fine, rambling old house sheltered by huge trees, and the home of Deacon Harris. He ruled his household with an iron hand. No food could be cooked on the Sabbath, no child could play on a swing, no one could whistle a tune. The only reading allowed was the Bible and the *Maritime Baptist.* Nevertheless, the Deacon had one failing. He loved a fast horse. After he had acquired a great stallion that could go like the wind, it was his delight to hitch it to his buggy and set off for Yarmouth five miles away. With the reins tightly gripped in his bony fists and his long gray moustache swept back to his ears, he would pass everything on the road.

Many years after the Deacon passed on to a better land, Mr. and Mrs. Jack Porter bought the place and fitted it up as Green Tree Inn. The stable became a fine dining-room, and the adjoining workshop, now filled with Mrs. Porter's five looms, was the huge box stall where the stallion fortified himself with oats and sleep between jaunts to Yarmouth. Jack Porter is a versatile man who can do most anything and do it well. Besides training his cooks to serve wonderful food, he writes poetry, paints, and makes beautiful lamp shades. Mrs. Porter is a handicraft expert and an authority on antiques. Back in 1936 the Porters were enjoying a serial entitled "The Silver Cow Creamer" by P. G. Wodehouse. Mrs. Porter, intrigued by what she learned of cow creamers, decided to start a collection through knowing that cow creamers, made 250 years ago in Great Britain, Holland and Germany, were extremely scarce and ranged in price from twenty-five to seventy-five dollars. She explored an auction room in Halifax and located her first cow creamer there. A search of the rest of the city was fruitless. Then Mrs. Porter asked friends in New England, New York and Pennsylvania to help her in her quest. In Lunenburg, she found two more creamers.

So, one by one, Mrs. Porter has gleaned creamers from unlikely places. She never passes an old shop or second-hand store without investigating. Her friends in Pennsylvania secured some fine specimens brought over by German settlers. But she got to know that the English had produced more than any other country, and has obtained some creamers of great value. She has a fine Delft specimen from Holland, an Iron-stone specimen, a beauty from Switzerland shaded in pink. One item had only the head of a cow. At another spot she found a bright red bull, the only one known to exist. Oldest English creamers had cows with hollow legs and as these were in daily use one wonders how they cleaned the inside of the legs. A few rare creamers came from Czechoslovakia and, strangely, these depicted a cow sitting up like a dog. During the last war Mrs. Porter found a creamer with its side covered by adhesive tape and the antique dealer let her have it reason-ably. She was afraid it might have been damaged but when the tape was removed it showed a picture of the Rhine. The dealer had obviously tried to cover the fact that it had been made in Germany.

Three cases of cow creamers are displayed in the dining-room, only part of a collection that is the largest in America. And there are other treasures as well, oldfashioned duelling pistols, an Egyptian sword with a gold inlaid hilt, a Kentucky squirrel rifle with a barrel as long as a horse. Along the great handhewn beams are long spearheads once used in the Holy Land. On the wall hangs a ceremonial rug made in Formosa five centuries ago, and by the entrance is a collection of forty-five bell-jars containing flowers and wax fruit. The infinite charm and grace of the house is a delight to people who visit it. They gaze at the wealth of beautiful ruby and blue glass, rare old china and other items, become fascinated by the cow creamers that adorn that which was once the Deacon Harris' stable. We slept soundly in the old spool bed and had a fine breakfast in the morning. It had been coolish overnight but lighted oil lamps had the dining-room pleasantly warm and the food was delicious. We left wishing there were more Green Tree Inns along our way.

Yarmouth is a grand old town with a live Historical Society to retain memories of the past. We saw their museum—marine—which they are setting up in the original library, second oldest in Nova Scotia, and the ships models and other items are simply fascinating. The Museum is emphasizing the good old Yarmouth days of wooden sailing ships. We wandered around the town and found there is much that intrigues. At the funeral home in Yarmouth North—the Sweeney—for instance, there is the oldest can of lobster in the world. Away back in 1849 100 cases of canned lobster were shipped to England, but were returned as the English people were afraid of ptomaine poisoning, the art of canning food being then in its infancy. What happened to the shipment is not known but one tin was given to an ancestor who operated the Funeral Home and there it is still on exhibition.

Harry R. Daley, a retired railway clerk, has the entire story, and pictures, of the first bringing of deer to Nova Scotia in 1894. His father launched a personal campaign and in February, 1894, brought in seven does and four bucks. Nine were placed in the Lake Jolly region twenty miles from Digby. Two were exhibited in Yarmouth a few days and then released. Thirty-five years later an average of over four thousand deer were being shot each hunting season. The deer cost fifteen dollars each.

A shop clerk directed us to the home of Sheriff Jack Baker and soon we were looking at the finest collection of rifles, guns and pistols in eastern Canada. These go back many years but ninety-five per cent of the relics are in working order. There are 132 pistols in the collection, everything from flintlocks and percussions to the latest automatics, from 22 BBs to 70 calibre. There are eight cannon including one from the local Bunker Hill Fort at the mouth of the harbour, and one from a British frigate sunk and later raised in the Savannah River, Georgia. His eighty rifles include muskets, musketoons, matchlock, cartridge and flintlock, with calibres ranging from twenty-two to a blunderbus that looks big enough to kill an elephant. There are early Springfields, Moorish rifles, a French fowling piece and others dating back to 1700. There are fifty edged weapons, such as swords and cane daggers. Sheriff Baker has his own repair shop and every item is catalogued according to date, name, serial number, where obtained and any other reference. The new ferry plying between Bar Harbour and Yarmouth arrived as we reached the pier, and a citizen produced from his pocket a letter from Nova Scotia's premier and published in the Yarmouth paper. It read:

Nova Scotia is of the sea—historically, physically, and by happy inheritance. It is fitting that the name, which so proudly symbolized the maritime pre-eminence of the Province in the days of sail, should mark today, the newest evidence of Nova Scotia's economic progress. The *Bluenose* is more than a name—a ship or a service. It contains in its eight letters something of the heart and life that flows by the waters of Minas, Fundy and the restless Atlantic. It designates a people—and lives in their blood. It stands for a race of mariners and tidewater landsmen who, although they have become industrial-minded and have added production knowledge to their lore of the sea, still harbour in their innermost thoughts a secret communion with the sea and a love for the salt-encrusted path along which they came to maturity, and greater accomplishments. May it ever be thus for the *Bluenose*, the people and the Province of Nova Scotia.

Henry D. Hicks

In a community that has long been noted for its green lawns, freshened continually by ocean mists, its fancy shrubs and colourful flower gardens, Yarmouth folks showing off the beauties of nature to interested visitors never miss taking them to see "Rock Cottage" and the "Lupin Trail." Rock Cottage is really a show place and its extensive grounds, once containing a gun emplacement, is probably photographed more than any other flowery spot in western Nova Scotia. Moisture laden climate keeps the delicate blossoms in all their glory for a long period, and local taxi drivers take willing fares to have a glimpse of the lavish beauty. The Lupin Trail has long been one of the most interesting drives near Yarmouth, and roadside and fields are covered with blue, white and pink lupin. There is also a fine view of the Tusket Islands, and Chebogue Point itself, end of the lupin trail, is the spot where the first English settlers of Yarmouth County landed on June 9, 1761. A plaque situated in the cemetery stone wall tells the story.

There was a road sign pointing to Wedgeport but we did not take it for we were told in Yarmouth that for some mysterious reason the blue fin tuna were not showing as they had in past years and the Annual Tuna Tournament had been quite a fizzle. This is a shame as when the first International Match was organized back in 1937 there were fish galore and soon the fishing fraternity around the world knew about the famous Soldier's Rip, a shallow maelstrom where the huge tuna came to feed on herring. And big game anglers, somewhat akin to big game hunters who go to Africa to shoot lions, flocked to Wedgeport and fought long, tough battles with giant fish that set world records. Anglers came from eight different countries to take part in the Tournament and Wedgeport guides had enough business to make up for the many lean years they had known before. Now the blue fin is lunching elsewhere but all the experts say it will be but a matter of time before the tuna are back and the Tournament resumed.

It was lovely swinging along Highway 3 on a summer morning with the sea a glitter, gulls on the wing, and the glory of flowers splashing colour in almost every front lawn. We reached the Pubnicos, and there are nine of them, the world's oldest Acadian holding, stretching ten miles around Pubnico harbour. Nearly half the people are d'Entremonts, and every farm has oxen which they work as long as the flesh is willing, and then sell for beef. The Acadians are a careful people, dealing shrewdly, saving, working hard, and the farms are without mortgages. There is no crime, no local taxes, no jail, no police force, no poverty, no great wealth, no divorce, no lawsuit, race prejudice or class distinction, and everybody is bilingual. The man with the most patience must be the postmaster as there are only four surnames and the majority have identical Christian names, sometimes identical middle names. And he must be careful with the old-age pensions which arrive in numbers for the good folks of the Pubnicos, like their oxen, live to a ripe old age. We saw old-fashioned box wells with their buckets hanging on rolled-up winches. Now and then one would have the bucket attached to a long pole, and we knew the depth of that well was not great. A pair of oxen were filling in as lawn mowers at one place so we stopped to get a picture and the man came out to speak with us. He said the oxen could do a better job at cutting the grass even than his old machine, which he had used for sixteen years.

"I will get a new mower this year," he said, "when there is a sale on in town, and I would have had one last year except that my wife died and there were many expenses."

"They are terrible," we agreed.

"But less here than anywhere," he said proudly. "The community owns the hearse and we each pay five dollars, no more, when we have a funeral. Also, we pay seven dollars a year for our fire department. We have cooperative stores, a credit union, community telephone, lighting and sewerage systems."

He told us so many things about the Pubnicos that they seemed to be a sort of modern Utopia. And when he urged that we see his home we went in. His daughter politely showed us her new electric washing machine, the frigidaire, vacuum cleaner, mixmaster and other gadgets, then pointed to the television set in the living-room.

"That has been grand for me," she said. "Before we had it there was always one or another of my father's friends dropping in to talk about the Yarmouth boat and the new motels and how things used to be when they were boys. They all wanted to talk at once until one night my mother got tired of so much noise and took in the alarm clock. She set it for one half hour and told our caller he could talk until it alarmed, then father would have his half hour, and always after that there was the alarm clock fetched out from the bedroom for the evening. It worked very well, that plan."

The father looked at us sheepishly but made no argument and soon we were on our way again. At Shag Harbour gulls rose in clouds around the wharf where fish were being unloaded. Roadside boulders and many trucks made parking a chore but we found space and after some dickering got a boat to take us over to Bon Portage. As we drew near the Island we had to get into a dory and then be rowed to a wide ramp of peeled poles on which the lightkeepers haul their craft. It was hard to keep balance on the slippery crossbars but Morrill Richardson, keeper of the light and husband of the famous author of *We keep a Light*, was there with a helping hand and soon we were walking the trail to the light. Raspberries fairly reddened the sides of the path and we ate handfuls. Broken lobster traps and debris of the sea littered the stony beach and was jammed and crammed into clumps of scrub bush farther inshore. We had lunch, looked at Evelyn Richardson's scrapbooks and, under her guidance, visited the lighthouse, climbed the tower and with the aid of powerful binoculars surveyed the realm of sea and islands and coastline. "I love the lighting-up time," said Mrs. Richardson. "Off there, twelve miles to the west, is Seal Island's rather irregular beam. Eight miles south-east is Cape Sable's bright white flash; not so far away and due east glows West Head's warm red; while nearest us, only two miles away, is the twinkling little harbour light of Emerald Isle. On fine evenings these add to the beauty of the sea but on stormy nights when the lighthouse rocks and the metal lantern vibrates like a taut wire under the rough fingers of the wind, they are like friendly smiles of comrades."

We heard many stories of wrecks that occurred in fog and foul weather, of salvage taken by shore people. One ship had a cargo of cheese and that winter every home along the South Shore had two or three boxes of cheese in store. One cargo was frozen beef and one man had the walls of his barn and house hung with beef quarters. A neighbour passing called out: "I see ye got some o' the wrack meat, Joe. Be it good?"

Joe spat, shrugged, and said grudgingly. "Good? Ay-ah, I das' say it'd be good all right. If ye c'ud git enough of it."

One wreck carried thousands of boxes of oranges and lemons. Homes along the shore kept lemons in puncheons of water and had delicious pies and lemonade all summer. Children carried home all the oranges they could pile into baskets. Even the sheep feasted on the fruit.

"There were hundreds of sheep those days," said a fisher-man on shore when we mentioned the incident, "and man! you talk about eatin' oranges. But the lemons they didn't like. They'd git a lemon in their mouth and come down hard, then what a face! You should'a seen them screwin their jaws around to git rid of that lemon. But after a while they got to know an orange from a lemon by the colour. Man alive, you could see nothin' but sheep eatin' oranges."

The Richardsons often have lobster from storm-thrown traps that are heaved up on the shore, but wrecks are very few today and much of the sense of isolation has gone with the daily use of a telephone to Yarmouth. Many birds live on the island and Mrs. Richardson knows them all, and is famed as a bird watcher. Her husband took us back to Shag Harbour and on we went and reached Barrington Passage where a combined rock, vegetable and flower garden demanded a visit. We were invited in for closer inspection by Mrs. Warren J. Nickerson, wife of the local customs officer, and found that she was a most remarkable woman. Her husband had wheeled in rocks and she had built a stone wall that was at least one hundred feet in length and very eye-catching. She calls her home "Beacon Knoll" and it has a fine view overlooking Barrington Bay. When the house was built she did her own interior decorating and mixed her own paint. She braided the rugs for her home and, to be sure she always has flowers, maintains a small greenhouse and keeps approximately thirty plants blooming in the house. She took a year's instruction in painting in Philadelphia and now has a large number of paintings which are much admired.

A number of men and boys were crossing the highway carrying long-handled nets so we stopped to see what was going on and found they were "dipping" fish from pools in the Barrington River a stone's throw from the road. These fish are called "gaspereaux" in the Annapolis Valley but in Barrington they become "kiacks." In watching the dipping process we became aware of an ancient structure nearby and discovered we were looking at the last mill of its kind in all of Canada, a woollen mill operated by water power. In the long ago it was kept busy carding, spinning and twisting wool into yarn for clicking needles that would produce socks and sweaters and scarves and mittens and gloves. But now such articles are mainly purchased at stores and the market is almost gone. A side channel diverted from the river keeps the horizontal wheel turning twelve months of the year and provides power for the machines. Most of the flocks that supply wool for the mill are on islands off the coastline and this wool is particularly good for the one big market left. Sheep raised on the islands produce wool that is unusually good for fishermen's mittens. The white yarn is used pure and explains that which puzzles many landlubbers who wonder how fishermen can haul lines hour after hour in the freezing winter weather without their hands becoming stiff with cold. These mittens of island-wool get a first wetting and it seems to insulate them as after that the heat of the hand keeps the mitten warm and the freezing water is unable to penetrate. We walked around the old mill, climbed to the top floor and saw fifty bags of wool all washed and waiting to go to the picker. Downstairs were two carding machines and running the length of one wall was a row of spindles where the wool is spun. On the ground floor it is twisted into various thicknesses. We asked Mr. Doane, the proprietor, why the island sheep produced the best wool and he said it was because the sheep eat a lot of kelp and seaweed on the islands, and that where there was no scrub bushes as protection from sea winds the sheep had the best wool of all. Only Mr. Doane and a helper were running the mill, and in the old days it gave steady employment to twenty men. On a board on the wall old orders were inscribed. They forbade talking or whistling while at work, and no one was to leave his job without permission from the foreman.

On we went and arrived at Shelburne. It was quiet and sleepy along the main street while we ate and no one was in a hurry as we made our way along streets laid out back in 1784 when thousands of Loyalists from New York arrived by ship and proceeded to carve homes out of the sheer wilderness. Soon they had schools, two newspapers, churches and a society that had balls and banquets in style. The prosperity was short-lived as when the three years of government bounty ended people began to go away. Two Scots had arrived, however, who were not Loyalists. They had come to set up a trading business and soon they had acquired a building. An addition was built on and the upstairs was to be a storeroom so a strong derrick was placed over a large door on the second floor and casks of molasses could be hoisted up there, rum and other articles. The elder brother lived below and more or less ran the business. The junior had the upstairs. Two slaves were kept in the cellar kitchen as cooks, and iron bars on the windows made sure they would not get away. At night they slept high up in a small room with a great lock on the door. When the brothers entertained guests entered the big house and went up to the second floor. A powder room for gents was there. Each pushed his head in the opening of the small room and a lackey inside powdered his wig in good style for the occasion. Today the old house is as sturdy as when it was built, and has become a showplace and museum. The iron bars are still in the cellar windows and we saw the fireplace where the slaves did their roasting and baking. Upstairs we saw the door where the hogsheads were taken in, and great racks where the old militia of the town used to keep their muskets. For a time the house served as a school, and it was a post office for some years.

There are many items of great interest on display on the ground floor, and we saw one of the most elaborate baby carriages ever made. It was constructed for some aristocrat by a skilled workman, is very large and must have cost a fortune. We saw, too, the old "wreck chair" that was the pride of Gilbert Nickerson of Shag Harbour. All the legs, slats, seat, back, etc., are of pieces of wood from noted wrecks and we noticed names like *Win the War,* stranded on Bon

Portage in 1922; *North Star* wrecked on Green Rock in 1919; *Viking* foundered in Lobster Bay in 1917; *Aberdeen* lost on Limb Ledge in 1923; *Express* stranded on Bon Portage in 1898; *City of Monticello* foundered off Yarmouth in 1900; *Harland* wrecked on Black Point in 1905; *Castilian* wrecked on Gannet Dry Ledge in 1899. There are a great many other pieces in the chair and all are from some wreck that was headline news in the past.

We wandered along the little streets running to the harbour edge, looking to see how many of the original "town wells" remained. They were dug in the streets so as to be easily reached by all in the area but only two of these old veterans survive. At an old house a broad bench was placed in the shade and there sat a man who looked very old and wrinkled. We said it was a nice day and he retorted that was nothing unusual in Shelburne. So we asked how long he had been in the town.

"Around eighty-six years," he said, "and my old father was older'n that afore he died. He could remember away back when his folks had a queer hate for the Indians, especially the squaws. They smelled of wigwam smoke and grease they put on scabs and cuts, and they were always beggin'. But I liked 'em, the Indians, and used to hang around their camp in the spring and they'd give me baskets they made. And don't forget them Micmacs knew more cures than the doctors we've got today. They gathered all sorts of wild roots and pounded them up in mixtures that would cure boils and the like almost overnight. One spring I went to their camp and they had such a mess of trout that after they'd eat all they could hold they took a tubful to the nearest neighbours. There was all kinds of game in the woods then, lots of moose and bear. I used to see moose reg'lar when I visited an uncle two miles out of town but the things that scared me most was the foolish face and the poppin' eyes of them little

screech owls. They were all over the place then and scared
the livin' daylights out of me.

"What say? Are we a hardy people like them oldtimers?
Not by a jugful. They didn't have to have half the heat we
need in a house today, and they could walk ten or fifteen
miles like it was nothin'. That reminds me there was a piece
in our paper this week about Mary Adams out at Port La
Tour. She had six children and she's sixty-five and drew the
unemployment insurance for fishermen's benefits last winter.
Does she fish? Man, she runs a boat and operated fifty lobster
pots, and she won't weigh over one hundred pounds soakin'
wet. She's worked in the herrin' factory. She mows her hay
by hand, she splits her own firewood, and she gathers peat-
moss. This last spring she bucksawed and split four cords of
wood, and the paper said one chore she did was backin' a good
size stove from some camp in the woods two miles to her
home. Ain't too many men want to tackle a job like that.
She's walked thirteen miles a day round trip to the bush and
cut down and got home and sawed and split twenty-one cords
of wood in one spring. She built a stone wall around her
place, she digs and plants her own garden, she's snared
hundreds of rabbits and taken them on her bicycle to town
to sell. No, sir, folks ain't like they used to be but Mary
Adams is one of the old kind."

It seemed wise to get a paper and read the story ourselves,
which we did, and all he had said was true. Moreover, at
the little bookshop we heard of an old sailmaker, the last
craftsman of his kind on the shore. His name is d'Entremont
and he now does odd jobs like bits of sail for yachts, sea
anchors and awnings. He has tools like splicing fids, palms
and needles used by the masters of his trade, and books like
*A Ready Reckoner for Sailmakers and Sea Captains.* He
learned his trade in his father's loft in West Pubnico, and his
father learned the trade in turn from the grandfather. There
**are only two other "lofts" in the Maritimes, one at Lunenburg**

and another at Saint John. We looked in briefly but a hot
discussion was under way as five men sat around the loft
where the smell of rope and canvas dominated.

A man who had listened to some of our questions advised
we make a call on Otis D. Orchard. We found him snug
in his small garden, a veteran of nearly half a century spent
in lighthouses. He had served twelve years at the Gull Rock
Light before taking over at Cape Roseway, he said, and Gull
Rock was the worst spot on the coast. "We had four dories
and a power-boat for fishing," he said. "We pulled them up
on a landing of posts and timbers leading to a shed at the
rear of the lighthouse tower. I was green at first and thought
it not so bad as talked about but that year there come a wild
night when the sea went up like boiling water and waves
twenty feet high smashed right over the island. The boats
vanished and the landing was smashed to splinters. By
morning the sea had swept the rock bare of everything but
our tower and I thought sure it was going. No, I didn't quit.
Work was scarce them days and after a time you get used to
everything. You go out fishing and the wind kicks up and
you have a near go of it, escape drowning by the skin of your
teeth. You shiver and sweat and get back to the island, but
the next morning is quiet and you put out again and forget
all about your scare. I suppose I was near death twenty times
around Gull Rock but I learned to let each day take care of
itself. I saw a fishing schooner pile up on the rocks one
night and in a few hours there was nothing but a few smashed
timbers yet we managed to save every man. I was mighty
glad to leave the Rock and get to Cape Roseway for it seemed
like a village to me. Seven families lived there then and there
was always fishing boats and fish buyers around. Worst was,
the landing and post office are the other end of the island,
making it two miles to go. We had to use oxen to get in our
winter supplies. Now the families have left and it's a lonesome place with just birds and deer and rabbits and squirrels

for company. Does swim from the mainland to have their fawns and get real tame. We had humming birds at our flowers as if we lived on shore, and pheasants by the pair. The worst nuisance is herring gulls. They get so tame we have to kick them from our path or they'll go in the house with us. But I hated most the number of birds that killed themselves against the light. One night they hit the glass steady and in the morning I picked up over six hundred small birds with greenish backs and yellow breasts, and there were plenty others I didn't get. Coot and ducks get killed regularly, both black ducks and eider. Once a pair of loons were dead under the light in the morning. No, I don't mind that I spent my life lonesome. Me and the missus were healthy, and I get a small pension. It could be much worse."

The next stop was at Sable River and we talked with a lumberman who was past eighty. He told us of the many mills along the streams when he was young, and all of them were powered by water. Then he showed us where a mill was still operating on the Tom Tigney River no more than two hundred yards from the highway. Tourists would love to get colour pictures of it if they knew it were there.

"Away back forty years ago," said the veteran, "an American company come here to cut lumber. They built their own narrow gauge railway seventeen miles into the woods with camps on each side and their mills sawed the logs up into boxwood. The company shipped it to the States to a shoe manufacturer who used it for packing cases. They made good money on the railway, too. The rails cost eighteen dollars a ton when they laid them, and when they quit operations they sold them at seventy-eight dollars a ton. Wood used to be piled in stacks fourteen feet high for eight miles along the track. No, nothing unusual ever happened up here, though they had a hotel back then, and while the stage coach was operating they did fine business. Best story I know was about the time that Bill Dunlop ran a hotel at Sable River.

Those days travellers went mostly by horseback and one night a chap came in and said he had rode from Liverpool.

" 'That so!' says Bill. 'How'd you get across the river?'

" 'Why across the bridge, of course. How else could I come?'

" 'I'll show you in the morning,' says Bill.

"He took the fellow there and showed him they were replanking the bridge and the workmen had taken off every plank the afternoon before as travel was very light. They hadn't bothered to put a lantern as a warning, either, and that chap's horse had walked over on a stringer. The shoe marks were there in the timber, and the man so scared he could hardly talk."

We were leaving when our informant suddenly grabbed us. "Did you ever hear about Sammy Small who lived on ten or 'leven miles from here, and advertised for a wife?"

No, we hadn't heard the story, we said. "Well, Sammy, he's a hard worker and in the log woods a lot but he pure hated coming out a Sat'day night and having to do his own washin' then, and get his own grub. So he fixed up a sign and nailed it to a hemlock tree near his house. It read: 'Sam Small is willing to wed a working woman his own age. Any time. Just send word.' Well, not long after word come from Lockeport that a woman there was willing, and Sat'day night Sam took up there first thing he got out of the woods. He was told that Bella Cowby was her name and had to ask a lot afore he found her. She was only on a visit from Boston but she'd heard of the chance. When Sam arrived she was dolled up to taste with gold ear bobs and a yellow scarf caught over her shoulder. But she was fat. Glory, she was. And she had sprouted quite a fair moustache. She waddled like a duck when she walked, her slippers slap-slapping, and though she'd spread enough perfume to sick a horse, Sam said her odour was strongest. She said she was handy with a needle and recited about a dozen stitches she could do but Sam backed out the way he come in, saying' 'No thanks, ma'am.' He hustled back home and put some more writin' on the sign. '140 pounds or under.' Next week an old coot from inland saw the sign, figgered it out, and fetched his bony cross-eyed daughter that Sat'day. 'You say one forty or under,' he said to Sam. 'On account her eyes I'll take one-thirty, but half has got to be cash.'"

At one of the stores we stopped to make some further inquiries and were told of a fine place to have lunch.

Next we knew we were at Lockeport, and still thinking of the fat hopeful. The town is sprawled along white sand beaches and not too tidy but we found the people kindly and eager to talk. We heard tales of American privateers coming to rob the place and the ladies throwing red shawls and red petticoats over their shoulders and parading shoulder to shoulder with brooms as their muskets. From out at sea they looked like Johnny redcoats and the Americans cleared off. Then a man told us we should go and see the Firth Museum. Questioning, we found the way to a yard and were taken up a ramp into an old wooden building that is filled with wonders. Away back, Louis Bunham was one of the best block-makers on the South Shore and he began getting every type and pattern of ships-block ever made. That started a collecting bug and when he died his son-in-law carried on until his death. The efforts of the two men is stored in the building we invaded and if properly catalogued and displayed would make an excellent marine museum. There are photos of celebrities, a chest containing a quarter century of the *Eastern Chronicle* in excellent condition, a brass sun dial, cavalry swords, muskets, pepper-box pistols, muzzle-loading Colts, greased cartridges from the Indian mutiny, brass candlesticks and snuffers, a shillalegh, a spoon horn from Iceland, A Norway pipe, an Italian hair iron, a boarding pike, sea shells, a high-wheeled bicycle and so many other things we could not list them. We sincerely hope the good people of

Lockeport will soon get this museum moved into a fireproof building and there show the items to advantage.

They call Lockeport Station "Allendale" and there we saw the sign "Ragged Islands Inn" and entered the yard, parked and wandered into an old house with a small but very attractive dining-room. Miss Dorothea C. Arnold operates the place and finds it fun after busy years in New York. The living-room invites you to take the weight off your feet and settle down with good reading, as there are many books and many objects of interest Best of all, are the meals. We had lunch and it was far and away better than anything we had got in grand hotels, served hot and fresh. The waitress was no gum-chewing girl looking for tips but a neat person whose sole ambition was to make you satisfied, and we had a meal we talked about for days afterward. It is a pity that more folks do not find this little inn.

A sign by the road said "Port Mouton" and we remembered reading Nova Scotia history that said the place was named by De Monts in 1604 when a sheep they had on board jumped from the deck into the bay, apparently in an effort to get to shore. So the water became "Mutton Bay" and now is Port Mouton. It was very quiet along the main way and a man who had been doing some chore was placidly seated in a wheelbarrow he had been using, and having a smoke. We stopped and asked if anything of note had happened in the place.

"I'll say there has," he exclaimed. "About seventy years ago. I had an uncle who was out in a double ender fishing boat that day, handlining for cod. During the summer months the men along here used to fish cod close to shore. They used to split the fish, pack them in salt and dry them, then ship them south by schooner. Trade with the West Indies was good back in the old days. At the time I mention a Hunt's Point fisherman name of Frellick was also out fishing. He had a twenty-eight-foot boat and it was early in the morning when he noticed a ripple in the water about one hundred yards away. He thought it might be a tuna—horse mackerel they called them then—chasing a school of herring, but as he looked an awful creature reared into view and terrified him so he couldn't hardly move. It had a head bigger than a horse's and rigged about the same except it had no ears, and its neck shoved that head up more'n the length of his boat, so you can figure how much body there must have been under water. Frellick watched it swim away from his boat and after a time it went below the surface and he sure lost no time getting to shore. He said the thing was light tan in colour and that much of it seemed to be coiled just below the surface. Frellick was a good church man, Methodist, and everybody believed him when he told about the sea serpent. More than that, some people were in bathing at Mersey Point that same day and they saw the thing. It was quite a distance out at sea but it scared the daylights out of them and nobody went in bathing there again for twenty years. Yes, sir, this is one place on the Atlantic where we had a real sea serpent."

On we went to Liverpool, home of the famous Captain Godfrey who was such an amazing sea fighter and whose exploits earned him an invitation to accept a commission in the British Navy. We were directed to old Fort Point, once site of an Indian village, where De Monts and Champlain landed on May 12, 1604, our guide said, and where a cairn bears a plaque with the following inscription:

In memory of the privateersmen of Liverpool Bay, who maintained and defended their trade with the West Indies, and waged successful war upon the enemies of Great Britain in ships fitted and armed at their own expense. Foremost among them were: Alexander Godfrey of the brig *Rover*, who routed a Spanish squadron off the Spanish main and captured its flagship, September, 1800; and Joseph Barss, Jr., of the schooner *Liverpool Packet* who, in nine months of the War of 1812, captured more than 100 American vessels on the coast of New England. They upheld the best tradition of the **British Navy.**

From there we went to visit the Simeon Perkins' house on the main street, a notable structure constructed in the simple New England style of the Cape Cod pioneers. The timber came from sawmills of the district and the plaster was brought from Windsor on the Avon River by one of Perkins' ships. The New Englanders who settled Liverpool back in 1759 were direct descendants of the Pilgrim Fathers and the Perkins house dates back to 1766. Perkins built ships and shipped lumber to the West Indies. He had a hand in starting a leather factory, was a leading merchant, a farmer, ran a sawmill, and became a magistrate. At the time of a smallpox epidemic Perkins was able to get a vaccine from Boston and halt the spread of the disease. He kept a diary faithfully, now one of the most prized records in Nova Scotia, and records his dealing with privateers from Salem, Mass., who wanted to storm the small fort but were talked out of it by Perkins through an exchange of prisoners, a barrel of biscuits, and rum. Bloodshed was thus prevented. The old house is extremely interesting, with the upstairs timbers hewn on three sides and the rough bark still on the fourth side. The ceilings are low and the closets are about five feet high, being close to the eaves. The oldtime furnishings make this an extremely interesting museum. Visitors who view the copy of the diary will remember many of the items that so quaintly picture for us the thought and doings of that day. During the smallpox scare he made this entry: "My wife, Lucy, Eliza, Mary, Simeon and Charlotte, are inoculated by Mr. John Kirk, all in the left hand between the thumb and forefinger, not in the loose skin but in the hand, by making a small incision and laying an infected thread into it about three-eighths of an inch in length. He then put a small square rag doubled, and over that a bandage to keep it in place. My wife stood the operation very well. Some of the children were faint."

The curator was an interesting fellow and told us about an old Customs Book owned by a business man in Liverpool carrying entries from 1821 to 1840, showing what items were brought into the port, and proving that those early settlers were a thirsty lot. In 1821 alone 64,306 gallons of rum were landed in the port as well as 39,723 gallons of West Indies molasses. Brown sugar, cotton and coffee were other favourite items. He told us about an eighty-five-year-old veteran of the sea in the town who makes ships models in half size and mounts them against the back of a shadow-box frame; and about Dexter's Tavern, built in 1763, still in use, used as a court house, as auction hall, and banquet room in the good old days.

# 4 | Houseful of Clocks, Bathroom Trapdoor, Buried Treasure, and Bear's Den

BROOKLYN IS A SMALL VILLAGE a short run from Liverpool, home of the great Mersey Paper Company and when we stopped by a small store and asked if there were anything of unusual interest in the place a man pointed to a house a few yards from where we parked. "Just knock at the door," he said. "You'll see."

We had some doubts about such a procedure but took the chance and a smiling man invited us in at once. "I guess you've come to see my clocks," he said.

His clocks were everywhere we looked. His name is Henry Maillete and he has two rooms filled with timepieces of every description. Moreover he has an amazing knowledge of them, has put each and every one into proper working order, and sometimes on summer days will have the whole lot going at once. It takes him three-quarters of an hour to wind them all so he has to be careful to set them at the right hour. His average clock is one hundred and twenty years old. He has a sun dial by the door, then an hour glass, and the final item is a small clock that will run four years on one dry cell battery. It all began some years ago when he bought a clock at an auction and could not find a jeweller who could make it go.

"So I got some tools and went at it myself," he said, "and I've been at it ever since, spending all my spare time and money for clocks."

The old clocks were made by firms with only a handful of employees and few if any spare parts were manufactured, so Henry has had to create fitting wheels, cogs, gears and springs as the demand arises. The older clocks work by weights suspended by catgut or twine wound on an axle, but he has clocks with lever spring movements. A small spring lies horizontally at the bottom of the case. When the clock is wound by key, two pieces of gut connected at either end of the lever spring pull into a bow. This tension keeps the clock going exactly thirty days. All his clocks are American made, mostly in Connecticut. He has them of every style and description, and now is hankering to get hands on European curios. No doubt when next we visit him Italian and French clocks will be chiming in his home. And remember one thing above all in regard to this remarkable fellow. He only has one arm!

It is a pretty drive from Brooklyn to Bridgewater if you like the woods and a winding road.

When we came to the bridge at Mill Village we saw a sign indicating that the Medway Inn was near at hand. Curiosity turned us on the dirt road along the river and in minutes we arrived at a most unusual setting, and fell in love with a fine old house built back in 1784. Some twenty years before that a 1200-acre grant was given to Samuel Mack who came from Connecticut to operate a lumbering business and to instal the first sawmill on the river. His chief clerk and right hand man was an Irishman—Patrick Doran. When Mack died Doran married the widow and prospered as the new owner, built the fine home that was then one of the show places of the County. It took four years to finish the house as Doran wanted it, and skilled craftsmen brought from Connecticut spent two years hand carving the panelling. The Medway River flows nearby and there is a small lily pond on the grounds. The river was used to float timber downstream to Port Medway and as there were few roads at the beginning one family moved to a new home by raft, piling on all their possessions and placing the children in a puncheon for safety's sake.

Bernard Woollen of Toronto now owns the place and its twelve acres of land. He is clearing away invading bushes and has found flagged paths. He says he bought the old house because it reminded him so much of some fine old pubs in England. There are twelve rooms and in one is an old china cabinet that is finely carved. Off the hall is a small room used for storage but at some time it must have been the "counting room" as the walls are lined with cupboards and drawers. The wall panels in the living-room are all different in size. The doors were made with wooden pegs and still swing on hand-wrought hinges and have large brass locks. The basement walls are of hand-cut stone four feet thick. While renovating the new owner discovered a stairway leading from a hallway cupboard to the bathroom above, the bathroom entrance being a trap door. He plans to convert the kitchen into a dining-room and make use of the ten-foot-wide Dutch oven fireplace. The food they serve is out of this world and visitors who discover the Inn go back again and again. The Inn was the happiest find we made in Nova Scotia.

Jays flitted across the open spaces as we left Mill Village and a lumbering porcupine complained irritably when we braked to a halt ten feet from it to save our tires. At last we rolled up hill into Bridgewater and down past a hospital and a steep hill put us on main street at the bottom. If one could not stop he would land right in a garage and we remarked as much to the lad who filled our tank with gas.

"Away back," said he, "when old Fords were the main cars around here, a giant of a fellow down La Have way was coming to town from Liverpool and just at the top of the hill something gave and his engine sagged down and hit the road. He was going very slow as his power had died and when he saw what had happened he jacked up the front and released the engine entirely, worked it free and put it in the trunk. Then he got in the car, released the brake and rolled down and into this garage. When a chap came out he shook his head.

" 'There's somethin' wrong with this here car,' he said. 'For the last ten miles or so she ain't got no power like she ought. See what you can do while I'm at the store.'

"The mechanic had seen the big man drive in. He raised the car hood—and gaped! He walked around in a circle and rubbed his eyes, came back gingerly and peered again. Then he rushed into the garage and told what he had seen. The others wouldn't believe him, and rushed to have a look. Finally the boss noticed the trunk cover was raised and located the missing motor. We still laugh about it."

Bridgewater is a very pretty town and its main street is parallel with the river. So the stores are one one side and you can park along the other. We were soon told that we should visit the museum and climb twenty-four steps they call a "Jacob's Ladder" to locate an old building in which the relics are stored. There is not enough space and it is a pity as there is much to see. About 1860 a young lawyer in the town, Mather Byles DesBrisay, started collecting anything of a curious or historical nature. He had made quite a beginning when fire destroyed the boarding house and all its contents. Not discouraged in the least, Mr. DesBrisay commenced collecting again and as County Court Judge, Member of the Provincial Legislature, and Historian of Lunenburg County, he kept up the good work. After his death Mrs. DesBrisay sold some items to the Halifax Museum but the bulk of the collection was retained and at her death became the property of the Town of Bridgewater. It had to be stored and there was no money with which to provide a proper building so the Women's Institute took the Museum under its care. There are countless items that were made by Micmac Indians, implements of wood, bark, earthenware and stone, quill work, costumes, etc. Early homemade farming implements show the skill and ingenuity of the first settlers, and half-blocks and models of schooners tell that the majority of the pioneers could build and sail ships to the West Indies. Old weapons speak of the War of 1812. A fire would wipe out all this treasure of the past gathered over a stretch of seventy years and we hoped that soon the town would make a drive for funds with which to establish a proper museum.

The highway from Bridgewater to Lunenburg is mainly along the water and there are some unusually fine views. The main street in Lunenburg is one way and it is a picturesque old town on top of a hill. There used to be a blockhouse on it and we drove up there and could see over both a front and back harbour. Parked down on the one way main street, we had conversation with several persons but an elderly gentleman wearing a straw hat popular twenty years ago was most eager to help us. He said if we wanted a picture of yoked oxen to go two blocks and we would find a man who kept a pair and tourists photographed them almost every day of the summer. He told us about the champion schooner, *Bluenose,* built in Lunenburg for fishing on the Grand Banks, that defeated the best the Americans could produce and was never out-sailed. Then talked about the champion dory mates of Lunenburg County who were world champions, having defeated the best from Massachusetts in match races. Then he talked about the trouble the first settlers had with Indians, the blockhouses built to protect them, and pointed out the location of the first cemetery that was once surrounded by willow trees.

"They couldn't afford tombstones like they have today," he said sadly, "so they either put up wooden slabs painted against the weather, or carried up smooth slate rock and carved names and dates on it. But we can't make out any of the inscriptions today though one stone shows the date plainly— 1761. Hot sun and winter storms erase the letters but when I was a boy I could decipher quite a few that were in German, as the first settlers came from Hanover. 'Geboren' is their word for born, and I made it out easily."

The old man shook his head.

"Times today are so different," he sighed. "There was much more fun and interest when I was young. If you go over to the Golf Course you can see the spot that was a dandy picnic place in the old days. Colonel Kaulback made a private park there as he had the money and the inclination. Fifty labourers from Cornwall were hired and a stone retaining wall was built around the entire shore line below the hill. The job took three years as the men only worked part time. Large granite slabs were hauled there to be used as seats, and are still there. They were quarried at Cornwall and hauled in during the winter when roads were frozen. They say it used to take six yoke of oxen to haul one of the bigger stones. When the old blockhouse at Battery Point was taken down the cannon came to Lunenburg and two were buried muzzle up at the entrance to the park. Soon after people started calling it 'Cannon Park' and that's how it's known today. Two more cannon were hauled to the top of the hill and you can see them when you drive over. Paths were made that led around the hill as far as the back shore and everybody went there on picnics. I used to think about them all winter. In 1900 a big whale was found floating off Rose Head and towed in. They extracted the oil from the carcass and the head and jaw bones were placed among trees on 'The Head' and hundreds went there to have a look at them."

We moved to a place where we could have a seat and sip a cool drink and our man never hurried or became tiresome in the least as he talked about the day the men from Massachusetts attacked the town and robbed everyone, about the Fisheries Exhibition they hold in Lunenburg every September, about the fine ships that have been built in Lunenburg shipyards, about Lunenburg having two of the finest homes in eastern Canada.

"Zwicker built a dandy," he said. "Gossip says it cost a hundred thousand. Overnight guests drive around the back of the hill and park their cars right outside their bedrooms. Then Morrow decided to go one better, and he did. We're used to millionaires here, and I've heard that only London, Ontario, has more wealth per capita in all Canada."

Then he talked about Earl Bailey, A Lunenburg artist cut down by polio when he was only three years old and doomed to a life in a wheel chair. He holds the brush in his teeth and every summer a large number of visitors find his studio. His work is of the highest order, brightly coloured Nova Scotian seascapes and marines that are cheerful and show the inate love for his native Nova Scotia that this extraordinary artist has.

An oldster, bowed as though he had carried a heavy yoke for years, paused beside us as we came from the tearoom and our friend immediately got him to talking.

"This man is almost ninety," he said, "and he was a farmer, went to sea, fished, has done about everything from cobbling to blacksmith work."

"I learned cobbling from father," said the oldster, "and never wore store shoes till I was thirty. We used to tan cowhide and it was tough. I was only fourteen when I made a set of sleds one winter when father was not well. He showed me how and all I had was an axe, a draw knife and auger, a handsaw, square and plane. I made a harrow, too, and flails with maple handles, a bit of green beech for a billet, and an eelskin to hold them together. I sold one to my uncle for twenty and one half cents. Don't look like that. We had lots of half cents back in those days. Everything was better than today. Now it's all sham."

He grumbled his way along the street from us and our friend grinned wryly.

"I tried to get him to watch television," he said, "but it was no use. He didn't want to watch anything that was what he called 'pretend'."

The afternoon had simply slipped away and so we drove down to the Bluenose Lodge for dinner. In the lobby we saw the steering wheel of the champion schooner, *Bluenose,* and three cups won in schooner racing. The dining-room is glassed around, light and airy. Everything is immaculate and the food the finest we had eaten in Nova Scotia. We talked with the propietor, Fred Glover, a real gentleman who keeps a close watch on everything and makes sure every guest is satisfied. The rolls were especially good and when we remarked about them he told us his wife made the rolls and pastry. There are plenty of poor eating places in Nova Scotia but you will go far across Canada to find a Lodge or Inn serving food as satisfying as Bluenose Lodge in Lunenburg.

"Don't leave this area without seeing the Ovens," said our friend.

"Ovens!" we repeated. "Bake ovens?"

"Hardly. Drive out a mile or so on Highway 3 and you'll see big signs pointing the way to Riverport. Follow them and soon you'll see signs leading to The Ovens. Back in 1861 some men working around the ovens, great holes in the rock where the tide roars in, found gold, and a regular rush started to take over the caverns or the land back of them. Eighty-two shore claims were worked and some lots sold as high as $4,800 each. From June to December they recovered $120,000 in gold without the aid of machinery, had a town there with shops, taverns and all. Then the gold petered out. Now the place is a park and you can walk down into an old tunnel where they dug, see all sorts of workings, and stand on a platform right over a huge cavern, so big that a local story has it an Indian paddled into it with his canoe, kept going and ten hours later emerged over on the Fundy shore. Sluice boxes, gold cradles, all sorts of relics are in the park museum, and the most amazing thing is that some go down and actually pan a few grains of gold. But this year they have the park fixed up in real style, with cabins, and places for trailers, camp grounds, even places to hold Sunday service. Don't miss it."

The evening was delightful so we drove along the water's edge to Mahone Bay, a winding road with constantly changing views of bay and ocean. High up on the hillside before we reached the town we saw a large old house, and there were cottages for overnight that looked most attractive. We drove up for we wanted to be away from the road and to have a fine view. They were called Lockie's Cottages and we discovered that the big house had been built away back when the first settlers arrived, that the cottages had been first built over on the famous Oak Island, then had been fetched over to the mainland. They held a spell over us after we knew they had been so near a huge fortune, and they were very clean and comfortable. After arranging for our night's lodging we drove to a place we saw open, "The Teazer," a shop that is a visitor's delight, filled with all sorts of handicraft, everything from woven, knitted and hooked goods to wrought iron, carved wood and birchbark. There is a marine atmosphere to the shop, and a back room filled with the unusual. No matter what you may be looking for to take home as something different, you'll find it there. We learned that the name of the place came from the fact that during the War of 1812-1814 an American privateer, the *Young Teazer*, was blown up by an English deserter as the vessel entered Mahone Bay. The deserter saw that the ship was going to be captured, and knowing he would be hanged if taken, threw a blazing torch into the powder magazine. The date was June 27, 1813, and one of the citizens of the town said many had seen the blazing vessel on that date, drifting in toward the shore. It is their biggest ghost story on the South Shore.

The same man who told us this story spoke to someone going past and asked if "Fishy Jim" was in town. We commented on the name and the man smiled.

"Jim's a hustling chap around here who comes from Lunenburg. He had quite a time getting started in his trucking business as he simply had to have a loan from the bank. Friends told him it added to your prestige if you rented a safety deposit box in the bank, as the manager would be impressed. Jim had nothing to deposit but he went in and rented a box, then applied for a loan. The manager turned him down cold. So Jim came along here and tried another bank. He got his loan without trouble, went home and got a ten-pound cod, wrapped it in brown paper and put it in the safety deposit box. It was July and after a time there were queer odours in the bank. Customers mentioned it but it was after a holiday weekend before the source was traced. When they opened Jim's deposit box all hands fled and two girls fainted. They had to close the bank all day and it was a month before the odour was entirely gone. Jim had gone to Cape Breton on a trucking job for the rest of the year and never answered a letter they wrote him. Since then, around here, some of his friends call him 'Fishy Jim'."

We asked if there were many of the old iron men from the days of wooden ships, and our informant nodded.

"I know one out at Oakland, named Langille, who's had his neck broken twice and though he was laid up five or six weeks each time he never bothered to see a doctor. He's around eighty now but only seven years ago he was tending his cattle when one ox slipped into a shallow water hole. The animal got excited and flung its head around unexpectedly, caught Charlie in the corner of the left eye and threw him about ten feet. He woke up an hour later, his face covered with blood, and was sure the ox horn had taken his eye out.

He got back to his house and they told him after there was a
hole big enough to put your thumb in, but he put a bandage
on it and it healed and the eye came all right. Two years
after a doctor examined his head and said there had been
a V-shaped fracture on top of the skull from the ox horn
which must have penetrated two inches. Charlie was only
nineteen the first time he broke his neck. The schooner he
was on was tied to the wharf and the crew was taking a
Labrador cod trap out of the hold. He jumped up on a gaff
to lend a hand when the halyard broke. He hit his head on
the hatch coaming and lay under a piece of canvas all night
on the deck. The next morning he started to work again
pain sent him home and he was two months in bed and
couldn't lift his head from the pillow, had to be fed every
mouthful. He vows his neck was broken. He was in his late
fifties when he fell to the floor in his barn and when he
became conscious his head flopped forward like on a swivel
and he had to use his hands to prop it up. Everything healed
after he was a month in bed but there's a lump on the back
of his neck where his shirts wear out first and he still feels
a grating once in a while. Charlie's one of the real old iron
men."

    We did not dispute the claim and were still thinking about
him next morning when we drove to Chester, another beauty
spot on the South Shore, a favourite with many American
visitors. Streets angle in several directions and each has a
variety of sea views. We got to talking with an elderly lady
who was working in her garden and were told they have a
Garden Club in Chester that really does things. "Right now
we're on the matter of making more of the old stone fences,"
she said. "There used to be many of them along the South
Shore and it is too bad that they've been pulled down and
carted away for cellars. Away back when this district was
first settled there were quite a few bounties to encourage the
people. They paid twenty shillings an acre to those who

cleared land and farmed it, two shillings a bushel bounty on grain, and at that time a man had to work all day to earn one shilling, and they sold firewood to New England vessels at two shillings per cord. Biggest bounty of all was for stone walls as they paid one pound, two shillings and sixpence per rod, and stone walls ran along most of our hills to cut down the slopes to road level. Where we have them today they are solid as the day they were built, and no cement was used. We're taking away the weeds and brush from them to show visitors what we have and it's a great pity that we haven't all the original fence that was built by such back-breaking labour. Personally, I think stone fences add much to a landscape."

She worked so energetically at her garden despite silver hairs among the gold that we felt she must be a direct descendant of those hardy old timers who handled rocks through sheer strength and hard labour, and we agreed heartily with her ideas.

"We're getting soft," she said. "Think of the work men could do without machinery back in the old days. If you want something to write about go along to Western Shore and take a boat over to Oak Island. Nearly all the world has read about the buried treasure there, and they've been digging for it since 1795. Whoever put it down dug a hole fifteen feet across and about 160 feet deep, and then drove water channels four feet square out from the bottom of the hole to the beach. Think of that, and them with only picks and shovels."

"How would they get air in the tunnels?" we asked.

"They drove air holes up to the surface about fifty yards apart," she replied. "And they covered the sea entrance with foreign seaweed held down with stones. When all was finished they put their iron chests and wooden chests in the hole and filled it in, leaving the timbers they'd used as props at every ten feet. What was funny, though, was that they used a lot of putty apparently, as about thirty or forty pounds of it was found on one floor when they dug down the first time."

"Why didn't whoever dug get the treasure?" we queried.

"Because they knew nothing about the water trap and when they were down about one hundred feet the water come in and drove them out. If them that buried it come back the first thing they would do would be to plug up the sea entrance. Then it would have been simple to take out the earth from the hole and lift up the chests. But they sunk one hole after another all over the place until nobody knows for sure which one was the original. And it was years before they discovered the water flooding was salt, and located the source. Then they found one of the air vents through a cow falling into it and instead of doing a proper blocking on the beach they dropped explosives down the air hole and that only made matters worse."

"You really believe there was a treasure down there?" we quizzed.

"I was ten years old," she said, "when they drilled right through two of the chests and brought up links of a gold chain and some bits of sheepskin that had letters on it. Had that crew kept working and used horse sense and blocked the water they would have had the treasure. But they spent all their money in digging more holes and couldn't keep the water out and after a time the whole cache shifted through water pressure and a dozen or so holes and tunnels down there. Now it will have to be located again. But I am sure that if somebody with enough money and brains comes along he'll unearth the treasure."

"Where's it from?" we asked gently.

"South America or Mexico, where else?" she flashed. "And either pirates or Spaniards put it down. Personally, I think it was Spaniards."

It was nice to dream about the treasure, as we motored on through Western Shore and along a winding road lined largely by bushes to Halifax. We saw the new paved road leading to Peggy's Cove but did not take it as our time was limited. Highway 3 enters Halifax by way of a Rotary at Armdale and traffic was heavy as we finally parked by the Public Gardens, dating back to 1872, when they comprised six acres, two for flowers, two for lily ponds and two just swamp. Twelve acres were added and the swamp drained, a bandstand erected to celebrate Queen Victoria's Golden Jubilee, and a fountain was put up ten years later during her Diamond Jubilee. The flowers and walks were beautiful and there were trees of all sorts from Europe, Asia and everywhere. Sailors and soldiers were strolling about and almost every seat was taken. It seemed amazing that such a delightful spot could be there in the very heart of the city.

One of the gardeners told us Halifax was more than 200 years old, was named in honour of the Earl of Halifax, and the name means "holy hair." It was given the English city because the head of a murdered girl was suspended by its hair from a tree in one of the streets. He said we should go up on Citadel Hill which is being made a famous sight-seeing spot, so up we went by a new smooth road and entered a narrow passage leading into Fort George. There was ample parking space and soon we were exploring the stronghold and its surroundings.

In the long ago it was a higher and steeper hill, densely wooded, with the harbour and its gulls on one side and a pine swamp on the other, and the Indians called the slope the "place of many pines." When Louisbourg had become a famous bastion of French might in North America, an expedition set forth from England to establish a stronghold on the Atlantic that would serve as a counterpoise to the French holding. Its leader gazed at the hill after he had entered Chebucto Harbour and selected it as a natural defence, and on the slopes below the hill he built the only fiat town on the continent and named it Halifax. That leader was the Honourable Edward Cornwallis. He had the trees cleared from the hill and erected there a rude palisade enclosing log quarters for the garrison. Sentries on duty watched British warships and transports assemble in the harbour for action against Louisbourg in 1758, and the next year saw General Wolfe sail from Halifax for his final adventure on the Plains of Abraham.

The American Revolution created a panic amongst Halifax citizens and there was feverish activity until a new system of trenches and battery positions had been constructed on the hill. But when hostilities ceased forgetfulness set in and the hill was in sorry shape when Prince Edward, the ambitious six-foot soldier who was never in favour with his father, George the Third, came to rule the military with an iron hand. He set every man available to work on the defences—sappers, soldiers and militia. His men cursed and groused as they toiled with spade and mattock under the hot sun, sweating their systems clean of West Indies rum, and lamenting the fate that had brought such a tyrant to command them. He took fifteen feet off the top of the hill and made a better site for a fort of timber banked with sod. Twenty cannon were placed on the new defences, and two flagstaffs were erected, one of which served in the chain of visual telegraph stations that extended to Annapolis Royal and around the Bay of Fundy to Fredericton. The Prince gave no one rest until he had such communications arranged, for on him depended the defence of the Atlantic Provinces. When the work was completed he named the stronghold Fort George in honour of his father, but this made small impression in London where those in power viewed with alarm the prodigal expenditures of the Prince. So he was called home and his final suggestion was that a town clock be erected, as he stressed punctuality.

The clock was erected duly and is there today keeping time. There were other constructions on the hill, and a final work went on for thirty years. Seventy-five different British garrisons of famous regiments have served time at Halifax

Citadel, and today the great walls are much as they used to be, with gun positions facing seaward. From the interior the visitor sees the entrances to three museums. The Maritime Museum has a striking figurehead by the entrance, and inside we saw models of German destroyers, submarines and other craft from the famous *Bluenose* to well-known liners. All the museums are in ancient casemates and such a situation is unique. The entrance to the Military Museum has a miniature model of old Halifax showing the early blockhouses, Government House, first streets, Grand Parade and Citadel Hill. There are displays of small arms, ancient arms, bayonets, pistols, muskets, gas masks, machine guns, uniforms, medals, badges, and the colours of three Nova Scotia units.

The Cavalier Block was built in 1830 as the higher part of the fort and was planned to house 322 men. The casemates are ideal for the Provincial Museum which has taken over the entire building. There is a Pioneer Room, an Indian Room, and a Handcraft Room. The visitor goes from display to display through arched stone passageways, and is intrigued by the surroundings.

We climbed a stair to the top of the defence wall, saw the moat deep below us and then gazed far out to sea over the harbour and George's Island and a dozen ships. There is a wonderful view of all the city, and of Dartmouth across the water, and of the Angus L. Macdonald Bridge, second longest in the British Empire. We were shown the spire of St. Paul's Church, oldest Anglican Church in Canada, the big Common where children play all summer long and where troops had quarters in World War One, the Dockyard, Fort Needham, a Memorial Park, Point Pleasant Park, old Province House, and a score of other attractions. There is no other view quite like it and some visitors were sitting on rugs they had spread as they took hours to drink in the details of all they could see.

It was quite a thrill to drive over the Angus L. Macdonald Bridge on our way up Highway 7. It is of the suspension type, has two traffic lanes, a sidewalk, and rests on solid rock, the foundation for the main piers being found at sixty-two feet below low water. Two hundred and twenty-five railway carloads of cement were used in the construction of the bridge and each of the main cables weighs 475 tons.

Dartmouth is almost as old as Halifax, and has a hundred tales of the beginning of the town including Indian attacks and whaling ships and Quakers. No one who simply drives through in a car will see much of note and it is far best to roam around on foot with a copy of *The Story of Dartmouth* in your hands. Dr. J. P. Martin, the author of this book, is one of the old-timers and has spent a life time uncovering unusual facts about the town. He tells about a pioneer industrialist of Dartmouth who established a chocolate and soap works and made three-quarters of a million by giving strict attention to detail. One of the buildings he occupied had been used as a prison for Frenchmen taken during the Napoleonic Wars. But the first big boom that reached Dartmouth came with the Nantucket Whaling Company from Massachusetts. The Company supplied many British firms with whale oil while it had existed in the colonies, but now that the colonies had become the United States the product would be charged a heavy duty in Britain. So the Company moved to Dartmouth to avoid that handicap and houses were built, wharves and a factory, and for a time there was prosperity. Then over went the whalers to Wales and the whale of a time had ended as far as Dartmouth was concerned. Many of the employees of the firm were Quakers and they had their own Quaker Meeting House, long since gone.

The whalers were gone but a Dartmouth man started making spring skates about 1863 and they were so appreciated that for years he kept improving his patents and customers sped over the ice on his invention in almost every northern country of Europe as well as across Canada. Final honour for the skate company was a special appointment by King

Alphonse XII, making the firm skate makers for the royal house of Spain.

When we saw the name "Westphal" on a sign we knew that somewhere near there had been an humble home in which two lads were born bearing the name Westphal. Both became admirals in the British Navy, one served at Trafalgar aboard the *Victory*, both were wounded several times, both lived to be over ninety.

Highway 7 along Nova Scotia's eastern shore is one of the prettiest drives in eastern Canada. The first few miles are past lakes and villages and filling stations and canteens but presently there is the sea to the right with inlets and coves and bays and the road follows the shore line so closely that in places you can see across the neck of water the road you will travel once you have "turned the neck." We paused at a spot where a trail led off to a low point and a queer little pier at which a boat was tied. A man looking bent with hard work and hard years was there cleaning some fish and a flock of gulls was hovering about him, alighting on the shed, on the pier, on his boat. He looked up as we approached and seemed glad to have company.

"Fishin'? Yes, around fifty years now. I were too stupid to learn any other way to make a livin'. Yes, born right down there half a mile, where you see that housetop over the trees. Seven of us and some had to git out, so I was one of the first. Went to sea when I were thirteen, and never slept home again. Can't say I'm real sorry I didn't try to get work in town. Never could stand the noise of cars and trams and the stink of them breweries. No, sir, give me the sea for clear air and clean air. Sometimes I figger I'd sooner been a farmer, but it takes a lot of money to buy machinery and cattle, and I never had a lot of money. But we've had some comfort, and our flowers. My woman is careful with a dollar as the next one but she will spend it on bulbs and the like. Wish you were along earlier to see our lilacs. My woman says that's

what she remembers most of where she lived in the Valley—
the lilac bushes in the spring. And we've peonies by the
kitchen window, and bee balm for the humming birds. What,
you never heard of it? Well, my woman had, and we've
always had a bunch of it blooming and humming birds
around it."

He upturned a tub and sat on it and we used his bench
for our seat while he talked of his boyish delight in seeing
the West Indies, of a trip to Spain, and one to Australia, but
we could sense he had a deep content with life, more than
the old age pension he and his wife were drawing. For he
began talking in his own way about the enjoyment he had
from spending an afternoon once or twice a week in his
back lot where he grew potatoes and garden stuff. He liked
to stop his hoeing and just stand, listening to the small sounds
of bumblebees in clover, a song sparrow on a fence post,
robins scolding a cat, or a crow calling to its mates. He liked
to listen in the evening of a June day when the breeze begins
to freshen just before a rain. There are trees to shelter his
modest home and as the wind reaches them he imagines he
hears the sweet tones of violins and the haunting melody of
the cellos.

"We both enjoy music," he said wistfully, "my woman
and me, though she's a lot smarter'n I am. She does word
puzzles in the paper and sends them in, always hoping she'll
get a prize. Some day she will, too. There's smartness in all
her family. She's a brother who goes to church reg'lar, never
drinks or smokes. He's the quiet kind and where he lives
everybody knows he had no gun and don't go hunting. But
he has more pheasants and partridge to eat than any of them
that goes chasin' around the woods half the hunting season.
You see, he puts out feed in the winter, gets the birds used
to coming to a little clear back of his place. Then he gets
a brother-in-law in Halifax to buy him a bottle of rum. When
it's open season he makes pellets out of meal mixed with rum

and puts them in his little clearing. Gunners has chased the birds to his place, which he keeps posted, and they gobble the pellets. The rum makes their wings and legs useless and they flop around and he wrings their necks. It's as simple as that. No shooting at all. I 'low he and his wife eat more birds than any other pair in that part of Nova Scotia."

It was very pleasant out there on the tiny wharf but we had to leave him and go driving on, winding around the cove fronts, seeing lobster traps piled by other small piers, boats bobbing out at sea, gulls perched on old pilings or following some fishing boat to shore. We coasted down into a sheltered Ship Harbour where a dozen people stood around a car with a Massachusetts license, climbed a hill and rolled along to Tangier and Pope Harbour and Spry Harbour. Our next stop was at Sheet Harbour where we got gas and talked with an elderly woman who had white hair and a complexion you cannot buy in a drug store. She had lived seventy-odd years along the Eastern Shore, she said, and wouldn't want to live anywhere else.

" 'Course we folks here ain't different from any others," she smiled. "We have our failings and our fallings out, but we get along and nobody holds a grudge, well, hardly anybody."

"Are you thinking of some particular person now?" we asked.

"Two of them," she owned, her eyes sparkling. "They're old, and sharp with the tongue, married to cousins, and jealous. We had a young preacher come to us some time back and when he heard about them and their spats he was quite put out. So he got them both to his house for supper and talked nice to them and got them to make up and promise to be friends. Everything seemed all right and just as they were leaving one said to the other, 'Well, good night, Lizzie, maybe we've done what's right. Anyhow I wishes you all you wishes me.'

" 'Ah-hah!' snorted Lizzie. 'An' who's saying nasty things now!' "

Mosers River, Marie Joseph . . . We drove slowly, drinking in the beauty of sea and rock and weathered wharves, miles and miles of green-clad sprawling slope wedded to the sea and only divorced, much of the time, by the wide ribbon of pavement that delights every motorist. Then we saw a sign Harbour View Hotel—Belle Baker, and drove a short distance down a gravel road and reached a spot restful to the eyes and body. There are a few cottages on the slope above an old house that looks as if it has always belonged, and we sat in big chairs and breathed salty sea air until a voice said we could eat. What a meal! It's just like going home to the farm, no bigger than a big farm dining-room, with two or three tables, but the food was something we still remember, and Mrs. Otis Baker is a person you'll remember. Cheerful. kind, having that magic in a kitchen that makes pies and pastry taste so different from the ordinary, always serving the right relishes and pickles and sauces. Everyone knows about her meals, we learned, and often the only way you can get dinner there is to phone ahead and make a date. She seems to do as much work as two women and without any fuss or flurry, and when we asked her what she did during the winter she smiled.

"I close up the place and go to Boston," she said. "I take myself a real holiday down there."

We supposed she took in all the shows, visited the big stores.

"No," she smiled again. "I've spent many winters there. But I go because I have so many friends there, and we play bridge. I hope you folks do, and that some time we could have a hand."

It was easy to think that she would be a master if she held good cards for anyone who can plan meals and serve them like Belle Baker will succeed in anything that is tried.

Next there was Liscomb and then we saw four deer on our left standing side by side and gazing at our passing as calmly as barnyard cattle. There were a few miles through bush and next we knew we were crossing a bridge and rolling into Sherbrooke. The main thing they talk about in the little town is the St. Mary's River for it is one of the best salmon streams in Nova Scotia. We found the usual old timer after a brief scouting of the main street and he proudly showed us a newspaper clipping naming him as having shot the deer with the finest spread of antlers in 1953. He said he had shot bear and wild cats, and eleven moose in his day.

"Fact is," he related, leaned against our car, "that the best hunting I ever did was getting a bull moose back over towards Wine Harbour. Dozens had been chasing him for four-five years but he was cute and kept places where there's a lot of scrub bush and rocks and cradle hills and it's next to impossible to get close to a deer or moose. This old bull knew every inch of that ground same as I did, and he favoured a spot where he could stand in a hollow and see all four ways at once. I spotted him there along in the afternoon and all I could see was the top of his horns. For about an hour I studied the lay of the land but couldn't see any way to get to where I might have a shot at him, and no matter which way I come at him, he was where he could keep cradle hills and old stubs between us when he started to get away. Then suddenly I had an idea. From the way his horns rested I knew his head was faced toward a rock crest that was chock-full of loose earth and gravel and old sticks, all at his eye level. The more I studied the more I could see that if I could drill a bullet against that granite so it would carom like a billiard ball I could knock a load of dust and small grit into the bull's eyes. Ten to one he'd be so surprised and blinded he'd stagger out in sight shaking his head, and that's my chance. So I sighted a time, moved twenty yards or so more right, rested my rifle on a rock and took the shot.

It couldn't have been more perfect. There was a burst of
grit and sand like somebody'd blew with big bellows and
next that old bull was up in plain sight, hanging his head
against a bush to get so he could see. I dropped him with a
bullet just back of the shoulder, and had him. Yes, sir, that
was some shot, 'round a hundred forty yards, I'd say."

A garage man had stopped to listen and he winked at us,
and some other old cronies came along the street. We said
we had to be getting on but think that if ever anyone wants
good hunting or fishing stories they'll find the finest ever
being told around Sherbrooke.

The drive from there to Antigonish, forty miles, was like
a dream. We went first along the river for quite some distance
and though it was warm there were occasional anglers at
various pools. It was very still. Now and then we could hear
a bird call but there are no trains up in that area, and traffic
was comparatively light. When we left the river the road
wound up through hills and soon we were out again by
beautiful vistas bordering Lochaber lake. They cannot be
described adequately. You simply have to drive along Highway 7 on a day in late June when the day is warm and
cloudless and everything is still. The entire farther shore will
be mirrored exactly to every tree and blossom, and we counted
seven cars with foreign licenses stopped along the way as men
and women with colour cameras were taking shots from all
angles. We saw how enticing it was but experience has taught
us you can never capture the beauty on film. You'll get a
picture, but never reproduce anything as striking as what
you see.

Antigonish is a college town, and Scottish. We saw advertising about their annual Highland Games, heard bagpipes
somewhere beyond the campus. Cars were parked both sides
of the main streets and farmers and their wives filled the sidewalks. Off the main street a few yards, we saw an old-
fashioned hotel, the Royal George, and a man we spoke to

said it had been the best eating place for miles around as far back as he could remember. He went on talking when he saw we were more than willing to listen.

"We've got a paper with a name you won't find any other town in North America," he said. *"The Casket.* That's the way everything is here—different. The college is a small one, compared with others, but we put out hockey teams and football teams and basketball teams that take all the championships from the big ones. All around here was settled by the Scottish and there's some mighty good farming country, too. Used to be lots of bears, and the like. Stories? Sure there are. You get a book by Dr. Murphy, I think the title is *Wood, Hay and Straw,* or something like that, and you'll learn what it was like. Two big lads, Scots, were out hunting a lost heifer, and come across a bear's den. It was a dark hole down under an old windfall and one was anxious to see if there were any cubs as a man had offered five dollars for one. His brother, Donald, had an axe, so he asked Donald to stand by and not let the old mother bear in if she should be near. Donald didn't like the idea but down went his brother without waiting for agreement. He found two cubs in the hole but when he tried to get hold of them they set up a terrific squalling and the old bear came charging from the bush so suddenly Donald had the axe knocked from his hands and just had time to grab the old bear's tail before she was at his brother. He was one of those big-boned powerful men and dug his heels in and hung on. The opening was narrow and the bear could not turn around but the man, down with the cubs, shouted: 'Donald, what darked the light?'

" 'If'n her tail gives out,' panted Donald, 'you'll soon know what darked the light.'

"The bear's rage melted by the powerful tug at her rear, and she lost her grip on the dirt, was hauled backward, swung around and plunged back into the bush. The brother, sensing what had happened, scrambled from the hole, and Donald retrieved his axe. Away they went through the woods and thereafter no reference was made to the incident. That's the way those old fellows were."

We asked if the people on the sidewalks and in parked cars were an average crowd in town.

"No," he grinned. "There's a one-cent sale on at the drug store. The most of them don't need any pills or the like any more'n my cat, but they'll buy some, and scented soap, and toothpaste, and first-aids and the like. Antigonish county people will drive ten miles to save twenty cents, and burn twice that in gas. I guess they like seeing each other. They always turn out for a picnic or public meeting or the like."

Everyone we saw seemed to be laughing and talking as if having a good time and we remarked about it. "Sure," grinned our man. "You can't find friendlier people though some of the women can be sharp if need be. Last week I was just about here when two who looked middle-aged met. They glanced at each other, slowed, then one peered. 'Is it really you, Maggie?' she says. 'Gosh, I haven't seen you in donkeys' years, and you look so much older around the eyes I didn't know you.'

" 'Is that so,' bristled Maggie. 'Well, I wouldn't have knowed you either, if it hadn't been for that hat and coat.' "

We turned right leaving Antigonish and soared over rises and down into low places and were at South River in no time where there is a large overnight place and a large eating house. Many cars were parked at both places so we knew it was getting on but on we went throught Heatherton and Tracadie, the highway following along the railway, winding and winding, and dipping down now and then to distant sea views. Soon we were at Havre Boucher, quiet in the late afternoon, and pretty with neatly-painted houses. On we went to Auld's Cove and saw Cape Breton on our left darkly blue against the water of Canso Strait, only it was no longer a Strait. We slowed to arrive at the Canso Causeway and saw where thousands of tons of rock had been taken from old Porcupine, a high hill, to fill in the great water channel that so many said would never be conquered. They said the channel was too deep, the current too strong, but there we were driving over the wide road with the railway alongside and the Strait no more than inlets on either side.

On the Cape Breton side we found a fine information bureau in a fine setting with a memorial to Nova Scotia's best-loved premier, the late Angus L. Macdonald, alongside. Soon we were on Highway 19 and riding along a smooth paved road halfway up the hillside. To our left was the sea, blue and dark in the sunlight, and on our right the hills and we went on and on in varying scenery but always following the sea. The houses were more scattered and there was not so much paint in evidence but the air was clear and it was as if we had entered another country where times were a bit harder. Half an hour or more and we were in Port Hood with small stores and trucks and filling stations and young folk eating ice cream on a tearoom veranda, both boys and girls in slacks and both hatless and their hair tossed and unruly. After that we rode on to Mabou, seemingly a repetition of Port Hood, watching on our left the long dark outline of Port Hood Island, for we had been told at the Information Bureau that the stone for old Louisbourg had been quarried there, that once a causeway had reached the island and had been washed away, that the best sea bathing in Cape Breton was at Port Hood, that one of Canada's greatest men, the late Sidney Smith, long the President of Toronto University, was a native of Port Hood. After we left Mabou it was as if a spell were descended on us, the spell of seascape and great reaches of wild beauty, of sparsely settled country and a different atmosphere. There was a sense of driving northward, of getting away from the world beyond the Canso Causeway, and when we curved over many grades and entered the long main street of Inverness, now almost a ghost town, we understood why a Cape Bretoner, no matter where he may be or what success may be his, remains at heart a native of his home island.

There were many cars in Inverness but we found no old-timer with a tall tale or history. Instead, we were told about closed mines and hardship and lack of co-operation by authorities and hard times and some families with little to eat. But the youngsters we saw looked happy enough and hardy enough and we hoped that some day coal mining would start again.

## 5 | *Wool Pictures, Sugar and Spice, Gaelic College, and Old Canal*

MARGAREE FORKS, the Margaree River with tall elms and an artist busy painting as the shadows began, and anglers at a salmon pool, and then we were at Margaree Harbour and stopped by an unusual building and inspecting an unusual eating place and seeing an unusual picture for those carrying cameras. It is called the Paul Pix Store, the big building, and carries the largest stock of handcraft we had seen in our travels, besides all sorts of coloured prints from post cards to large pictures for framing. And on the walls were some superb specimens of portrait tapestry. Elizabeth LeFort, of Point Cross, Cape Breton, specializes in this art and she had made a twenty-five by thirty-one inch tapestry of Queen Elizabeth in which she had used fifty-eight shades of coloured yarn. She was hoping the tapestry could be presented to Her Majesty during the Queen's Canadian tour. A native of a small village on the Cabot Trail, Miss LeFort has studied the intricacies of portrait tapestry for over a quarter of a century and she received much publicity when President Eisenhower accepted a framed tapestry portrait of himself which was displayed for five weeks at the Canadian Travel Bureau in New York. Miss LeFort worked from a colour por-

128

trait of the President and completed the tapestry in less than a month though she had to use more than 160,000 stitches. Kenneth Hansford, the genial proprietor of the Paul Pix Shop, discovered Miss LeFort, one of nine children in a farmer's family, while he was driving around the island looking for hooked rugs of the quality of a generation ago. "I was astonished by the high quality of Miss LeFort's workmanship and by her skill at dyeing the wool—far beyond anything we had in Nova Scotia before," explained Mr. Hansford. "I began framing her wool pictures and showing them in my shop. They sold quite well and soon we were getting commissions for pictures."

We heard an amazing story of success. This Acadian woman, descendant of fugitive Acadians who reached the Cheticamp area as a hiding place during the Expulsion, has caught the attention of the world with her skill in dyeing and her beautiful creations. She has sold enough to be able to spend her winters in Arizona and there can observe life vastly different from existence in the snow and cold of north Cape Breton during January and February.

There is much to see at the Paul Pix establishment. A fishing village in miniature is laid out for the tourist with a camera, and a platform at right angle enables the photographer to take a picture that looks like the real thing. Just a few yards beyond an old veteran schooner of the north Atlantic trade has been hauled close ashore and fastened there. It is easy to go on board and where the dories swung and fish were landed has been converted into a very high-class restaurant where fish foods and steaks are served by waitresses in sailor rigs. Diners glance from the windows and the sea is there below them and a bit of imagination will set them swaying with the tide. Many go aboard to eat and it is something quite different.

From there we drove on to Cheticamp and the entire distance is through Acadian settlements where the French language is spoken and the people possess the outstanding traits and natural culture of their Norman ancestors. We passed through Belle Cote, meaning "beautiful hill," saw a chap with an old Ford pulled off the road and the wheels blocked with stone as if the car brakes were not good. He had an old-fashioned tire pump and was working away, bobbing his head and shoulders ceaselessly as he tried to inflate a flat tire. Nearby a trio of crows sat on a fence rail and watched operations curiously. The next place was Terre Noire, meaning "black ground," and after that came Friar's Head, so named because a great boulder bears some resemblance to the cowl of a monk. A man was driving two cows across the road so we slowed, then stopped as he had trouble with a red giver of milk that had unique white markings around the eyes.

"Thank you," said the man. "Some day somebody will hit that damn Marie as she always acts up when something is near."

"So her name's Marie!" we said.

"Sure. I name her on account she's just like my wife, looks like her, only I don't mention it in the house. But Marie, that's my wife, she always acts up when company comes, like this cow when there is a car. Why—because she wants everyone look at her, give her the attention. Sometimes she jus' wrap a rag around her finger and they will say 'What you do?' Then comes big story about having to fix chicken coop or like that, like I can't drive a nail, and they say what good worker she is, and why I don't do more 'bout the place. Me, I can't say nothin', though some day I'll pull that rag off and tell the truth."

The back door of the trim little house opened and out came a woman with something in a basket. She proceeded to the clothesline which ran near the road but never glanced our way. Then she pinned a towel on the line.

Our friend winked and spoke from the corner of his

mouth. "She can't bear not to know what you want. That's my Marie."

We looked and saw she was wearing exceptionally wide glasses with large white bows. They gave an appearance of white marks around her eyes, and it was easy to think of Marie, the cow.

"We'll drop by again some time," we said loudly, "and you can tell us more about her." Our friend looked startled, then shrugged and winked as we drove away for the Marie at the clothesline was frozen in position, holding a clothespin an inch or so from the line, and listening.

"St. Joseph Du Moine" read the next village sign, and then we were at Grand Etang, the first large community along the way, with many boats at anchor, many children playing by tiny wharves, and many odours from the old nets and traps that lay about. Because evening was setting in and the breeze had gone we were more conscious of the atmosphere of this place. At other fishing coves we were aware of a light wind strong with ozone and sunshine and salt and sea-lapped timbers, and in many such locations the smells are high for gutted cod drying on flakes of peeled poles do not affect the nostrils like roses. A lobster pot, too, has a smell of its own; so have clam flats when the tide is out. Old dories smell strong and rank, and huge iron pots with their mysterious brews for fishing nets emit their own reek and flavour.

A man going to his supper stopped and chatted with us about lobster fishing and lobster canning, and changing times. He said the village had been far more prosperous ten years ago. He talked about extensive natural cranberry bogs in the area, of excellent oyster beds that existed when he was younger, and said the parish we had come through was dedicated to St. Joseph, hence its name, that down at Friar's Head when there was a big storm the wind, if onshore, would throw salt spume on the roadway until it looked like a field of snow. He had started fishing when he was fifteen, had his own boat when he was twenty, went out in all kinds of weather, and could not swim.

The outline of a big church was etched against the sky as we drove on to Cheticamp, a long village sprawled either side of the main road making the main street nearly two miles long. Soon we were admiring the fine structure, St. Peter's Church, built of freestone quarried on Cheticamp Island. Cheticamp is a fishing town, and famous for hooked rugs. Over the years hundreds of American visitors have driven to Cheticamp to select hooked rugs for their homes and at one time they were able to purchase these at a ridiculous low figure. Now the people know more about the industry and charge accordingly, and sell just the same. Some years ago an order was received for a very large rug, and this became a community effort. Each day the women went to a building where there was room to put up frames large enough to start the masterpiece, and each woman had her place and worked away with a will. It took a long time to finish the project but the result was a rug large enough to be used in a hotel lobby, and every woman was paid her share of the proceeds.

We saw the "Foyer du Souvenir." The proprietor is Louis Philippe Chiasson, and he sells all sorts of items in wood and leather in addition to the famed rugs of his district.

We stopped one mile north of the main centre of Cheticamp at Laurie's Cabins, and were very glad we had made the choice. The cabin we had was clean and comfortable, the bed just as we wanted it, and we were off the highway on a hillside, away from traffic noises and with a fine view of the sea. We went to dinner in the dining-room and got the very finest in food, and quick service. No visitor to Cheticamp will make a mistake in stopping at Laurie's Cabins.

After dinner the moon had risen and we strolled down to the water front and out on a pier where swordfishing boats were anchored alongside. We noted the "pulpits" constructed

far forward for the use of the man who throws the spear
into the sworder, and judged he must be sure of hand and
arm and sure of footing as any unexpected lunge of the boat
could put him from the pulpit into the sea. Others came along
the pier and the beauty of the night and the tang in the air
made us want to just walk about and enjoy the scene. Then
a lanky man who looked henpecked came along and peered
at the boats as if something out of this world. He asked
questions eagerly of a man who was seemingly a member of
the swordfishing crew, ejaculated "Well, I declare," and came
away as if everything belonging to the pier were out of this
world.

"Come far?" we asked.

"Me? No, I didn't." He grinned. "I'm from the Valley,
here in Nova Scotia, but me and the wife ain't ever been in
Cape Breton before. Fact is, we ain't ever been anywhere
much. It's hard work to make a livin' on a farm, and we
raised five youngsters. The oldest one's been working up on
that Dew Line, whatever that is—he said we'd never understand the rights of it—and he come home and bought us a
car and told us to go take a trip while he looked after things
for us. He's a mighty good son, our George, past thirty and
not married yet. He used to go with a girl some but she got
notions from readin' women's magazines and plucked her
eyebrows and painted somethin' scand'lous, so he quit her.
Then he had a trip to Boston where he has some second
cousins his age. One's a girl and she said she'd meet him at
the boat, and for him to wear a ten dollar bill in his lapel and
she'd pick him out easy. From what he said when he was
back them's the only kind of chaps she wants, them with ten
dollar bills stuck out in sight. But she didn't get too much
from George, and he come home ahead of time."

"He's a mighty good boy," broke in the lanky man's wife
who had come alongside. She looked stringy and tired but
there was acid in her voice, and we figured we were not

wrong on the henpecked idea. "No gold digger will get George."

It was very evident that our lanky friend liked to talk with strangers and he kept with us as we roamed down the street on a tour of inspection. He talked about the Canso Causeway, the fine paved road all the way to Cheticamp, lobster fishing, the number of American cars he'd seen, his experience in eating at hotels and restaurants.

"We've a daughter married and livin' in Windsor," he confided, "and once or twice a summer they get us with their car and we visit a day or so with them. My son-in-law's a grand lad and he sends us the Windsor paper. My wife don't know folks up there 'cept our daughter so she don't bother with it but Jim, the son-in-law, tipped me off to read a column in it called 'Sugar and Spice' by a writer name of Bill Smiley. I've the last one with me. I cut it out and used the paper to light the fire so's the wife won't know. She's nosey, like wimmen, and kind-a strait-laced. I'll say you and me is goin' in to have an icecream, and that way I can show you the paper."

This was done and soon the lanky one and myself were at a table in a small icecream parlour and he took the paper from his pocket, watched and grinned while I read:

I started thinking about busts while I was watching Brigitte Bardot, the little French sex-pot, in a film the other night. That may seem like a silly thing to say. It's like saying you started thinking about music while you were watching an orchestra play. But it was merely a coincidence. And just to make things perfectly clear, I don't mean busts of famous men, done in plaster. I mean busts on ladies. It was my first view of the young lady. I understand she is the second citizen of France, after General De Gaulle. Certainly her pictures appear in the paper more often than his. And I'm here to tell you she is definitely better looking than the General, though somewhat shorter. After watching her a few minutes with some interest, I became first embarrassed, then mildly

disapproving, then bored, then plain sleepy. About halfway
through this process I had sense enough to say to myself:
"Boy, either you are ready to be put out to pasture, or you
need a dam' good spring tonic." And it was dismal to learn I
had nodded off, and my wife had to drive me in the ribs at
the point where the celebrated Miss B was making a monkey
of the censors. It was at this point I started thinking about
busts. Don't ask me why. What's with this bust craze anyway?
Mammalians of mammoth proportions create headlines every
time they take a deep breath. High school kids practically
break their backs trying to stick their chests out an extra inch.
So who's impressed? Other girls, maybe. Not men. Men have
been marrying women for thousands of years, and busts have
nothing to do with it. Let tenderness, humour and sympathy
show in your face, let goodness and pity and love shine in your
eyes, and you'll get your man faster than if you had the biggest
bust this side of Bali. Busts cause nothing but trouble. I knew
a girl in college called Betsy. She had a vast bosom. I always
called her Busty to myself. One night I was dancing with
her and inadvertently called her "Busty instead of Betsy."
Know what happened? She bust me. Right on the nose.
And maybe that's why I've been a little psychological about
busts ever since.

I gave the lanky man back his treasure and we got out
just in time as his acid-voiced partner was on the doorstep
peering in.

We had a glorious morning as we left Cheticamp and
started around the Cabot Trail. The road is very good and
when we soared up the first long grade and the views became
breath-taking we came upon workmen widening and paving
the road. Every provision had been made for passing traffic
and we had no difficulty whatsoever. Up and up we went,
going in to our right and then coming back toward the sea
around the face of a bold headland. And ever up. The
Trail offers one of the most exhiliarating rides I know. And
on that western side of Cape Breton you can take all those
grades on high gear so well have the highway engineers
planned and constructed. Then we were at the top and for a

few miles crossed a great tableland of wilderness. Signs tell you to beware of deer crossing but we did not see one until at the far side. Then a doe and her fawn took small notice of us as they ambled over a clearing in search of better feed. A sign asked us to put the car in low gear and down and down and down we went, around turns that were outsize hairpins but perfectly safe as they were so wide and we had the car in control. Over our left the land dropped sheer away to the sea and ahead of us stretched the farms of Pleasant Bay. We learned later that until 1927 the village could only be reached by boat or by a footpath over the mountain.

It was quiet down in the straggling road that wound in and out of dips and hollows and we failed to find a spot where some rugged feature would warrant photography. The whole Atlantic seemed to roll outside and the general view was one for a panoramic camera. As we turned to come away a man with sandy hair and a wind-reddened complexion appeared from nowhere and asked if we were looking for anything in particular. We explained we wanted some story dealing with the area.

"Not much ever happens in here," he said. "We had a terrible fire seven-eight years back when the whole mountain was burning and sparks dropped around here like rain. It was the worst I ever saw. Rabbits and deer come tearing down fast as they could go and took off toward the sea. If you look back from here you can see the blackened stubs yet."

We spotted them easily, and then he went on.

"I don't know what you can put in a book," he said, "but until last Hallow'een we had an elevated outhouse that was quite a story. It was away back near the last place on this trail and the man who lived there goes away most of the winter on a job. This time he was away till Christmas and when he got back there was about four feet of snow on the level and the wind had piled it in seven feet or more back of his house. His woman was terrible ugly over it as she couldn't get to the outhouse 'thout she shovelled a couple of days. Well, the man looked things over and saw how that drift had settled and rain-froze until it was hard as old ice. So he went to a man who moves buildings and hired some hoisting jacks. Then he got a fellow to help him and somehow got the jacks under the building and put it up ten feet on a framework of posts. He even got a box to use as a step and after New Year's went back on his job. Another storm come but only a foot or so of snow piled up but in the spring when the thaw come it was another story and when he got home his woman was using the barn ladder to get up to the out-house. She wanted it back to earth level, of course, but he'd gone stubborn after the work he'd done in the ice at Christmas and wouldn't do more'n stake the ladder so she wouldn't have a fall, and there the shack stayed till kids out on Hallowe'en sprees toppled it over."

The road from Pleasant Bay climbs steadily but the Lone Sheiling on the right was a lovely spot to take a breather. The trees are tall around the building and five cars were parked there. A woman was taking pictures and others were just going around the paths or examining the structure that is an exact replica of the places shepherds have in the highlands of Scotland.

Up and up and up we went with the great valley on our right an ocean of tree tops of varying green and the height of land on our left. In places the road had been gouged out of the hillside and a stone wall ran on the outside for the protection of motorists. At different spots we found wide spaces and there cars were stopped and tourists were taking pictures. We talked with a couple from Connecticut and they told us they had never imagined there was such magnificent scenery in Nova Scotia. Down and down and down we went on the far side and at long last emerged on a small plateau in Sunrise Valley. Now the moutain ridge was away from us and glorious in contour and giant hill. Far off, in a haze, we saw the ocean. Two deer were down on the level below us and three hundred yards from any bush or woods.

On we went and at long last were on a ridge where there were overnight stopping places and a sign urging us to see Cape North. It was a dirt road we took but it was amazingly smooth and as full of curves as a Hollywood entertainer. We enjoyed the rollercoaster effect of small hills and the still air of wooded areas. Finally we arrived at a spot where two cars were stopped and saw they were examining a unique memorial to the first cable that ran from the mainland to Newfoundland. A portion of the old cable was embedded in cement on the top of a cable post. One of the tourists told us that the road through on the right led to another memorial and we drove carefully down a lane and into an open park-like space where a car from Massachusetts was left with all four doors open as father, mother and three children wandered over to the water's edge. We swung around in a wide circle and saw an ideal picnic spot, prepared for one, and a small rugged tower of stone bearing a plaque saying this was the spot where John Cabot had landed back on June 24, 1497. It gave us a queer feeling to stand there and gaze out over an endless expanse of ocean and think that one morning in that long ago a queer little ship had been anchored by the shore and Cabot and his men had been exploring the area.

The American and his wife came back and began taking out baskets to have a picnic. "It's a wonderful spot," he said to us. "I think we'll spend the day here. Lookit the kids. I told them they might find Cabot's tracks if they hunted around."

It took but a short time to get back on the paved Cabot Trail and then we were headed down the eastern side of Cape Breton island and soon had reached glorious seascapes that simply made one pull to the parking places arranged and drink in the beauty. There were cars all along, and signs urging motorists to be careful of deer crossing. At some parking places, right off the road altogether, there were paths down the rugged shore to the water. These places gave way to others without number and the drive down through North and South Ingonish has no rival in eastern Canada. Presently we rolled into a spot where we saw the imposing headquarters of Cape Breton Highlands National Park, and suddenly realized we had seen the signs back above Cheticamp telling us we were entering the Park area. Cars were stopped by the buildings as many tourists had camping-out equipment and we heard them getting directions of campsites within easy reach.

A road in the vicinity took us out on a promontory called Middle Head and there, in ideal location, is Keltic Lodge. The view from in front cannot be described; it has to be seen to be appreciated. Old Smoky towers like a great guardian of the whole Ingonish area and blue water reaches far into corners that are blue-green alcoves of evergreen growth hanging over the water. We stopped for lunch and the food was as wonderful as the surroundings. The Lodge is new and beautiful in appointment. Every visitor there was relaxed and happy and the management would do anything to enhance such a feeling. Manager Fred Irwin is always friendly and smiling, exuding hospitality, ever ready with suggestions to make things even more pleasant.

"The deer are bothering the gardens," he said, "and they are out on this neck of land. Why don't you take the hike that goes out to the point. The scenery is worth the effort."

So away we went after lunch, taking our time, following a well-worn path that many must have taken. He had given us good advice. It was one of the finest hikes we have had in a very long time, and the scenery will enthuse the most jaded soul. More than that, you can play hide and seek with pretty white-tailed deer for half a mile through scrub bush and up and down cunning glens right out of Scotland.

There is nothing to worry about in driving the Cabot Trail. The grades are easy. And you can climb old Smoky from the northern side in high gear almost all the way. Be sure and stop at the top because you have a view only duplicated in the Rockies, and the Rockies do not have a great expanse of shimmering ocean to furnish startling contrast to great heights and bald mountain. The Trail is very wide. Put the car in low gear and you can descend without the least trouble as there are constant turns and half the time you are gazing at one sort of view and then away from it to inland vistas of tree tops and cliffs. Down and down and down is a very long way and the glimpses you get when making outward turns often cause a gasp. You seem very high in the air. Then, when you make a turn far below, glance upward, and have another thrill. But the whole way is absolutely safe for any driver who is sober.

Down from the mountain, the road runs near the coast and there are occasional small communities such as Wreck Cove and Skir Dhu and Briton Cove. Seven miles out from Briton Cove are the famous Bird Islands, and if the weather is right boats may be hired to take anyone interested out to the Islands to look at the thousands of birds that nest there such as the herring gull, Arctic and common tern, European and double-breasted comorant, Leach's petrel, razor-billed auk and puffin. The inner island is known as Hertford and the outer one as Ciboux, on which a lighthouse is located. Best time to visit the islands is July and August.

The Trail swings along through North Shore and Indian Brook then turns inland and crosses North River bridge. There is new paved highway here that is smooth and perfect and you roll up grades and soar in and around the hills until suddenly you glimpse the sea again and are at St. Ann's where the Gaelic Mod draws thousands every summer. The situation is ideal. Gaelic College is here, the Giant MacAskill Museum and many other features. By the entrance three great millstones form a unique picture as they are placed in concrete to support a plaque honouring the memory of the famous Rev. Norman McLeod who was the founder of the settlement. McLeod came from Scotland with a load of Scottish settlers away back in 1817, and arrived at Pictou on the mainland after a very strenuous voyage. Grants of land were given at Middle River and soon McLeod and his flock had a tidy settlement and McLeod's unusual ability in and out of the pulpit soon had his name known far and wide. He received a call from the state of Ohio and when he answered that he could not leave the people he accompanied across the Atlantic he was advised that if they came with him all would receive free land in Ohio. This seemed a very fine offer and it was agreed that a ship would be built to take all families and their possessions to the distant promised land.

All those not in McLeod's congregation dubbed the vessel the *Ark* but it was completed in due course and then every family went on board with all personal possessions. It sailed from Pictou in 1820 but after passing throught the Strait of Canso encountered a terrific gale. The ship was driven off course and northward along the coast of Cape Breton Island as those in charge tried desperately to keep from being driven on the rocks. At last the *Ark* veered in spite of all efforts and then the people were devoutly thankful to note they had reached a haven of sorts—St. Ann's Bay. They wanted no more of the sea and McLeod could not blame them. So they and their goods were landed after the shore had been explored and the ground found fertile. The area was unoccupied and the people learned they could obtain all the acres needed for a very small sum. All thought of Ohio vanished and the trees were cleared, dwellings erected and, the next spring, the land was tilled and seeded. Crops were very good. The Bay was found to be fairly filled with fish and everyone was happy. A school and church were soon built. The Rev. Norman McLeod was schoolmaster as well as preacher, postmaster and justice of the peace. He ruled with a rod of iron, would not permit so much as a whistle on the Sabbath, delivered sermons hours in length, forbad any woman of his congregation to so much as display a ribbon on her bonnet. But the sterner his discipline, the better they seemed to like him.

Legend has it that he did relent in some matters, such as deciding the champion of the district. There was a large and brawny Scot in McLeod's group, nearly six and a half feet tall and built accordingly. But down Baddeck way another giant had developed, not quite as tall but even broader, and one fall it was arranged that the two men meet and decide who was the better. The encounter took place two miles from the settlement so that the wives and young folk would not be terrified, and the Baddeck man won because he was wearing sheepskin moccasins with the woolly side out. This footwear prevented his slipping, while the St. Ann's man wearing cowhide, slithered on the torn grass and sod, and lost his footing once too often. The fellow from Baddeck made a mighty leap and landed amidships with three hundred pounds of bone and muscle and the great man of St. Ann's was too caved-in to continue. Before that ending blows had been struck that would have felled a steer, and it is said that neither man fully recovered from the encounter.

McLeod had a son who became a sailor and eventually reached Austrailia. From there he sent home a letter telling of the wonderful opportunities in that new land. It was a year when potato blight had ruined the crop at St. Ann's and although the grand old man, McLeod, was past seventy he announced that they all should make the voyage to a land free of ice and snow. His carpenters set to with vigour and built two ships to carry the population. One became frozen in the ice before the move could be made, but the Rev. McLeod, with 130 of his people sailed on October 28, 1851, and arrived at Adelaide, Australia, on April 10, 1852. It was not the land they had visualized. True they found it was summer instead of winter but all the rush was for various gold areas and lawlessness was rampant. So when the ship arrived that had been frozen in the ice the two vessels set sail again and early in January, 1853, reached Auckland, New Zealand. They were immediately offered good land and much assistance at the Waipu district, 100 miles north of Auckland, where they settled and found everything to their liking. Five other ships were built at St. Ann's and by 1861 the whole settlement, 883 persons, had left St. Ann's and made a new home in New Zealand.

We wandered around the grounds of the Gaelic College and saw many lassies in gay kilts parading slowly in various spots as they learned to draw sweet music from the pipes. An instructor kept going back and forth and looked as if he had a pleasant task.

It was not far from St. Ann's to Baddeck where we went to spend the night at Inverary Inn. We were installed in a fine cottage situated well away from highway traffic and beside a growth of small trees alive with birds. Dinner was exceptionally good and we were happy to have found another top-notch eating place. We recommend Inverary Inn without reservation to any traveller, fussy or otherwise.

In the morning we explored Baddeck and found it a beautiful, historic and delightful place where world history had been made. Visitors roamed the streets and all carried cameras. Yachts in full sail glided on the blue water on which the town faced, and far over the way loomed a great hill that looked a first cousin to Old Smoky. We went into the courthouse and were shown the office where a well-known Cape Bretoner had served as county clerk for many years. His name was Charles W. K. McCurdy and his prized possessions, we were told, were a cutlass of great age and a twenty-four-pound cannon with a one-inch bore. Both weapons were said to have been uncovered at Cape North when a farmer removed a strange mound from the middle of his plowed field. The late Mr. McCurdy, we were told, always believed the weapons to have been left buried in the field by John Cabot and his men. This could be fact as both weapons date back to the sixteenth century. Other items he had in his office museum were a gold toothpick with an "ear digger" at one end; a carved lamp from Siam; a model outrigger canoe from the South Seas; a strange chest from a Siamese temple; a Chinese camphor-wood chest; a Masonic pitcher brought from Scotland over a century ago; a vase from the old Chinese Imperial Palace; a Cape Breton map of 1789 which showed the island divided into ten counties; the sea chest of Captain Lawrence, commander of the ill-fated *Chesapeake*, which was worsted and captured by the famous *Shannon* off Boston Harbour; a huge mahogany and rosewood chest that had been in the family four generations; an original seal of the Island of Cape Breton signed by the Colonial Secretary during the reign of George the Third. There was a twelve-pound model of the famous *Silver Dart*, the plane in which the former Lieutenant-Governor of Nova Scotia, J. A. D. McCurdy, made the first flight in the British Empire, taking off and alighting on the ice of Baddeck Bay. There were old guns from the Tower of London, a flintlock from Dublin Castle, a Gurkha head-hunter's knife, a German Iron Cross, and many old coins. A little further along the main way we turned left into spacious grounds surrounding the Alexander Graham Bell Museum. This is an odd-looking building and is a delight to look at and a source of enjoyment inside. Although Bell was born in Scotland he was long a resident of Canada. His name is always associated with the invention of the telephone but he had genius that carried him farther into scientific reasearch than most people realize. He made important contributions in medicine, aeronautics, marine engineering, genetics and eugenics. He did extensive research in electricity, in sound and speech. He was a teacher and, perhaps above all, a great humanitarian. We could spot his fine estate known as Beinn Bhreagh on a headland across the bay from Braddeck, and there he built a famous laboratory and workshops that produced many of the items now on display in the Museum. We went from one exhibit to another, amazed that one man could know so much about so many different problems. He constructed kites in various forms to acquire basic knowledge regarding air flights, and specimens can be seen. It would take a full day to examine every interesting item in the Museum and our time was limited. To us, a most curious arrangement was one for extracting fresh water from salty sea water, this for use by such as sealers and fishermen who get adrift in dories every spring and have no fresh water with them.

It seemed too nice a morning to miss seeing Baddeck from the opposite hill so we turned right outside the little town and soon were climbing a quite narrow road that wound up and up and finally let us emerge in a clearing where we parked and had a most wonderful view. Baddeck and the Bras d'Or Lake spread away below us in a magnificent panorama and in the clear air we could see even small boats away on the far side and probably six or seven miles distant. The graves of Dr. and Mrs. Bell are there in a secluded spot on the hillside, a most beautiful location.

Back on Highway 5, we reached Ross Ferry and waited for the boat to come over. There were five cars waiting and a friendly man with a twinkle in his eye came over and began talking with us about Cape Breton Island, which he considered the showplace of the east. He said he had been around the Cabot Trail but had left it at Barasois Bridge and motored over to Englishtown.

"I wanted to see the spot where that Frenchman, Captain Daniel, had a fort away back more than three centuries ago," he said. 'I read about it when I was going to school and somehow it struck my imagination. Fancy those old-timers away back then walking around in armour and having only spears and swords and battleaxes to fight with, and then staying the long winter in this land with only Indians to get them fresh meat. No wonder that men so cooped up got to having crazy notions so that one officer killed another. Then I wanted, too, to see the grave of Giant MacAskill. It's hard to imagine a man seven feet nine inches tall and weighing four hunded and twenty-five pounds. No wonder he toured Europe with Tom Thumb and they told me he made good money. Another thing was his strength. I guess he was more more noted for that than for his size. A huge professional boxer came to fight him one summer and Giant Angus laughed and reached to shake hands. When he let go the boxer's hand was so crushed he would not be able to fight for months and that was that. There was a woman from Connecticut in a party looking around his home and visiting his grave. She absorbed all the stories about his size and when she joined us at the ferry I asked her if she had seen all she wanted. 'I certainly did,' she said. 'And he was every bit as big as they said. Do you know they had to cut him into three pieces to get him into a grave. I was there and saw the headstones.' There are two stones, one each side of the Giant's grave, marking the family lot, but she had figured for herself what had happened and I didn't try to correct her."

Another man said he was from Wolfville and when we asked about his apple crop he shrugged. "Best yet," he said, "but where can a man sell his fruit when it's ready. Last year we had bushels of apples go to waste. We had a lot of windfalls and the wife got to thinking maybe we should share ours with apple-hungry people who might not want to buy first-class fruit. So she got a nice basket she had bought from the Micmac Indians at Millbrook, filled it with windfalls and put it at the edge of our lawn with a cardboard sign pinned to the rim reading 'Help Yourself.' Nobody did. Some cars slowed and then went on so she made a new sign the next day after I told her people were suspicious of anything for free. It read 'Five pounds ten cents.' Just one car stopped and the driver asked how she weighed the apples and seemed uneasy when she dumped about ten pounds in his car. Then our mail driver came along and said she was underselling folks down the road so she got some paper bags and filled them with apples and put them in the basket with a sign '25 cents a bag.' She sold three lots the next morning and then an official of the apple plant at Cold Brook stopped and said she was selling fruit too cheaply, that even windfalls were worth twice her figure. Out she went and put a new sign on the basket '50 cents a bag.' She looked out just in time to see a fat woman taking the last bag, and hurrying so that she tore the sign and only '. . . 50c.' was on the cardboard. After supper she filled more bags and went out but the basket was gone and fifty cents was lying on the board to pay for it. And that basket had cost her two dollars and fifty cents at Millbrook. So we went out of the apple selling business."

The ferry arrived and we got on board, had a short run across and headed for Sydney. Much of the way was a nice drive and then we had to go through the mining towns of Florence and Sydney Mines. Next was North Sydney and then we were waiting our turn to cross bridges on the way to Sydney. We turned left at Sydney River and not long after saw a most remarkable church. It is not remarkable in appearance but has a story without parallel in Canada, and the man we talked with was filled with pride.

"This place has been growing over the years," he said, "and we felt there just had to be a church, but there were Anglicans and Presbyterians and Baptists and United, so what could we do. Then all hands got together in a meeting at the hall and we decided to build a church that would do for everybody. That was back in '51. We talked around after that and a big firm, Bairncroft Inc., sold us the land we needed for a mere nominal sum. That was a good start. We wanted the rest of the ground to the river for picnics and the like and they let us have it on a ninety-nine year lease for one dollar a year. That was that. Then we got the Rev. Dr. A. A. MacLeod, past seventy and retired but a native son of Baddeck who knows the Island and our people, to come and get us going. He got a grant from the United Church and we held meetings in the hall, had 150 at communion, then formed a Board to handle the church building. The Chairman was an Anglican, the Treasurer a Baptist, the Clerk of the Session a Presbyterian, and the Chairman of the Stewards a United Church man. The Chairman of the Building Committee was A. E. Sibley, local manager of the Municipal Construction Company, and our main help with the plans and specifications was John A. MacLeod, Chief Engineer for Dominion Steel Corporation. He superintended every detail of construction. The actual work of building was done by men of the congregation, practically without any outside help whatsoever. They made sacrifices of time and energy that can't be measured in dollars. They got the site bulldozed and had two mixers, a carload of cement and about forty men, many of them office staff. They came after a day's work and rigged lights under the stars and ran the wheelbarrows and did the hard manual labour. Never was so much done for so many by so few. In a year and four months it was finished to the last detail of modern kitchen and minister's office and washrooms, all equipped with modern plumbing, electrical installation and gas heat. A bell was put in and when the job was done there was a church worth over $150,000. Five hundred people came to the first service, and the men kept right on with the work, built a fine manse and bought ten acres for a cemetery. There were seventy-two Protestant residents in the area when the church was begun and five years later there were 511 members with 426 attending Sunday School. This made an extension necessary and again those men pitched in with time and money and built a two-storey extension ninety-six by twenty-two feet. The church is filled every Sunday and there is no mention of anything but Protestant, that's what they all are. The Roman Church is that one right there, and nights when they have a turkey supper we turn on the lights so they can use our parking lot, and they do the same by us. Tell me where can you find another area where all hands are together as one, like here?"

We couldn't. We could only admire the people of Sydney River and wish them the very best.

Driving into Sydney we saw tall grey towers of an unusual building etched against the sky as we drove along King's Road. So we pulled to one side and began asking questions of a man who was stopped with a delivery truck. It is not often such a person is a mine of information but this man evidently had taken pains to know about the building. He called the structure a castle and said the wooded grounds around it consisted of ten acres, that there were thirty large rooms in the castle, that it is heated by two steam furnaces, fourteen fireplaces, has seven chimneys and twenty-one flues. The main hall has a ceiling forty-five feet high, a stained glass front, and wood panelling bearing crests and standards. A wide semi-circular stairway, elaborately carved, is another feature, and each stairway is guarded by a beautifully carved gryphon holding a lantern. There are thirteen bedrooms, a sewing room and billiard room upstairs in addition to the tower. The original owner, Arthur J. Moxham, was born in South Wales in 1854. When fifteen years old he moved across to Kentucky and got work in the rolling mills, learned the business of making iron and studied engineering. In 1878 he went to Birmingham, Alabama, and designed, built and organized a plant for the Birmingham Rolling Mills Company which he managed for several years. By 1895 he was head of a steel company in Ohio where he built the original Moxham's Castle. Retiring, he took a trip around the world in his own yacht, met the man who was promoting the building of the Dominion Iron & Steel Company of Sydney, agreed to become manager, built the

Sydney Steel Plant and put it into operation. His wife didn't like to leave her home so he said he would move it. It cost $350,000 to take the Castle down and ship it by rail to Sydney where it was reconstructed stone by stone exactly as it had been in Ohio. His oldest son was killed in the Steel Plant, and Moxham resigned in 1902. He died in 1931. The Castle was used as a hospital during the first World War, is now the home of Mr. and Mrs. W. N. MacDonald and couldn't be constructed today for less than one million dollars.

We stopped at the Isle Royale Hotel, and looked around the city, built on a peninsula and facing one of the finest harbours in the world. Wentworth Park is one of its showplaces, having a lake stocked with ducks, geese and swans. We were told we should see St. George's Church, fourth oldest in Canada, built in 1786, and possessing a chair from the wardroom of Nelson's ship the *Victory* and presented to the church by him when he was in the harbour with a fleet in 1795. There was a pleasant man at the church and he said they had something far more unique than the chair. It certainly is, and it is doubtful if it can be duplicated anywhere else in the world for it is a quit claim to a man's affections and was duly entered into with legal formality. The story is that a young blood of Sydney was paying attention to a young lady and after courting her with serious attention noticed that her sister had even greater attractions, so decided to switch affections. But the sister was wary and before she would consent to become the man's bride she demanded, and got, a quit claim deed from her sister to the effect that she would not interfere in any way with her future husband nor exercise any undue influence on his affections by reason of their former association.

A tablet on the post office bears the following inscription:

Joseph Frederick Wallet DesBarres, 1722-1824. A distinguished military engineer, who served in the mid-eighteenth century wars in America. Afterwards employed by the

Town Square, St. Andrews-by-the-Sea

Reversing Falls, Saint John

THE DEICHMANN HOME, SUSSEX

Fort Beauséjour

Magnetic Hill, near Moncton

SHAD NET TWO MILES FROM SHORE AT MINUDIE

FORT ANNE, ANNAPOLIS ROYAL

START OF INTERNATIONAL FISHERMEN'S DORY RACE, LUNENBURG

MILL COVE, ON ST. MARGARET'S BAY

UNIACKE HOUSE

PEGGY'S COVE

THE TIDE REALLY GOES OUT ALONG THE BAY OF FUNDY

LITTLE FISHING COVES LURK AS SURPRISES ALONG THE SHORE OF NOVA SCOTIA

The Canso Causeway connecting Cape Breton Island with the Mainland

Inside Citadel Hill, Halifax

CAPE SMOKY, ON THE CABOT TRAIL

THE BELL MUSEUM AT BADDECK

Festival of Arts, Tatamagouche

Louisburg National Historic Park

Fort Edward, in Victoria Park, Charlottetown

Queen Square, Charlottetown

GOVERNMENT HOUSE, CHARLOTTETOWN

TONGING FOR OYSTERS

HUNTER RIVER

COL. E. W. JOHNSTONE AND ONE OF HIS MINIATURE CASTLES, BURLINGTON

GREEN GABLES

CAVENDISH BEACH

CHRIST CHURCH CATHEDRAL, FREDERICTON ·

GRAND FALLS

SALMON ANGLING IN NEW BRUNSWICK

British Government to survey and chart the eastern coast of North America, he gained great fame as an oceanographer. First Lieutenant-Governor of Cap Breton, 1784-1787, founder of Sydney, Lieutenant-Governor of Prince Edward Island 1804-1812. Erected in recognition of his public service.

Every school child in Nova Scotia probably knows that Sydney was first known as Spanish Harbour, that DesBarres was of Huguenot descent, served with Wolfe at Louisbourg and again at Quebec. He spent ten years surveying the coast of Nova Scotia. On September 1, 1785, he formally proclaimed Spanish Harbour as the island's capital and invited settlers, naming the place Sydney in honour of the Secretary of State for the Colonies. The woods was cleared, the town marked out, and barracks commenced for six companies of soldiers. DesBarres, being encouraged by authorities, offered settlers provisions for three years, clothing, building materials, tools and implements, and 3,397 persons responded to his offer, the majority being from New York State. The winter was a severe one and suddenly the military authorities decided not to issue food supplies to the settlers. It is hard to know, at this date, what such fellows had in mind. Without food, and no transportation available, they would simply have starved to death, every man, woman and child. DesBarres gave orders but they defied him. Then he learned that a ship bearing supplies was frozen in the ice at Arichat. He mortgaged his property, sent a party to purchase both ships and supplies. The vessel was chopped free of ice and sailed to Louisbourg, from whence the supplies were dragged on sleds by hand. So the people survived and DesBarres won lasting popularity.

He was known in many quarters, acquired land at Tatamagouche, Windsor and Minudie, had several mistresses, the most noted being Polly Cannon who looked after much of his business, danced on a table at age of one hundred when a party was given in his honour at Halifax, and died at the age of one hundred and two.

All roads were leading to Louisbourg. All the papers were carrying headlines about the great celebrations about to be held at the site of what was once called "The Dunkirk of America." In the Sydney paper we read:

History-saturated Louisbourg! Ruins that are headstones to an era! Ancient fortress of the days of New France! In its keeps you will find yourself looking around for a footstep you thought you heard, for today Louisbourg is the deserted stage upon which great dramas were enacted. In its grass-grown redoubts you will sense a melancholy brooding, accented as much by desolation as by the green-sworded fleur-de-lis growing among spectre-haunted rocks.

It is only half an hour's drive to Louisbourg from Sydney. We found the route well marked and the road paved all the way. Much of the ride is through wooded country but there is beauty around Mira River and then there is the town of Louisbourg a mile before you reach the Historic Park containing the ruins of the old stronghold. Celebrations were going on for it was the 200th anniversary of the final capture of the French stronghold that might have defied much had the situation been different. But it is doubtful if even Quebec saw as much graft and wholesale robbery of the public purse, as much drunkenness and debauchery as reigned at Louisbourg. Many of the garrisons were imports, Swiss and others, hired soldiers eating poor food, sleeping on flea-ridden hay mattresses, forgotten on paydays so often that one fall the soldiers went on strike, stood no guards, scared the officers from their quarters and daunted the citizens until they could walk into a grog shop or any sort of store and take what they wanted without payment. There were great balls that lasted all night, enormous feasting, enormous drinking bouts, and officialdom was so corrupt that it did not keep many records. The officials danced and drank and played with their mistresses, using the funds sent out from France for the strengthening of the defences. So that each time the British came the garrison had small appetite for battle, were ill-prepared in every way. Brash New Englanders, untrained, uncouth, reckless, unused to discipline, took the fortress the first time, were left there for the winter and, hating the eternal fog and mist and chill, drank to stupidness and death. Eight hundred of them were in their graves by the time May brought sunshine and warmth the following year.

We drove around to a fine museum on the grounds and inspected countless relics that have been found during excavations, then went out and roamed over what is left of the massive masonry and defences. The town can be traced by the cellars of the old street and the youngsters with an American car from Ohio were having a grand time climbing in and out of undergrounds and chasing sheep which grazed where French soldiers had stood guard. The sea was rolling in strongly so that there was much surf and we saw the site of the first lighthouse in America. A man who was going around the park with some official stopped a moment to chat with us.

"We've started a ten-year plan for Louisbourg," he said. "We're going to build a seawall cribwork to protect the entrance to the grounds from erosion by the sea. Who's we? Why the Associated Boards of Trade of Cape Breton Island and the Cape Breton Historical Society. Then we're going to take down all the poles and have the wiring underground. We're going to restore the west gate and a section of the wall there to demonstrate the old fortification. We're going to beautify the grounds, publicize the place each spring, restore the grand battery and explore the harbour for any sunken ships or cannon we might recover, pave a road direct from the Park to Arichat down the coast, and include Wolfe's Landing into the Park. We're going to restore every street with cobblestone, restore the King's Garden with the same flowers as the original, restore part of the King's bastion to include the chapel, restore a few of the dwellings to show how the people lived, construct a part of the hospital, a seawall along the harbour side, preserve the cemetery, establish trailer camps and camp grounds outside the park, and have roadside tables and benches for those who want to picnic on the grounds. Yes, sir, you wait another ten years and Louisbourg will be a 'must' for every tourist who comes to the Maritimes. It was the finest fortress of them all, saw more fighting than the others. So why not make it a standout?"

We agreed with him and reluctantly turned toward the Canso Causeway and followed Highway 4 from Sydney. It was up hill and down dale a time, long swoops to the valley and up curving slopes and then we were beside the Bras d'Or Lake and having magnificent vistas of water and evergreen borders with blue sky above, fit for any painting. There was East Bay and Big Pond and Hay Cove and Soldier's Cove, with schoolhouses here and there, wayside canteens and filling stations and Americans invading the country in Buicks and Fords and Oldsmobiles and all the other makes. Here and there among the traffic were small cars from overseas that cost less and run many miles on a gallon of gas. Cape Breton Scots know the value of a dime and many of them drive the little fellows.

St. Peter's Canal cut across our way but we crossed the bridge and parked and walked about and tried to visualize the place away back when it was said to be named "San Pedro" by the Portuguese who visited a great deal around Cape Breton. But the first white man to make something of the area was fine old Nicholas Denys who cleared land and planted crops and set up a fur trading station. He had a small fort and got along famously for a time until some of his own countrymen raided him under false pretences and carried him off prisoner. Denys managed to get the ear of the government in Paris and was released and took his place back but fire destroyed all his store of furs and he moved away.

Years later the French built a fort in the clearing and then an Englishman came and took the stronghold and burned four schooners lying at anchor. Six years later Count de Raymond was at Louisbourg and felt that St. Peter's might become a fine trading post so had a road made at the expense of 100,000 livres and hoped brisk traffic might begin between Louisbourg and St. Peter's. But those in Paris were wild with rage when they knew what had been done, saying the road would be used by the British when they came to attack either point, and de Raymond was removed from command. In 1793 an English colonel came to St. Peter's and built a strongpoint which he named Fort Granville. It was not maintained for any length of time but as we explored a trio who came from a car parked further along showed us the site of the fort and told us about the cutting of the canal away back almost one hundred years ago. It saves vessels seventy-five miles if they want to enter the lake from the southwest. We learned that the canal follows the old portage of French days, that it was begun in 1854, completed in 1869, and enlarged twice after that.

"Are ye American, now?" asked the oldest of the trio, who flourished a red nose like a road signal.

We assured him we were not.

"I'm glad o' that," he grunted, "as it's effort for me to stay polite and I have to do that if you're not native. Four fine lassies there were up Iona way and you might say I had my pick, being there first, but three of them away to Boston with boys who came for a holiday and bewitched them with stories of a lovely land back home. So I had to take the fourth, and she's been jealous of them ever since, and plagued me because I haven't the ambition to go and live up there. Twice she's dragged me into making the trip. The first time we took what they called a short cut up there in Maine, a roller coaster through the woods, an 'Idiot's Delight,' I named it, and more than the hop-step and jump they said it was. Two flat tires

I had before we reached Bangor, and a fog closed in and I near run down folks a dozen times through them riff-raff walkin' in a haze and daze and me tryin' to make out road signs. Finally we put up and I was hungry enought to eat horse meat. So my better half ordered steaks and cooed about being at last in a land flowin' with milk and honey. The steaks came, well done, the waitress said. It was us were well done. I could hold mine up and read the menu through it, but not a word would the wife let me say. The bed was good that night and the weather cleared and we reached her sister's, a square boxy little house on a corner where traffic roars day and night. We told her about our loss with the Bangor steak but blowed if she didn't have a thousand things for supper—like we do here at home, beans. Only ours is done proper with molasses and pork, crisp and yet not dry. While hers were from a can—in fact all we eat out of was cans the three days we were there. So we moved on to another sister and her big idea was to take us out to a Babylon-on-the-beach. I saw more liquor drunk than in Glace Bay on a Saturday night, more half-naked women than you'd believe, and the sun was hot, the ice cream slimy, and you hadn't room to change your mind. The wife and her sister jumped on me when I mentioned any of them things and said it took all kinds of people to make a world. I told them I was darn glad I wasn't one of them. So we moved on to the third sister and she was a day's drive the other side of Washington and hotter'n a place our patient old Presby'erian preacher named when he talked about a meddlesome Methodist who wanted church union. They had Judas trees down there, and talked about them all the time, and they had more insects than I knew were made, and hot nights and no peace, and the same traffic misery as around Boston. And the sister had a Judas peep hole in her back door and heard me relieve my mind a few times so we cut our trip short and come home and I slept three days and nights in a cool climate just resting. In fact I slept so much I was like one of them three-toed sloths the wife finds in crossword puzzles. And that ended my going there for vacation until I went to a place back of Portland to see a cousin I went to school with. He's had more bad luck than two men. Married the wrong woman to start off, took the wrong job, went to the wrong place to settle down. He's had the seven-year itch twice, to hear him tell it, been in three car accidents and broke his leg. It made me feel bad just to hear him tell them things so I didn't stay long, and now I'm on vacation here."

"Vacation?" we echoed.

"Right. Each summer the wife goes to visit her sister for three weeks, and I take three weeks off and have a mighty good holiday here. You'd understand more if you met the wife. I call her 'honey' most of the time as that's the only sweet that doesn't agree with me."

"Don't let Sandy make you feel bad," said the second man of the trio, a thin fellow with reddish hair. "He's from Iona, and you know what they're like. Most Scots are decent fellows, college presidents and mine managers and the like. And good soldiers, too, for they have lots of courage. They show it when they wear the kilt. This while back I've noticed how the influence of the pipes and Highland dancing is spreading. I'd hoped they'd keep it to the back part of Cape Breton but last summer I saw kilts swinging and heard the pipes in Glengarry up in Ontario and blow me if I didn't see a Chinese girl on television dancing the fling and wearing the kilt like a natural out in Saskatchewan. It's spread like a disease and that big Scot at the border is great advertising for Nova Scotia."

"They're to have a Highland village in Iona," announced the third of the trio, a dark and swarthy fellow with hair in his ears. "You know they speak the Gaelic there as they did one hundred and fifty years ago when the Scots came there from the Hebrides. They've had a real battle over the site

for those Pictou Scots and their tales of the *Hector* seemed in
line for it. But it's in Iona, down the 'Road to the Isles' that
they'll put up an authentic old Scottish town with cottages of
field stone, a miniature castle, a post office and a museum.
The roofs will be of straw and heather, and it's fitting. For
Iona is a spot where the Gaelic is really a fireside tongue."

They talked like old cronies and told us about old families
and old houses and old Scottish belongings that would go to
fill the museum and seemed so happy that they were to see
the village a reality before going, as Sandy said, "to higher
ground." He gave us a few more details about his house-
keeping while "honey" was absent and let us know that the
red-haired one washed the dishes and the dark man got up
first and made the porridge. So we figured it was a threesome
in honey's kitchen and there might be some cleaning-up to
do when she was home again.

They wanted to treat us to icecream but we drove on and
reached Grand Anse, debated a trip into Arichat, voted
against it, and keep on through Cleveland to Port Hawkesbury,
turned right there, stopped a time and talked with a man by
a filling station and heard the tale of the first circus that
came to the Island, pitched tents at Hawkesbury, attracted
hundreds who came on foot and horseback, and tried to
overcharge and shortchange customers. You can't do that
with Scots. So there were some broken heads and the tents
downed and cages upset and some animals got away and
there was, in the man's words, "hell to pay." The sheriff
established some sort of order after a time and the circus was
reloaded on the vessel but one of the monkeys could not be
found. Back over the ridge from the town two old neighbours
had been at odds for years. Crusty old Maggie had never
married and distrusted men folk. Crusty old Jock was a
shrivelled little man with a bald head and had small liking
for the fair sex. So the good constable of the town was greatly
concerned when Maggie came to him at next daybreak with

the report that Jock had scaled her woodshed and tried to get into her bedroom. It was not very light, she admitted, but there was enough moon for her to see him. "Him it were," she persisted. "I made out his bald head, and him wi' no shirt an' a'."

The constable dare not even accuse Jock of such adventure but investigated on his own—and found monkey tracks leading to the shed roof. The animal hung around the area for several days but killed some hens and had to be shot.

# 6

## One Thousand Babies, Rambling Reminiscences, the Eight-Foot Woman, and Saw-Whets

BACK OVER THE WIDE CAUSEWAY and away we went to Antigonish where we stayed the night at the Gael Motel, fine accommodation, with a delightful little breakfast place across the way. There we lingered the next morning for an oldtimer was telling about early days when the town was named "Dorchester" and surrounded by woods. One of the first settlers was Jane Pushie, the midwife of the district who had a vast knowledge of herbs and Indian remedies. She worked hard, was a small woman, lived to be one hundred and three and it was said she brought over one thousand babies into this world. Legend has it that the beautiful wide main street of Antigonish is really an old path blazed by Zephaniah Williams and an Indian, Joe Snake, through the dense woods. Back in 1794 the land around Antigonish was sparsely settled and there were no schools but Williams' wife was determined that their six-year-old son should be educated. She heard of a school at Truro and resolved the boy should attend it but there was no road to the place. So the boy was made ready and with his clothing and some money accompanied his father and an Indian guide who blazed a route to Truro, a route by which the boy came and went for various terms. After a time

160

the guide trail became a regular footpath used by those going to Truro. Eventually the footpath became a cart road, and, in the town of Antigonish it became one of the most beautiful wide and shady streets in the Province.

There are many in Nova Scotia who have hobbies of one sort or another but there in Antigonish we learned of a woman who collects unusual surnames from all over the world. Mrs. Thomas F. MacDonald can show any interested visitor her books in which she has listed the names and the information she has gleaned from authentic sources. She watches newspapers carefully and has become an expert on names. She says that in the beginning there was Joseph Owns Land, and this was shortened after a few generations to Joe Owns. Finally it became slurred to our present "Jones." Names were created, she has found, and it makes one wonder about her list of "Savage" and "Nutt" and "Swain" and "Twaddle" and "Fraud." For religion there are names like Pope, Bishop, Dean, Rector, Priest, Creed, Temple, Chappel, Missions and Divine. There is Spring and Somer, Fall and Winter, Daye, Knight, Morrow and Weeks. In food she has Hogg, Bacon, Lamb, Trout, Curry, Pye, Pickles, Roast, etc. Really unusual are Turkey, Duck, Apples, Onions, Tea, Coffee and Cream. The names are in black-covered books and they go from Mr. Love and Mr. Hope and Mr. Faith, Byers, Sellers, Nickel, Dollar, Penny and Sale and Profit and Beard, Foot, Bone, Graves, Grieve, Coffin, Kidney and Rump to Mr. Goodenough, Mr. Bothersome, Mr. Barefoot, Mr. Wellbeloved and Mr. Gotobed.

The morning was grand if a little cool for the time of year and soon we were driving through James River and Marshy Hope and had arrived in Barney's River. An oil truck tried to take the corner bridge at top speed, swung around and jammed tightly in the middle of the bridge. A bus headed for Boston was held up on the eastern side and irritated passengers erupted forth and expressed their opinion of the truck driver in very loud voices. Four or five men gathered with various tools and set about freeing the truck. A man in coupe crossed over the grassy bank on the left and looked down to the stream which was only a few inches deep. He saw a gravel bed and noticed the low bank on the far side. In a moment he was in his car edging over the slope. Down he went into the stream and shot across with a thin arc of spray and tore up the other side, wheeled onto the pavement and sped from sight. A fellow with a panel truck on the western side, seeing how easily the coupe had crossed, edged his vehicle down the low bank and into the stream. But he acted without thinking. The side the coupe had descended was quite steep and the panel truck gouged its hind wheels deeply in the gravel and stayed right there, its hood pointing skyward. So we parked and walked back among gathering onlookers, noticed a few oldsters and began making conversation.

"It's the third time a truck has come down that hill too fast and got stuck" said an indignant old man with a cloth cap on and watch chain across his vest that looked very solid. "Too much speed. All they is today is speed. Hurry and hurry to git somewhere, then sit down when you're there 'cause you've got nowhere to go and nothin' to do. But break your neck to git there."

He sounded very peevish but we had brought a packet of strong Scotch mints and when he had sampled one he was almost smiling. "Them's the kind I like," he pronounced, "only you can't get them hereabouts."

We thrust the packet into his hands and assured him they were too strong for us and he was more than welcome. At that, he thawed more and began talking about the place, named, he said, after a first settler, Barney McGee.

"They were tough, those first settlers," said our mint friend. "There was John Sutherland who come to this country wearin' a kilt and never put on pants no matter how cold the weather or how deep the snow. He lived over ninety and had ten children. I reckon half the Sutherlands here to Pictou is his get. Over the other side of the bridge on that flat part is where them first comers had a log fort. They feared the Injuns for quite a time as one of their women found an old buck drinkin' cream out of a bowl she'd set out to cool in a log shed. She slapped him hard and threw the rest of the cream over him, and he vowed he'd have her scalp. The settlers dug a long deep cellar in the ground and built their fort over it and word we used to hear when young was that they had grub enough in that place to live on for six months. They had a well in the cellar, too, so the Injuns would have a time waitin' them out."

"Are you a native here?" we asked.

"Yes, and no." He took his fifth mint in a row, and grinned. "I were raised over at Merigomish, but I were born here. There was six of us boys in the lot, and an uncle over at Merigomish had three girls so I went there to give a hand with the chores. That way, I hadn't much schoolin' as my uncle felt that chores included lobster fishin' and farmin'. Lobsters was plenty back in them days and we didn't git much for them so had to catch a lot. They didn't have dry ice them days like now. They ship 'em by air in seaweed and dry ice and they're alive and kickin' when they git to Toronto or New York or any place. Then they git boiled, as most visitors do to them big cities, and make good eatin' and fetch teetotal prices. Lobsters is the homeliest things that swim, and about the stupidest. There ain't nothin' else will swim into a trap headfirst and then try to back out. He can't do that because his claws won't let him but he never thinks to turn around and swim out. So all we used was a bit of dried herring for bait. We'd make traps in the winter. Late years the price has went up so and many rules about fishin' that some folks along the shore make easy money havin' a few traps set. They line up a tree and a stump or barn corner and know jist where to reach for the trap, but no inspector could find it. 'Course that's not strictly 'cordin' to law but them there high taxes they put on us ain't right, either. Folks not used to lobsters lose a lot of the best eatin'. They fork the meat out of the tail and claws and leave the rest alone, never knowin' the best tidbits is hid in the main gear or that they kin suck the meat out of the legs. Wimmen here a year gone said lobster legs was juicier an' better'n frog legs. Me, I don't know. I never et frog legs."

Someone had brought a heavy jack and they were freeing the front left bumper of the truck. The bus passengers were watching with moody impatience and the bus driver was eating icecream placidly.

"I did two years with a lightkeeper," informed our friend, absorbing more mints. "Last night I had company from Sheet Harbour and we were looking over an old book of instructions I had." He pulled a thin volume, rather greasy with age and handling, from his shirt pocket. "Have a look," he invited. "I'm takin' it over to a friend of mine."

We scanned the faded print and learned that lamps were to be alight from sunset to sunrise, in fog and "during darkness from other causes." Wicks were to be trimmed and chimneys cleaned every four hours, and lanterns kept free of snow and sleet. Spare chimneys to be kept on hand. The lightkeeper might go ashore to draw his pay or attend church service, but not for any other reason without permission. Under a heading "Sickroom Instructions" we read: "Room heat must be from 60 to 65 degrees. A screen must be used to keep out draught. Sheets must be changed more frequently than when in health. There must be no despondent remarks or whispering. Milk and beef tea must be served." There was no reference to the means for securing the milk. Instructions ran in long detail regarding the treatment of Constipation, Piles, Diarrhoea, Indigestion, Whooping Cough,

Measles, Smallpox, Scarlet Fever, Dropsy, Worms, Toothache, Burns, Scalds and Sprains. Also "How to Feed and Wean Infants Bringing up by Hand." Medical stores to be kept on hand included Blue Pills, Castor Oil, Tincture of Iron, Syrup of Squills, Spirit of Nitre, Spirit of Peppermint, Epsom Salts, Ginger, Quinine, Nitrate of Silver, Mustard, Bandages, two Surgical Needles, Mortar and Pestle."

A small woman with a rosy complexion and gray hair came along and stopped by us. Our friend immediately presented her with a few mints.

"This here's our poem writer," he said. "She's written pieces for everything from weddin's to sick horses."

"Now, Jim," protested the old lady. "I just made up one jingle to tease a neighbour when he had a sick horse. Don't heed him too much. He likes to tease me. All I do are jingles to amuse some of my friends but we do have some good poetry in Nova Scotia. I happen to know Mrs. Hazel Goddard down in Dartmouth and I think she's good as any in Canada. I learned one of her pieces to say at an Institute meeting." We begged to hear it and she obliged.

### COUNTRY SPREAD

Dabs of gold sunlight butter the brown crust
Of well baked pasturelands which warmly lie
Like leavened loaves dredged in midsummer dust
And left to steam beneath a bowl of sky;
On the blue line of which spoonfuls of cloud
Windwhipped as country cream, swing in the breeze,
In scalloped islands high above the bowed
Sun-reddened crests of laden apple trees.
Stacked amber cones of dried sweet clover tent
The toasted fields at intervals, and stand
Like old stone crockery, their thick lips bent
Downward unto the ripened harvest land,
Whence meadow creatures hasten to the spread
Of apple float and honey on fresh bread.

"I'm sure," said the old lady, thanking us for compliments we meant, "you will be well entertained. Jim has been everywhere."

"Boston and New York and the West Indies and Australia ain't everywhere," said Jim. "I've been around some but all I kin say is give me old Nova Scotia any time and I'll be happy. I have two Acadian knives we dug up at Merigomish, and I've showed a lot of people where the old Acadian settlements were, 'specially their blacksmith shop. Some folks have crockery they dug up, and one man has a shovel."

We noticed the oil truck was free and was being driven through the bridge. The bus went on its way and we said good-bye to our minted friend and followed after and into Sutherland's River, where we saw a fine large school, and on to New Glasgow. There we stopped for lunch at the Norfolk Hotel, and had a walk down the one-way main street with shops on the right having a large parking space at the rear. Not many towns offered such accommodation, and it was free parking. Being a Scottish community, such a feature would be appreciated, and when we mentioned as much in a book store we visited the lady clerk smiled and said a standard story in the town was about an elderly Scottish couple who entertained at tea occasionally and always passed a sugar bowl with tongs—and granulated sugar.

We asked about some special feature and were told about the new hospital but wanted something different.

"I think we have it," smiled the clerk. "We have a veteran printer with our paper, the *Evening News,* and every time he has a birthday they let him have a piece in the paper. I have a copy right here in the office. The man's name is John William Fraser."

### RAMBLING REMINISCENCES

And still another year has fled with magic swiftness o'er our head; and now this scribbler reappears with term of nine and fifty years. Can you recall the former days when we were used to cruder ways? We rarely thought conditions bad but were content with what we had. Our neighbour we could safely trust, and slept the slumber of the just; our snoring hours secure and tight, we rarely locked our doors at night. The wage received for hardy toil would make all union folk recoil; and steelworks men of brawn and power received but fourteen cents an hour. The family's soiled and dirty duds were cleansed with scrubbing boards and suds; and women had a hectic day, their knuckles almost worn away. Now window screens were rare and few, mosquitoes could get quickly through; and with that narrow-pointed nose he'd scent us underneath the clothes. How could a human being rest when scourged by this unwelcome guest; when morning came we'd count our bites and pray for frosty winter nights. Why should some narrow-minded bloke consider it a standing joke 'cause we had nightcaps on our heads and crockeryware beneath the beds? No squirming in a torture chair for "permanents" to crimp the hair; few women's gowns with open backs nor teenage youngsters wearing slacks. And then those outside four-by-fours with hook inside and drafty doors; we sat and shivered half to death, emitting steam at every breath. It was not proof against the weather, but hurriedly was thrown together; its lumber was not tongued-and-grooved, appearance might have been improved. Its knotty boards were common spruce, warped and twisted like the deuce; we can assure you, kind sir, it was not built of Douglas fir. 'Twas neither anchored down or pinned but rocked and swayed with every wind; we wondered oft how it could last when battered by a wint'ry blast. We still can sense that upward draft, its dire effects were most abaft; no toilet tissues soft and clean, but pages from a magazine. This rendezvous for daily use was oft the object of abuse, but worst of all we've often seen it toppled o'er at Hallowe'en. We are on Easy Street today, we've mostly quit the old-time way; no more those days and nights of gloom, we boast a cosy upper room. With teas and sales we weekly strive to keep our favourite church alive; and then, a monthly rummage sale will net a neat amount of kale. Our chicken suppers hit the spot, we serve each order piping hot; we want each customer to say: "I'm coming back another day." We have an apron on the round, a money-maker we have found; just take a moment of your time, sew in a nickel or a dime. Why fret your principles away, we're living in another day; don't raise objectionable scenes, the end will justify the means. We keep our church's future bright when all in harmony unite; and thus with free and full accord, we're raising money for the Lord.

It was not far to Pictou. We had left Highway 4 after following it from Sydney, and branched to Highway 6 at Alma, a small place with a filling station. The road was interesting all the way and at a sharp turn beyond a bridge we saw an old stone house at Lyon's Brook. A tourist we met at Antigonish had stayed there the night, as it is known as Taylor's Stone House, and said there was a nice display of Nova Scotia handcraft for sale on the ground floor. Up through Lyon's Brook the road wound and across the railway track, to the left, sharp right and into old and tired Pictou. At least it looked tired to us. We stopped at an ancient stone building and talked with the sheriff in his office about the good old days when there were two glassworks in Pictou County and plenty of work. The sheriff said he had a glass cane as a relic from those days, and had owned a glass chain.

The sheriff told us about the memorial to Sir William Dawson that was unveiled the previous autumn. Sir William was born October 13, 1820, in Pictou, and once had quite a collection of geological specimens he collected. He also collected and mounted birds native to Nova Scotia but gave his collection to McGill University. And in the old house he occupied he wrote lectures he delivered to the Literary and Scientific Society of Pictou. He attended Pictou Academy and continued his studies at the University of Edinburgh from which he graduated in 1842. He became interested in geology when he returned to Nova Scotia with the Scottish geologist, Sir Charles Lyell, and they searched the Province for specimens they needed. In 1850 Dawson became Superintendent of Education for Nova Scotia, became Principal of McGill

University in 1855, discovered the first reptile in the coal formations in America, investigated the fossil forests of Joggins and wrote much material on his findings, lecturing through Canada and the United States for forty years. He was created a C.M.G. in 1882 and elected the first President of the Royal Society of Canada, was knighted by Queen Victoria, and died in 1889.

We were not long in Pictou before several old-timers were telling us about the town and its people. "We've even had a book written about us," boasted one old fellow who looked smart with a blue bow tie. "It was called *A View of the Town* and made out that our newspaper fellow was a joke, that our celebration back in '23 was another joke."

"A book?" scoffed the man near him, who wore a very old straw hat. "Five or six books is more like it. There's Patterson's *History of the County*, *Pictou Parade* by Sherwood, the *Pictou Book* by George MacLaren, and Frank Patterson's *Founder of the Town*. And there's been more doctors and preachers gone out of Pictou than any other town its size in Canada. The first settlers here come from Pennsylvania and Maryland away back in 1767. In 1773 the *Hector* came from Scotland with a load of settlers and though they had a mighty rough time the first years, they were of good stuff and made this a grand old town. It's gone down some lately but it'll be back. We used to have a Lobster Carnival here every year until some of the boys got drunk and threw some Mounties into the harbour."

"And now we're branching out with a Campsite and Wildlife Park" said bow tie. "There's over three hundred acres bought for it and we have deer and racoons and beaver and rabbits, and plans made to have a better place or zoo than down at Shubenacadie. We're getting trailers too, and fitting up to service them right. Our member in the provincial House, Harvey Veniot, asked for a Wildlife Park the first time he made a speech in the legislature, and he's got the

Federal helping him, or did have until the end of May.
They've a caretaker's cottage so the man is always on the spot
and more and more tenters are coming. There's been paths
cut to the bathing beach and we're going to have the most
popular campsite in the east. There's a staff house and gravel
roads and twenty-four roadside tables built along with eight
stone fireplaces, a good well and lots of firewood."

"We've a grand hotel, too," said straw hat. "Pictou Lodge
is one of the best in the east, and we've got a good ferry to
Prince Edward Island."

"Don't go steering 'em over there," protested bow tie. "We
need all the visitors we can get. Our weekly paper is out and
it's another best we have. I take it, and my daughter takes
it, and my two brothers up in the States take it. It's the
*Pictou Advocate,* and the editor's wife writes a smart column
in it and calls herself Ann Advocate. I read it one of the
first things on account I'm always hoping she will have a
story of people up along the shore that wanted a house. At
that time there was a place that had been left vacant when
most of the family died, and the fellow who come to buy it
heard that it had been haunted just after the first family
was in it. Used to be folks walking around in it all night
and one shuffled like he was lame and used a cane. Well,
he bought the place just the same as he said they had to have
somewhere to go. Then he moved in and every time he and
his wife was in town to buy groceries they talked about the
ghosts. They invited some to go and spend the night with
them so they would know, but no one wanted the experience.
I had a cousin from Truro who knew them well and he
come over and stayed a night. Sure enough, he heard somebody go shuffling around after midnight and it kind of
raised his back hair a bit. His wife nearly went into fits
and they lit the lamp and woke the man and told him but
he said nothing would bother them. Next day the cousin
quizzed the fellow pretty sharp and as he knew him pretty

well he got him to own up it was pretty much a trick. The man took him upstairs and showed him how the base board would come away in his bedroom, and if he scrubbed around in slippers the noise went into the room where my cousin slept like it was real. 'What do you do it for?' my cousin asked.

" 'Taxes,' grunted the fellow. 'They haven't the heart to charge me more'n a token tax. I figure the ghost stuff is worth ninety dollars a year'."

Along we went to Toney River, with cottages strung along the shore, to River John built around a bridge and then on to Tatamagouche. The place was decorated with banners to a mild degree but a man in a store said that if it were the year before we would have been able to attend the Festival of Arts, that the Festival would be back the next year. He showed us a book by Frank Patterson telling the story of Tatamagouche from the beginning when the Acadians were there and carrying on quite a trade with Louisbourg, then took time out to show us where there had been an old fort, old wells, Acadian river dams and dykes. There had been a sea battle fought off the coast and all in all it is quite historic.

"Just a few miles from here, at Millbrook near New Annan, the biggest woman ever known in Canada was born and raised. She stood over eight feet tall and weighed over 350 pounds. Her name was Anna Swan and legend has it that when she was four she was big as a young woman and when a stranger saw her playing with a doll he thought she was mentally deficient. Word about her size soon spread around and P. T. Barnum got her to go to New York where he looked after her education and had her for his show. She earned a lot of money by going on exhibition and then she married a man who was an inch shorter but weighed 500 pounds. They toured this country and the States and then went to England. They had a special house built for them in the States, with high doors and big beds and furniture but

Anna died in the mid-thirties. Her clothing and a shoe can be seen up at the Green Hill Museum."

There are many fine views from Tatamagouche and it looked a pretty village. We drove on past many beaches where summer cottages dominated and then reached Wallace. Again we stopped and soon discovered there was a Wallace Bay, Wallace River, Wallace Bridge and Wallace Station, that the old name of the area was Remsheg, that a Loyalist group were first settlers and had gristmills, sawmills and a carding mill in operation, that eight stone quarries were operated and the Wallace stone used in building Province House at Halifax and public buildings at Ottawa to say nothing of banks and other buildings in many towns. There were also four brick-yards back in the old days. Now it is a quiet area favourably known by summer tourists who drive the Sunrise Trail, and famed for its panoramas of sea and island.

On we went again and reached Pugwash, the village that makes the headlines each summer when Cyrus Eaton, the Nova Scotia-born multimillionaire, comes to his summer home and invites celebrities from all over the world to join him in thinking exercises. No one in the county would call Pugwash a Highland word or say that many of the citizens have Scottish blood, but a few families who live there in summer have roused a Scottish tradition and each July 1 they hold the "Gathering of the Clans," a day given over to Highland dancing, piping, and the wearing of the kilt. More than that, they make sure that there is mention of Gaelic for sign posts of the streets bear Gaelic inscriptions as well as English. The celebration was almost due and many yachts were floating around the harbour and some booths were being erected. We were impressed by the huge tower of a new salt mine that is a feature on the landscape, and wished we might linger for a man who sat in an old buggy in front of the drug store chuckled when we asked him for a story.

"All around here," he said. "Just keep your ears open.

There's an old granny around the corner who has a son in the States. They come home every summer, the son and his wife and family. The son has three-four of them college degrees and the old lady is so proud of him she can hardly talk steady. She's just as proud of her grandsons and they come by the other day and a woman asked how old they were. 'The doctor's nine going on ten,' she says, 'and the engineer is eleven next week.' You want stories, go over to Tides Inn and see if you can locate Charley Hollis. He was through the First World War, was a Fisheries Warden and chased poachers all over this coast, played hockey till he was near fifty and is tough as square nails. Or get them to tell you about the old woman just a bit across the bridge over there. She had a place to rent and advertised it as being 'near salt water and overlooking well-kept grounds.' So a couple from Boston paid a month in advance and come. The place is near salt water all right, but there's a high bank and you have to walk half a mile to get near bathing. As for the well-kept grounds—that's the graveyard!"

A distance from Pugwash we turned right down a slope, crossed over a long narrow bridge and were soon at Port Howe. It was hard to believe our eyes when a red fox sat up impudently ten feet inside the roadside fence and watched us go by, so we were not greatly surprised to find one lying dead on the pavement where it had been hit by a car. A mile beyond we saw another within one hundred yards of a farmyard, pulled over and mentioned it to a farmer working his field.

"Sure," he nodded. "That fellow got a chicken not long ago. I'll have to load the shotgun and watch for him. Foxes are all over the place because they're not worth catching. And racoons are just as big a trouble. I had fourteen in my barnyard one moonlight night. I shot seven down in my blueberry patch. And there's skunks, lots of them. One got into the cellar of the manse in Pugwash. Another got into a cellar over Linden way and the woman of the house almost stepped on it when she went down for potatoes. It was sitting on the steps like a cat. In Tatamagouche last week Mrs. Clarence Lockerby heard a noise on her veranda early in the morning, got up and looked and saw a skunk with its head inside a tin can. It would stand up on its hind legs and feel around for something with which to pull the can off, then bump down on the veranda. She told her son who got up and took the garden rake and led Mister Skunk off the veranda a distance and then yanked the tin off. It walked around in circles a time as if it were drunk, then went to the back shed and went to sleep in the sun. This made Mrs. Lockerby wonder as she has a pet rabbit that feeds at night and so she looked out that night and there in the moonlight was Mr. Skunk enjoying the midnight lunch with the bunny. Not so long ago Mrs. Lockerby heard a knocking at her door and opened it to find a big sheep trying to get in. It was afraid of cars speeding by. So Mrs. Lockerby knew it must be a pet and began phoning around. She found it belonged to a farm two miles away, and the owner, a lady, came and got the sheep in her car."

We gossiped further and the man stared at me. "Didn't you get to see the Hopps Museum back at Bay View?" he queried.

We said we had seen the sign but had not investigated as twice we had visited places so advertised and found little of real interest. "But this is different," insisted the man. "J. R. Harper, the New Brunswick expert in such matters, came to examine the things Hopps dug up and declared they were Indian burial relics. It was just chance digging that uncovered them and there are large copper pots, axe heads, and whole lot of knives and daggers and swords, bundles of hides and birch bark. Mr. Harper thought the grave of a chief had been uncovered. There was an arm bone and a tooth to prove a human was buried there. He thought the burial would be back in the first part of the seventeenth century, and he said it was a matter of prestige with the Micmacs to give a chief an all-out lot of equipment for the next world, that the Indians had got the pots and knives from French fur traders. You should tell people about it because some are keen about seeing Indian relics."

"Certainly," we agreed. "You never know what a summer visitor wants."

"Lots of them are collectors, too," said our friend. "They stop and ask where they can get old clocks, dolls, shaving mugs, tobacco pipes, coins, lanterns, salt and pepper shakers, old guns and the like. Some of them will pay crazy prices for things, too. My father made a mat hook for mother. He used a big nail and filed the hook, set it in a wood handle with a top of a rifle cartridge to keep it firm. She used it thirty years or more. A tourist saw it when he called about an old lantern we had, and when she didn't want to part with it he offered her twenty-five dollars. So she took the money. She bought a better hook for a dollar and had the rest for profit. The lantern was brought over by some Loyalists, was tin punched with holes and you set a candle inside. The door had a mica front. It wasn't ours but was in the house when we bought it, and one day an American come and offered mother fifty dollars for it. She had a struggle with her conscience but she took the money. She said it seemed like robbery of some kind."

From Port Howe to Amherst on Highway 6 there are farms that look prosperous and farms that have been abandoned for years. There is the occasional church and school, some of the latter being closed, and stores at some points, along with filling stations. We saw three deer near an orchard of old apple trees, as if they were looking to see if there were any prospects of fruit in the fall. The house was gone and only a few lilac bushes and a gaping cellar showed where it had been. The old barn was still standing, weather-stained and gray, with a sag in the roof, leaning out of plumb, its doors flapped drunkenly on one hinge. We stopped to watch the prowling deer and wondered if some man in a remote part had been a boy around the place, enjoying a feeling of security as he tended sleek horses and placid cows, jumping from the scaffold to piles of hay pitched to the barn floor for supper feeding. Perhaps on stormy days he, with a pal from the next farm, made a tunnel in the haymow, or hunted the higher scaffold for nests where free-ranging hens laid their eggs. Of course he might enlist the neighbour boy's help with the chores of feeding the calves, cleaning the cow stable and spreading clean bedding.

It must have been good to go to the barn in the morning and hear the eager whinney of the horses as the door opened, the cows impatient in their stalls, to inhale the odours of hay and grain and livestock and manure and harness. The boy would carry a lantern winter mornings and be careful where and how he placed it. The light would be dim but enough for one used to the barn, and the lantern would be hung on a peg while the milking was done. Quite likely the farmer's wife hated the lantern but more or less respected it. It often leaked kerosene and she hated cleaning it, but it had to be kept in working order, was used in the henhouse and woodshed as well as the barn. Sometimes it was lighted, turned low and put under the buffalo robe close to one's feet in the sleigh when there was a long ride to the store and chilbains must be avoided.

We got out of the car and walked to the old cellar hole as the deer put up white flags and vanished into the woods. If you have any feeling for history, there is poignant meaning in old cellars that tell of yesteryear. They speak of a pioneer couple wearing their lives away in an attempt to make a fertile farm from too thin soil. The land was cleared, a garden made and an orchard set out. The boys and girls grew to manhood and the bright lights of big centres lured them from the long hours and hard work on the farm. Or friends brought word of stone-free rich soil in the west and the trek was made. And we could see a tangle of vines and bushes in the place where the cream bowls had sat in the cellar. By the spot where the kitchen steps had been a plucky peony was still making appearance each season, and we knew the old purple lilac spread its fragrance on the air each June. The apple trees looked gaunt and shaggy and some young hemlock and spruce were firmly rooted where the garden had been. We walked around and found three cherry trees and felt that robins would be calling us intruders for they surely must await the ripening of the fruit. Some time a wife had carefully watched those cherry trees, made cherry pies and put cherries in bottles for the winter. And it was more than likely that the daughter of the house, and perhaps the son, helped with the stoning of the cherries, a rather sticky but rewarding task—for who could say how many luscious red blobs found their way elsewhere than the bowl?

There were five or six more deserted farms after we had our stop at Linden and it did seem sad to think of the changes wrought by time and better modes of travel. Here and there we saw sheep, and pasture brooks that wandered around as if in no particular hurry to reach a larger current. By one we saw an ancient wooden trough up-tilted and knew that at one time cattle drank gratefully from it. It was one of those country streams that run full with the spring freshet and in hot summer dwindle to a trickle washing dark stones and gravel, and shallow little pools where birds bathed with tiny splashings.

Then we were back at Amherst again and as we made sure of right turnings to find the road to Cape Tormentine an old man at the filling station where we paused asked if we wanted to know anything about the town.

"You ever hear of the great Amherst Mystery?" he wheezed. "It was the biggest ghost story ever in this whole country, and I can take you to the very spot where Dan Teed's house stood. He worked in the shoe factory and in the house with him were two of his wife's sisters, Jane and Esther Cox. This Esther was short and rather stout. She was the pale sort but had curly hair. She was going with a young chap who worked in the shoe factory and they had a spat of some kind and he left town. Then things began to happen. Esther slept with her sister and the night after she jumped up and yelled there was a mouse in the bed. They lighted the lamp and saw something moving the straw in the mattress but there was no mouse. So they got back into bed—and something moved on the floor. They looked and it was a cardboard box filled with patchwork to make a quilt. Esther pushed it out from the bed with her foot and next thing it jumped in the air and fell over on its side. Jane picked it up and found there was nothing alive in it, put it down—and the box jumped again so that both girls screamed and Dan pulled on his pants and went to see what the racket was about. They told him but he shook the box out, found nothing and ordered them back into bed.

"Well, the next night Esther declared she was dying. Jane lighted the lamp and had a look at her. Esther was red as fire and all swollen. So Jane called Dan again and when he came there were sounds like shots from under the bed and suddenly Esther went back to normal colour and the swelling vanished. In the morning she had no appetite and that night the bedclothes flew from the two girls to a corner of the room. Both girls screamed and Jane fainted. Dan ran in and put the clothes back but they flew to the other corner of the room, and the pillow under Esther's head sailed up like a balloon. That was enough for Dan. He called a doctor.

"The doctor come and laughed at Dan's story, said Esther was suffering from nervous excitement. Just as he spoke Esther's pillow shot straight in the air, and the doctor jumped back. As he did the bedclothes were whipped off to the corner of the room. Before they could pick them up a loud scratching noise was heard. It sounded above Esther's bed and when they looked up they saw writing being formed without any pen or visible hand. The sentence read: 'Esther Cox, you are mine to kill.' Then a large piece of plaster flew off the wall and fell at the doctor's feet, while rappings sounded from under the bed. Dan quizzed the doctor but the medical man said he could not understand anything, that he would return in the morning with a strong sedative and other medicine.

"The sedative was slow to take effect so he injected morphia and a great banging on the roof began. Dan and the doctor went outside and it was if an unseen hand holding a big hammer was pounding the shingles. It was now too frightening a matter to be kept secret and a town minister, Dr. Tucker, heard the story and declared that Esther was a fraud. Dr. Clay, the Baptist minister, visited the girl and went away declaring she had become a human electric battery. He preached a sermon about her, defending her against the other preacher. Then the Teed's minister, Methodist, named Temple, came to see Esther. As he came in a pail of cold water in the sink began to boil, and articles flew around the room. People flocked to the place. Other doctors examined the girl, were mystified, and Dan packed her off to Sackville to a married sister there.

"Nothing happened while she stayed away but the night she returned she said a 'ghost' had told her the house would burn. Careful watch was kept that night and Dan, quite relieved when nothing happened, laughed about it as he got ready to go to work in the morning. Suddenly lighted matches began to fall from the ceiling and but for quick work by Jane a serious blaze would have resulted. Dan and his wife kept close watch that day and the next, then things seemed normal. The third day they smelled smoke, ran down cellar and found kindlings on fire. People were angry when they heard the

story as they said half of Amherst might have burned down
had the blaze got going, and they begged Dan to send the girl
away from his home. John W. White operated a restaurant
and had been greatly interested in the case. He offered Esther
work in his place but soon after she arrived the door of the
large stove he used for preparing meals refused to stay shut.
It bulged open despite props placed against it. A boy with a
jack knife yelled as the knife flew from his grasp and stabbed
Esther in the back. A box of groceries weighing fifty pounds
suddenly scuttled the length of the room, and that was enough
for White. He sent Esther home, but Dan did not want her
and she lived for a time with friends in Saint John.

When she did return, Dan had a visitor, Walter Hubbell,
an actor, who wanted to stay in the Teed home and observe
Esther. She was hardly home before Hubbell's umbrella, left
by a stand, flew fifteen feet into the dining-room. His satchel
was thrown ten feet. Fearful of what might happen next,
he sprang up as a large knife appeared on the ceiling above
Esther's head then darted at him. He avoided the knife but
a chair slid across the room and rammed the one he was
sitting in, almost knocking him clear. Other chairs slid
around when he escaped to another room. After lunch he
lay down on a sofa to rest. Esther came into the room and
a large glass paperweight rose from the shelf and whizzed at
him. It struck the arm of the sofa. He was scared but stayed
on and saw a large sugar bowl vanish from the dining-room
table at breakfast, then drop from the ceiling. He had enough
in short time and went away to write his book. Dan sent
Esther away and she got arrested for stealing clothing though
she had not been at the place, was sent to jail for four months.
Finally she was married and left the area. The book on the
Amherst Mystery sold like hot cakes and you can't find a copy
now, which is a pity as Hubbell had lawyers and doctors to
the house until he had sixteen witnesses to prove what was
going on in the Teed house. Yes, sir, sounds scary. It

happened just the time I was born and was all I heard when
I was a little tyke. Too bad  they took the house down."

Our friend had wheezed like an old leaky boiler and now
he coughed and coughed as he finished his story. The filling
station man said he had read the book and it was the *gospel
truth*. He was so in earnest we were half glad we did not have
to stay in Amherst for the night. Across the marsh we drove
and at Aulac swung right on New Brunswick Highway 16
and soon were at a corner where and old church stands. In its
steeple is the bell once used by the Acadians at Beauséjour.
It was not far to Point de Bute from the church at Mount
Whatley, but on the way we saw a stone gateway at the
entrance to an old cemetery so stopped and read the inscription on a plaque, learned that the first Methodist church in
Canada was built on the location where we stood, that it was
erected in 1788 and was a stone building with a thatched
roof.

We saw more sign boards erected by the New Brunswick
Government. One at Mount Whatley had said the spot was
where Colonel Moncton had his headquarters in 1755 while
his troops were advancing against Fort Beauséjour. The next
one, beyond the church site, called the spot "Camp Hill," and
said the rebel, Jonathan Eddy, had his headquarters there
when he led his ragged band of looters against Fort Cumberland.

On we went and came to a sign board reading "Pont a
Buot." It is about 400 yards from a spot where the French had
a small blockhouse as a defence for a crossing of the Missiquash
River. When Winslow marched his New Englanders up the
marsh from Fort Lawrence the French could watch him all
the way and knew exactly that he must use the log bridge
to cross the tide-ruled stream. But they did not destroy the
crossing nor come out to oppose his scouts. They chose to stay
under cover and fire their muskets but the New Englanders
charged over the bridge and chased the garrison back to Fort

Beauséjour. We parked and walked around the scene, trying
to visualize the marching New Englanders, slapping at the
marsh mosquitoes, cursing the warmth of the day that made
the slogging over the spongy marsh such an effort, and angry
as wasps to get at the Frenchies and the Indians in the background.

An elderly farmer came along in a tractor and stopped to
talk with us. He said many Acadian relics had been plowed
up and dug up by farmers along the ridge, and sometimes
they found Indian arrow heads as the road mainly followed
the old Indian trail, and the portage used by the Acadians.
He said there had been much travel along that way for many
years as the French had built Fort Gasperaux as a defence
on the other side of the Isthmus of Chignecto and as a point
from which to ship supplies to Louisbourg. One farmer had
uncovered a cache of seven old pewter plates in perfect condition. He said that when he was a boy an old well-like hole
had been discovered in a pasture. It was cleared to quite a
depth but water seeped in and the diggers were discouraged.
Rumour had it that the settlers in the area had buried
their coin in a deep pit at the time of the Expulsion.

"They used to tell, thirty years ago," the farmer continued,
"that a band of gypsies camped along the ridge for a week
and that it was a long dry spell. They had heard about the
money pit and they dug at it day and night. Old folks used
to say they could see lanterns around the digging all night.
When they were gone some people went over and the hole
was down more than thirty feet, and left open. The farmers
filled it in lest some sheep or cattle fall into the hole, and
nobody knows whether or not the gypsies found a thing."

He sat silent a time, chewing a timothy stem, then stirred.
"I've heard a lot about these instruments that will detect
metals," he said. "Many a time I've thought I'd like to invest
in one and use it along this ridge. The Acadians were thrifty
and they sold fat cattle here for half a century. They must

have had money, and it's almost sure they buried it for the time they would be back. Anyway, I like to dream about it, and it's cheaper to dream than buy one of them Irish Sweepstake tickets."

He was in no hurry to go and neither were we, for he spoke gently, as dreamers generally do, and when we mentioned the marsh and watched the mouse hawks over the dyke banks he began talking about the scare he had had when a boy and some screech owls nested in a grove near his home.

"I think every hair on my head stood straight up the night I was going home alone and one of them little fellows let out his screech. Worst was, I glanced toward the bush and saw his eyes. They seemed coming right at me and I ran faster than I was ever able to do again. Now I rather like the little fellows, especially the saw-whets. Mouse hawks? Yes, they've been here long as I can remember, flying over the dykes all day long, now and then catching a fat mouse. It beats all the way the mouse population keeps up. Last Sunday I was down by the marsh edge and it was nice and warm and enough wind to keep off the mosquitos. I lay back in the grass and soon I could hear tiny sounds. I pulled away some weeds and grass tops and there were three different mouse nests in view. There were five or six wee fellows in one and the old one came in as if I were not there at all—which makes me wonder if they have good eyesight. When she edged in to rest a while the little ones made tiny little squeals, and that was the sound I had heard. My wife used to tell me that on a still afternoon she could hear the fairy fiddle of the grasshopper, but I never have."

We hated to leave our friend and, in fancy, I could hear with him the tremulous call of the screech owl that seemed to fill the countryside on a still night. They like to sound their notes during a harvest moon, and the farmer said he had heard them tormenting a fox when it barked from some marsh cover.

It was but a short distance before another sign indicated: "Inverma Farm, owned by John Allan, co-leader with Jonathan Eddy of the Rebellion of 1776. The house was burned by British troops." It brought to memory a story in a paper years ago about one of the rebels hiding in the woods and living on potatoes that had been in the Allan cellar and were roasted during the fire.

# 7 | Wind Chain, Switchel, White Turkeys, and Burglar Alarms

IN A SHORT DISTANCE we saw another sign which read "Bloody Bridge" and knew it marked the spot where five soldiers of the garrison at Fort Cumberland were ambushed by a band of Micmacs, killed and scalped. The redskins had hidden below the bridge and in the surrounding gully, outnumbered the British five to one and took them completely by surprise.

A few miles further on we saw a woman working at her flowers and stopped to ask about the location of the old French road. We were looking over the marshes and trying to imagine a group of dark-skinned Acadian farmers driving cattle to a schooner waiting at Baie Verte. The lady was very gracious and said she was glad to rest her back, that her petunias were the best she had ever grown. When we asked about the old trail she cupped her hands and showed amazing lung power as she sent a high-pitched call barnward.

"History gives me a headache," she smiled. "They talk about who lived here one time, where the Acadian cellars were and that sort of thing. But I'm only interested in who lives here now, and the people of today. I don't even know who my great-grandfather was, and I don't want to. Why bother with yesterday? It's gone."

A thin man came from the barn. He wore overalls that had been laundered many times and were now a very pale blue, and he limped slightly.

"Hurt my leg getting over a fence," he smiled. "A neighbour's bull was after me and I was in too big a hurry. Can I be of help?"

He looked like a gentleman, and he talked and acted like one, and we had a most enjoyable time with him as he pointed out the trail used two centuries ago, showed us where part of the old French portage could be seen, where an old Acadian aboideau was located. He talked about the homes of a generation ago that had lined the road going into Baie Verte. All had had fine horses and fine carriages, and social events were taken seriously. "There were more dinner parties then than there are in town today," he said. "I can remember grandma in her silk that rustled whenever she stirred, her shiny black buttoned boots, her skirts right to the floor. Watch as you go along and you'll see some old elms and chestnuts and hedgerows along the way. There were fine homes back of them when I was a boy, and some rare old characters."

He carefully walked with us out of earshot of the flower lady and began to chuckle gently. "My wife is from another part of New Brunswick," he said, "where there is no history whatever, and she rather resents what she terms the 'eternal talk' about this area. You have to go down around Port Royal in Nova Scotia to find a region with as much history as this district. The Acadians came in the seventeenth century and had their villages all along. And this was their great road across the Isthmus, and there were two forts with garrisons. Then came the attack by the New Englanders, and both forts were captured. The Expulsion followed and there were Acadian fugitives in hiding all through this area. About fifty of them wintered in a place ten miles from here where the Indians had a camp. I have arrow heads I found there fifty years ago. It's too bad you didn't come around here about a book at that time. Fifty years ago there were real characters in every community. There was a choice lad who lived down toward Point de Bute. He had a big post at the entrance to his farm lane. There was no gate or bars, just the post, with a length of chain hanging from it. People who came to the farm usually asked George what the chain was for. That was what he wanted. 'It's very windy here on the marsh,' he would say, 'and we have to plan our work according to the wind. Every morning when I get up I look out at the post—and if that chain is out straight I know it's too windy to work on the marsh.' He was a rough lusty old lad who worked long hours and he was middle-aged before he thought of getting married. By that time he had his place in good order but he was no beauty, and knew it. So he courted a schoolma'am a bit past her prime, one of the sort who has high ideals and is choosy about a man. But her hopes had dimmed and probably she considered George somewhat better than a lonely old age. So they were married and after four or five years with George and three babies I think all the ideals had flown out the window. George never had time to go to anything, not even church or an auction, but Mrs. George had her way of managing him and one fall she got him to a revival meeting being held in the Baptist church. It was Thanksgiving time and the good man exhorted all to stand and give reasons for thankfulness. Some were thankful for improved health, some for good crops, some for visits from relatives not seen in years. It went on until nearly all had testified. Then the good man asked if there were no one else, and Mrs. George slowly rose to her feet. 'I am thankful,' she said in her rather thin voice, 'I am not a man. . .' She seemed to realize suddenly what she had said, wavered and sat down. There was a silence as no one knew what she had intended to say, and the good man looked perplexed. Then George, who had been to two or three school meetings, jumped and exclaimed loudly: 'I second the motion.'

"That ended the service. There was a hymn, loudly sung, and men and women shaking as they tried to control themselves, and George looking satisfied with himself, and poor Mrs. George looking at the floor. I'll not forget that meeting as long as I live. A year or so after a man from town bought the farm next to George, and George resented anyone from town. The town chap did not understand this and used to go over and ask how to raise turkeys, how to sow buckwheat, all sorts of questions, with George merely grunting answers. One day the man ran over to where George was plowing. 'Did you ever have a horse sick with the heaves?' he asked. 'Yes' grunted George, never halting his team. The man followed right behind in the furrow. 'What did you give it?' he asked. 'Turpentine,' grunted George. 'Thanks, ever so much,' said the man and hurried back home. The next afternoon he came again to George, looking quite depressed. 'Did I hear you right?' he asked. 'Did you say you had a horse sick with the heaves?' 'Yep,' grunted George. 'And you gave it turpentine?' 'Yep.' 'Well, I gave my horse turpentine, and it died.' 'So did mine,' grunted George, never checking his team."

Baie Verte was a sleepy little village with a very sharp corner and just beyond the corner we saw three large blue heron standing in shallow water not two hundred yards from the nearest buildings. One thrust like lightning and its head came back to reveal a small fish abut a finger length in its bill. It was but a short drive to Port Elgin and before we reached the village we saw a sign pointing the way to Fort Gaspereau. We drove in and found a lighthouse near the beach. A large boulder bore a plaque stating that this was the site of the fort, and markers showed where the powder magazine and store houses had been. A small enclosure had nine graves with headstones, the burial ground of a patrol of English soldiers ambushed by a large Indian party while looking for fuel. The old fort site seemed a lonely place and we visualized French sentries looking over the water from the ramparts on moonlight nights and dreaming of France. The only activity in the place then was the arrival and departure of trading schooners that came to get beef cattle and butter and other stores for the garrison at Louisbourg.

There was a bridge in the middle of the small town, and friendly stores. In fact, we found Port Elgin an amazingly friendly place. We were rolling slowly looking for a parking place when a man with a panel truck called: "Wait a minute. I'm going to leave." So we waited and he waved to us cheerfully as he went away. We went into a small drugstore to buy a daily paper, saw a soda fountain and went toward it. Immediately a woman with three children yanked one youngster from a stool to make sure we had seats. "He's really finished," she smiled. "He just doesn't want to get down."

We had milk shakes that were delicious, and listened with great interest to a wave of chatter around us as three men and two women came in to buy soap and shaving cream. "Maud likes to put on the dog," muttered one man to his friend. "She'd drive clear to Moncton to get paper napkins different from what you get here, and she's got her bathroom decorated with guest towels no bigger'n a wash cloth my wife uses." "I know," nodded his pal. "My wife sent to Moncton for some of them towel doodads, all colours of the rainbow and useless. She's even got toilet paper the colour to match 'em." "My wife's gone bugs on summer drinks," was the rejoinder. "She's bought them plastic cups with a tray and she has a pitcher with a slot you open with your thumb, and mixes grape juice with coke and the like. It don't taste like anything fit to drink." "I know," sighed the other man. "I tried and tried to get Nellie to make drinks like mother did. We had a great big red earthen jug and she put in cold spring water, a cup of molasses, a cup of vinegar, a handful of oatmeal, a teaspoon of ginger and two cups of sugar. She kept the jug in the cellar and boy when you came in and had a mug of that switchel it was worth while. In haying she'd make us a jug of just molasses and oatmeal in the cold water and we'd sit the jug in the shade and go to take swigs pretty often. It gave a man something to sweat out of his system and it tasted mighty good. There was a thick bush at the edge of our hayfield and I mind finding a woodchuck hole right where we were going to put the jug. I got a spade that evening and started to dig the chuck out. It was the hardest work ever and when I got down a few feet in them bush roots and my arms ached fit to drop off, found the chuck had a back entrance and was gone. Another time we had a wild morning when father shoved the jug into the shade of a bush and disturbed one of them big hornet's nests that was just overhead. I never knew he could run until then."

They moved away after finishing their icecream, and the third man, who was to one side, listening, grinned at us, showing a wide gap in his uppers, and great good humour. "Them fellers wouldn't marry girls around here," he said. "Had to go down around Sackville, and now they can't git enough ahead to buy a new tractor. Their wimmen spends it on clothes and the like, and they have a time to get them up in the morning. Well, that's life, and why I married me a girl from right the next farm. She knew how we lived, and she had no airs. She ain't no looker like them fellers' wives but beauty's only skin deep and my wife's worth a dozen of them. We don't run much more than a one-horse farm but we've got a dollar in the bank and no back taxes. My woman is up around daylight and she puts a real breakfast on the table, one that'll stand a man till noon."

We murmured inquiries as to what he thought constituted a good breakfast.

"Any farmer can tell you that," he shot back. "A mess of apple sauce, two, three eggs, boiled, biscuits or muffins with lots of butter, good tea and a piece of pie a quarter-plate size. And another thing. We don't turn on the radio to eat break-fast by. We're still friendly."

After Port Elgin the road stretched away through a less populated district with scattered farms and some fields looking untended. There was sense of sameness we could feel, a sort of countryside inertia, and we were to Melrose before seeing any variety. A large church loomed on the landscape but seemed far away from everything. We began meeting quite a string of cars and knew they must have come from Prince Edward Island on the ferry. Then we sighted water far ahead, saw we were in a speed zone, rounded a long turn and arrived at Cape Tormentine. We parked by a general store and were entertained by a genial merchant who had one of the old-time powder horns so rare today. He also owned a "goose" gun over one hundred years old, and told us about the geese and ducks shot in bygone years along that stretch of shore.

"You came in through Bayfield," he said, "and one time that was Cape Tormentine. Then the people got together and agreed to switch names. So this place became Cape Tormentine, and back there was Bayfield."

We asked him what the people did for a living.

"They fish," came the answer. "Mackerel mostly. They go out in their boats and set their nets and go to bed. Yes, they sleep in the boats. At daylight they begin hauling and will catch half a ton on a good run. It's a hard way to earn a living but we're used to that around here. As for us, we don't have to complain as many tourists going to the Island stop in to buy this or that. We thought there were a lot of them when one boat handled the traffic. Now we've got two boats on the run and often there will be cars left over. The Island premier has asked them to either build a cause-way over or get another boat on the run for next year. Now that they're getting fine paved roads over on the

Island, everybody wants to go there. No, I won't part with that old gun. It's been around as long as I can remember and it used to be taken to chivarees. Shoot her off alongside the window of a house, and it sounds like the end of the world. One place we were having fun the bride got very mad. She was upstairs dressing to go away on a trip that evening and she opened the window to throw a pitcher of water over the men with the gun and, somehow, let go of it. A man was pointing up to the window to warn the others and the pitcher came down so that his hand went inside. The blow almost broke his wrist but the pitcher wasn't even cracked and he carried it home as a souvenir."

The *Abegweit* was arriving at the pier so we hurriedly drove over and ours was the last car but two to get on board. We paid three dollars for a round trip ticket and thought the rate very fair, as it is a fine boat. It was nice up on deck to watch the long New Brunswick coastline recede and the dark-red banks of Prince Edward Island begin to loom nearer and nearer. Two men sat near us and they began to argue rather loudly about the good old days, and the present. One claimed that when fox farming was at its peak the Island had the best times it would ever know. The other declared that when a Causeway was built travel to the Island would double and it would become the greatest vacation land in the east.

Their talk ran on and on as we watched a line of green appear above the red band and listened to their tales of deep snow in the winter, the bumper crops of the old days and the size of average Island pigs we knew they were Island sons, and were to learn in the next few days that nowhere on earth are there good folk who can compare with the Islanders for clannishness and an attitude in general that almost makes them a race apart. Don't mistake my meaning. You will not find a kindlier, more genial, more hospitable people anywhere. They are always ready to lend a hand, will go out of their way to get you information, but you sense that in their heart of hearts they feel sorry for your hard luck in not being born on the Island.

We drove from the pier at Borden and every car seemed to be racing to get away first. Fine new pavement led out as a long ribbon laid between fields of varying shades of green, their cart roads reddish markings. Here and there were small woodlots and the gentle roll of the land was comparable to that of the Northumberland Strait we had crossed. Soon road signs loomed before us and we chose the route to Summerside. It would soon be evening and thickening light shed its glamour over a mosaic of garden squares blacked neatly in front of well-kept farm buildings. The houses looked small in comparison with the large well-painted barns but the whole was spread like a warm valentine done in bright colours. All the way along the places looked well arranged, as if nothing was out of place, as if nothing unneeded were there. And when we thought something might be missing it took us some time to discover there were no stones, no stone fences, no stone piles in the field. And seldom was there a grove near the roadside. It was getting late and we did not stop anywhere to chat or make enquiries but turned from the street entering Summerside where we saw a fine new motel on the left and close by an eating place. Luck was with us as a new wing to the motel was just being opened and we got a place for the night. The maid had to carry in chairs as the furniture was just being installed. Then we went to the eating place and had a fine dinner.

Later we walked around the town and found the streets rather rough. There are many small stores but Holman's was a large departmental feature. There was considerable traffic and many were going to the movies, something we had not seen around Nova Scotia. We saw nice playgrounds, a fine new civic auditorium, and several churches. It was nice and warm in the morning and we talked with several people in the town. We asked how the town got its name.

"A Daniel Green owned the site and for a long time this was known as Green's Shore," said a man in a store. "The legend goes that one day late in March a visitor who lived on the north shore came to visit Green and was struck by the strength of the sun on the southern side. He turned to Joseph, a son of Daniel, and said: 'Why, you are on the summer side here.' Joe repeated that story to everybody he met the next few weeks and soon people started calling the place 'summerside.' It was as easy as that."

We had no trouble parking but the meter would not take our money. We mentioned this to a passerby but he assured us there were many in such conditions and not to worry in the slightest. We asked if there were .any features we should explore and he said the town was like any other but maybe we should call on Golden Reeves who was a woodcarver and used maple wood exclusively. "Only he's out of town right now," concluded our friend.

There did not seem to be any of the usual rush we had noticed on the mainland. People had plenty of time. In the stores there was no impatience to get waited on, and outside it seemed that for every person working there were two idling on the sidewalks. An old chap with a bright red tie caught our eye as he peered at fire-blackened ruins on the main street.

"Carelessness," he was muttering. "Always carelessness. That's what makes fires."

Soon he was telling us of three fires out where he lived, all caused by carelessness. "That's why I've never smoked," he added. "Smokers toss matches around and leave cigarette butts where they start fires. Course, there was the cost of tobacco helped me decide. I've a cousin who has smoked enough to buy himself a tractor, and I tell him so. There he is now, crossing the street by that drugstore. That's Joe."

"Ah, yes," we said, feeling impelled to say something. "What's his full name?"

"His full name's 'Jack Dempsey'," chuckled our friend. "And it don't take much to get him full. Lost his farm three years ago. Couldn't raise enought to buy a horse now."

"Do they buy horses over here?" we queried.

"Sure do," snapped red tie. "I own two, and one's a good-enough roader. Don't have to get him licensed every year or new tires. And another thing, the model doesn't change. There's plenty got horses out my way."

"Is that far from here?" we asked.

"Not in a car," came the snappy answer. "I'm between Mount Carmel and Cape Egmont, and there's a road. You ever been out that way?"

We admitted we had not had that pleasure, and he shook his head.

"One of the best parts of the Island," he said. "Law abiding, as any, hard working, if there's good pay, church going, if the wife's got a new hat. Just like any good place. You a foreigner?"

"If Nova Scotia is foreign, I am."

"Any place off this Island is foreign," he shot back.

"What about Confederation?" we asked. "Aren't you part of Canada?"

"Son," he squinted his eyes seriously, "that Confederation you talk about never comes further than Cape Tormentine. We're the poor relations down here, and that's the way we've been treated. They write us nice letters sometimes, but they sure don't want to see us. They call us clannish over here, and I reckon we are. Not too far from here there was a man died last summer. He'd been head of the Children's Aid for years, head of the Sunday School. In fact he was up to his eyes in any good work there was, and he sold farm machinery, knew everybody, helped everybody. But when he died the paper printed a fine obituary, telling all his good works, then the last line said. 'But he was not an Islander. He was six months old when his mother brought him here'."

Our friend laughed and rocked on his heels.

"That's the way we are, but we like everybody 'cept them at Ottawa. You drive around and see this Province. We've got the finest climate in the world, the best sea air. You stay around a week or so and you'll be like that woman down in California or some place. She'd just divorced her fifth husband and a friend asked how she felt. 'Just like a new man,' she said." He cackled and rocked again. "That's how you'll feel," he said, and walked away as if he'd suddenly remembered something.

We drove from Summerside on Highway 1 and it wasn't the best pavement in Canada, but showed wear and tear and had the occasional break that made us drive carefully. Soon we were away from the better homes and farms and there were long gaps of scrub bush and often the homes were anything but signs of prosperity. Some seemed quite isolated from neighbours and there was not much traffic. We stopped at a small store and wondered what trade it enjoyed as there were only two other homes in sight. But a dirt road wandered away in the bush and perhaps some customers came from that direction. We went in and looked around. Two women in overalls, and hatless, were buying a few essentials like soap and salt and cigarettes. They eyed us with some hostility but the man back of the counter nodded cheerfully. He wore a dirty apron and he needed a shave, had needed one for at least a week, but he talked readily when the two women were gone. His entire stock would not have fetched two hundred dollars.

"Well, I make a sort of living," he said. "Most of the people around here haven't cars and they walk here to buy. Take me, I haven't been as far as Charlottetown in twenty years. I'll bet one of them women that was here ain't been to Summerside since she was a girl. Lots in this area don't earn much in the run of a year. The men work out wherever they can and they make a dollar last."

We asked how far we would go to reach another town.

"Clear to Alberton," said the man. "This part of the Island ain't settled much. In fact you take the whole Island and we haven't had an increase in population the last twenty years. It's going down, if anything. When I was a young fellow in O'Leary it was much bigger than it is today. You're looking for things to write about, eh? Well, I could tell you some in other parts to the east of here, but up this road there's nothing. One place I know was plagued with fellows writing on walls and fences. You know how it is around country schools in some places. They never could catch the fellow who did it but after a time the writing stopped and there was no more until a man in the village had bought a farm and was starting out for himself. His barn and wagon shed were across the road from the house and one day there was writing on the shed four inches high. It read: 'Wanted. A Wife. Healthy. Good Natured. Good Cook. This Place Mine. No Mortgage. Apply at House.' Of course people said right off that this was the fellow who used to write on fences and walls, and some said they ought to have the law on him no matter if it was a few years late. But darned if a woman didn't go to the house one day and ask to see the lad. She looked him up and down and asked questions and he did likewise and the upshot was he bought a license in Kensington and they were hitched. Then somebody, likely jealous of this woman's luck, told her about the writing on walls. She jumped on her husband about it which made him so mad he up and forced the real culprit to own up, and here it was the son of the preacher who had been on the place at the time. You never can tell, and you hadn't ought to judge."

We agreed wholeheartedly.

"Come to think of it," he grinned, "about seven miles on, past the first canteen, there's a woman who had ten gall stones removed. She has them in a bottle to show people and nothing would please her more to have you call. She was never in a hospital till the operation and she gives the details first to last with nothing left out."

It sounded interesting, we said, but we had to get to Alberton.

"An old girl back where I used to live went to the hospital last summer," said our man following us outside. "The doctor seen she was new to it all and nervous. 'I guess you've never been X-rayed before?' he said. 'No,' she answered brightly, 'but I've been ultraviolated.' Ain't that a good one! They tell it on the woman but I bet they got the story out of the *Reader's Digest* or the like."

Bushes and canteens and little traffic suddenly gave way to some fine farms and then we were approaching Alberton. There were plenty of cars and we saw five with American license plates in one block. The first man we questioned told us about the fine wood carving done by the Leavetts of Alberton and we were disappointed to find their place closed. One man we talked with was a photographer and worked for the Charlottetown *Guardian,* which, he said, "covered the Island like the dew." Another told us that Alberton was first known as "Cascumpeque," and was named after Albert Edward, Prince of Wales, later Edward the Seventh, who visited the Island in August, 1860. In another store an elderly man who was a customer became quite interested when he learned we wanted information and stories. "I can give you one," he said. "My father was a lawyer, and when he was a young man went to Toronto to college there. The residence was a wooden building with poor heating, and the partitions between the box bedrooms were thin as paper. Father roomed with another law student and next door was a lean, gaunt fellow studying theology. He had barely enough money to live on and that winter had a bad cold. He coughed so father and his roommate could not get to sleep and in the morning they told him he should see a doctor. He said he was very sorry he had disturbed them, but they said they were worried over his health. Of course he didn't see a doctor as that meant expense. Next night he was worse than ever and they made up a story, telling him they had consulted some medical students who said that such a cough might result in terrific spasms and men had been known to cough up their insides. The theolog said he was very sorry, he would try and control his cough. That night as they returned to the residence father and his friend met a medical student who had intestines taken from a guinea pig during experiments. They borrowed the parcel and that night when the poor theolog had had a worse spell of coughing than usual, and slept again, they stole in and placed the entrails on his pillow. Next morning he was very late coming down to breakfast and looked pale and shaky. "It happened,' he said in a hoarse voice. 'I coughed them up.' Father and his roommate were all sympathy at once, and half sorry they had played such a trick. 'Oh, I think it will be all right,' said their victim. 'With the help of prayer and a toothpick, I got them back in again.' "

We went out quickly to get fresh air after that one and were told that the main feature of Alberton was the turkey ranch of Jack Matthews. We soon had directions and drove to the farm. Mr. Matthews was more than kind to us and took us around all the buildings. There were turkeys everywhere, turkeys by the thousand — A. O. Smith Whites in medium size, and Thompson Whites in large size. There were one thousand birds in the breeding flock, and Mr. Matthews said he had begun his project with exactly twelve turkey eggs. He had raised 55,000 in a year. He had large wooden runs at the beginning but heavy falls of snow had wrecked these and they were abandoned. A lot of work ran hand in hand with raising turkeys. There had to be the cleaning of pens and weekly fresh litter. The old litter put out each time made enough rich fertilizer to plant fifty acres in oats and wheat, and because of the turkey manure he got sixty bushels of oats to the acre. He took in five hundred eggs a day. A brooder looked after four thousand birds at a time. There was running water on the various floors of the buildings and heat was regulated carefully. Turkeys were shipped to all parts of the Atlantic Provinces and elsewhere. It was turkeys morning, noon and night, week in and week out, but Mr. Matthews has built his business into large proportions and is having remarkable success. He studies every angle of turkey raising, is extremely careful in all he does, and gets top results.

After leaving Alberton we saw an impressive memorial by the roadside and stopped to read the inscription:

To the Glory of God in Memory of His Servants The Rev. George Gordon, 1822-1861. His Wife Ellen Catharine Powell, 1833-1861 and the Rev'd Jas. D. Gordon 1833-1892. Devoted Missionaries of the Presbyterian Church Who Were Slain as Martyrs By the Natives of Erromanga in the New Hebrides. Erected at their Birthplace by the Presbytery of Prince Edward Island 1955.

As we were stopped a man in a car braked and asked if we were going to Tignish. We said we were and he smiled and said: "Just a tip from a native—the back dirt road is the best."

We thanked him and drove that way, liked the view of farm and field and woods and shore line. Many cars were parked around the little town and nobody was in a hurry. We liked that serene Island atmosphere. No one gets agitated. Everyone nods and speaks with a stranger. A car with a Michigan license was in front of a store and we saw a clerk follow the man out and point out the way he should go. Then and oldster by the front door looked us over and asked mildly if we were looking for anyone in particular.

Yes, we said, we wanted some native who could tell us about Tignish and the area.

"Reckon you don't have to look further," he announced.

"I've got time to kill as my wife's making a call, and I know this country on account of having spent seventy-odd years hereabouts."

We said we had just come from Alberton and had visited the turkey farm.

"That's Stump Town," he said cheerfully. "If Jack keeps on we'll be hearing gobbles clean up here. My dad always called Alberton 'Stump Town' because that was it's first name. The settlers chopped a lot the winter they arrived and as the snow was deep they left high stumps. In the spring they were there in clusters four and five feet high and the first cart track circled and turned to avoid the bigger ones. After that first winter there were better times as the ship building began, and soon Stump Town was Cascumpeque. There was a man named Hill who lumbered the district and sent cargoes to England and the West Indies. He bought townships and leased them to settlers, beat them down in price when he bought from them, and charged the limit every time he sold. He set up a store and as he had no opposition made what profit he felt like. But he got some punishment. He had a hired man he trusted and this fellow began stealing from him. Hill missed his goods and had the man arrested. The fellow was proved guilty and hanged but it was years after when somebody took up the floor in the barn of the man who was hanged and found over a thousand dollars worth of goods, men's wear and harness and tools. Hill made his pile and went to settle in England and Sir Samuel Cunard got hold of most of his holdings.

"Well, after a few years Tignish got started by three families. Two more came but there was no road to Stump Town, just a blazed trail. Those first families were really religious, had family worship regular in their cabins and when a preacher come to Stump Town and got a church built the Tignish folks would start on Saturday and travel the shore trail, crossing Montrose River in a log dugout that was always tied up on the bank. They had two dugouts, and the rule was that one must always be left on the opposite side. The folks put up at the homes of friends, slept on the barn floor, the men folks, that is, and on Sunday attended both services. Them days a preacher had to be sound of wind and go an hour and a half under full steam or he was no account. Everybody had carried baskets of food with them and this would be gone by Sunday night. Monday they'd be up bright and early and headed for home. Mind you, they only did this during the summer. Nobody ever made the trip in the fall or winter. I've heard them tell many times that some of the firstcomers paid as high as a dollar for a single darning needle, and one summer down at Stump Town the only needle they had got lost and a man rode on horseback all the way to Charlottetown to get another. He was able to buy three and the day he got back after two nights in the bush, they found the lost needle. It's likely he was madder'n a wet hen."

"How about going to church these days?" we queried

"Fair to middling," said our friend. "I wouldn't say there were any heathens hereabouts. Now you must have heard of the black foxes on the Island? Sure. Well, did you know the business begun up here? A man named Dalton started the business, brought in the first silvers and raised them on an island down at Alberton. He and his partner split up and he came here to Tignish and by that time everybody wanted to get into the business. So he set his selling price at twenty-five thousand a pair—and got it. They even took options on unborn fox families. Dalton became a millionaire, got a title from the Pope and become lieutenant-governor of the Island. But mighty few others go rich though a mint of money changed hands and for a few years there were fox ranches from one end of the Island to the other."

Our friend walked into the road and peered towards a house some distance away.

"We've been down to Charlottetown," he shrugged, "and my wife will be telling all the new dresses and hats she saw, so I guess I've got plenty of time. We visit her sister-in-law, who come from the Old Country. The first winter she was on the Island she got excited when she looked out the window Christmas Eve and saw men carrying something into the next house. She rushed to tell her husband. 'They're taking in the Yule log,' she chirped. 'It's like home to see the old customs.' 'Customs nothing,' snorted my wife's brother. 'That's old Ned himself, dead drunk, they're taking in.' Now we've got more fame up here in Tignish. Not only did we have the first fox farming but we had the first Credit Union. We had a smart man here, Chester P. McCarthy, who was a fisherman and who went to college so he could have learning enough to help his fellows. And he certainly did. He got better prices and he got men saving the right way and running their own store. The Co-op's a big thing up here, and you'll hear on all sides that M. M. Coady down in Antigonish is the only man in Canada qualified to be Minister of Fisheries in Canada. Maybe I better go now, my friend . Could be I'll get a cup of tea though sometimes our friend makes coffee. She never saw any until she was married and the first tries she had were'nt very good. Her husband was troubled with them curly weed in his cucumbers and never found a way to get rid of them till he tried emptying the coffee pot in the patch. Every weed died. Now be careful and don't swallow any crazy stories, and go back by the gravel road."

It didn't seem nearly as far driving back and we decided to stay in Summerside another night, and spent the rest of the afternoon driving to O'Leary on pavement and looking around its streets. We parked without difficulty and liked the people we saw. There seemed more teenagers than any other place we had been and they were gay in manner, seemed to be getting a lot of fun out of life. There was a cluster of them around a car from Massachusetts, all girls, for there were two lads of the same age in the sedan, wearing very vivid sport shirts and trying very hard to appear sophisticated. At another corner we saw three girls together and one of them was playing a mouth organ with the skill they used to have fifty years ago before radios and television spoiled local enter-tainment. Soon the other two girls started singing and here was a trio who should be given a chance on some talent show. Near the barber shop on the main way we saw a man wearing a button signifying he had served in the 1914-1918 War and noticed how old he looked. We asked him if he were not middle-aged when he enlisted.

"Thirty-nine in '15," he laughed. "Told them I was twenty-nine and they never asked a question. Got sent to the Fifth Mounted Rifles, and was scared to death I'd have to ride a western horse, and a year later wished I had the chance. We've mud on this Island but nothing like I saw at Ypres or on the Somme. One fellow from here took a small camera with him and hid it in his gas mask. He got pictures right in the front line trenches, but I don't know what he ever did with them when he got back home."

We said we hoped that if ever they were published we'd get to see them, and asked if he had travelled the rest of Canada.

"I been to Ontario," he said proudly. "I go to Pembroke where I have a married daughter. It's a good town and my daughter's always coaxing me to go and live with them. My wife died six years ago. I tell her I'm too scared that people will talk about me when I'm gone. Like away back there was a woman lived here who pinched every cent she got in her hands. An uncle in the States died and left her a nice bit of money she had it all go to a bank in Summerside, and a lawyer there looked after everything for her. She got scared, how-ever, that word of her money would leak out and people be asking her to help this or that. Times were pretty good here that summer and she spread word around she was running a quiet bawdy house, then bought the clothes and things she wanted. Everybody was talking behind her back and shaking heads, that is, the women were, and the men were just trying to get a look at her girls. She had two summer boarders, women, and they left in the middle of August because everybody got so queer acting when they met them. That summer the men around here had to just about ask permission to be out for an evening and the women were all joined together watching the husbands. But the woman with the money lost her nerve in the fall and sold out. She moved to somewhere in New Brunswick and the lawyer in Summerside spilled the beans. You couldn't hear anything else but her name all that winter. No, sir, I don't want people talking about me when I'm gone."

We asked what he did, whether he lived alone.

"Nope, with my brother," he said. "I get the Old Age pension and that keeps me, and I've a few dollars put by. Mostly I read. Not magazines, but books. Sometimes I wish I could try my hand at writing, I've heard so many stories about the old days, rum-running, smuggling, all that. Back thirty-odd years ago a storekeeper here bought a hundred barometers at a sale over at Saint John, New Brunswick. He got them dirt cheap and they had a nice brassy finish. He never put them out in sight in his store but one day he got a chap in the back shop and whispered he had taken a dozen barometers from a chap that had smuggled them in from the States. The chap was excited right at once and bought one. He promised not to let on but next day a man came around and hinted he'd seen something at a friend's house, and he'd like one. So another barometer was sold. Do you know that before the week was out people drove in thirty miles to get that storekeeper in the back shop and buy a barometer. He sold the whole lot and could have sold more. That's one story I could write up. And over to the west of the Island a man bought a hearse that was past usefulness. He just wanted the axles and wheels but when he started taking out the body part he found he had a job on his hands. Everything was bolted solid and he got a big wrench and crawled inside and levered so hard he had a heart attack and died right there in the hearse. His wife was so upset she made them take the thing right off the farm, and kept the window blinds down till it was gone."

It was late in the afternoon before we got away from O'Leary, a fine, friendly village where young people seemed to have a good time.

Leaving Summerside the next morning, we drove on Highway 2 a distance and then took the new road to Charlottetown. Our first stop was at Bedeque where we got in conversation with an elderly man who was painting his porch. In all our travels around the Island we did not meet anyone more proud of his home place. To him Bedeque was the final word, had more history, had better living people, more famous folk, was better known, than any other community. When we questioned some of his statements he carefully wiped his fingers on his overalls, laid his paint brush on a post and went into the house. In a moment he was back with a green-covered book, *Historic Bedeque*, by George A. Leard, and soon found the chapter he needed. His claim was that Bedeque had the finest climate in eastern Canada, borne out by all who had visited the place, and named by the Indians as "Eptek" or warm place. When the Acadians came they, too, found it sunny and warm and called it "Bedec." The English settlers used it carelessly and soon "Bedeque" was evolved.

The Acadians arrived in 1750 and many who came had been forced from good farms in the Chignecto area by the fanatical English-hating priest, Abbé Le Loutre, who brought such sorrow and woe to his flock. They settled near the marshes and had only been there a few years when came the Expulsion and soldiers carried off the people and shipped them in vessels to far places. But the soldiers seemingly had short time to do their work for many substantial French homes were not burned and were there, fifteen or so of them, in 1782, though the cleared lands had largely grown up in small bushes again. Then the Loyalists came by ship from Shelburne in July, 1784, but over half of them left when they found the landlords trying to obtain too much money for the acres needed.

The Loyalists found the climate genial and some foods were plentiful such as bar clams, quahaugs, and grandfather lobsters weighing ten pounds each, the finest oysters on the continent. Those who explored the fresh water found it stocked with fat trout and salmon, and any who liked eels found them in abundance. This area, of course, took in what is North Bedeque and Central Bedeque today. John Baker was one of the first citizens and certainly the first blacksmith, and our friend proudly said he hammered axes that were used a century after. Times were hard for some of the settlers and there is a saga about a Richard Robins who took a shore trek to Charlottetown in February to bring needed supplies to his neighbour settlers, got caught in a blizzard and sleet storm and though he turned back in good time fell exhausted under the force of the storm and died there on the frozen ground.

Those firstcomers were men of great determination and though they had to work hard for all they gained took out precious days to erect a church. At least they put up the walls and a roof. The good man who came to visit could not wait for doors and windows and pews and pulpit but preached the first time to the people as they stood before him. However he loved such opportunity and the sound of his voice so one by one the older ones went down to sit as best they could on the hard floor and an old account, according to our friend, said the majority found it easier to sit back to back, leaning against each other for mutual support. One by one the families put in pews, thus clearing themselves of pew rents. However times bettered along the shore when ship building began in Bedeque Bay and men came in to run sawmills and stores and shipyards and a church was built at Lower Bedeque that had a gallery and boasted it could sit three hundred people. One family had a slave, Susannah, commonly known as "Sook," and she had a beautiful voice, led the singing for a quarter of a century in the old church at North Bedeque.

The first horses used were mostly for saddle purpose and oxen did the plowing. The women made home wines they took for their health, while port and peach brandy were on every sideboard. The taverns sold rum and whiskey cheaply and nearly everyone indulged, even when returning from church service. Our painter sighed and remarked that even in his father's day many a good man wasted all his wages on drink. The great Miramichi fire in 1825 filled the Bedeque air with cinders and smoke and brought sorrow to some homes. Bedeque had sold potatoes to Newcastle as well as oats, and several young men from Bedeque had gone to work for lumbering firms in the Miramichi area. John Wright from Bedeque was at Newcastle when the fire occurred and kept ferrying people across the river, and found one family almost under water—up to their chins most of the night to avoid the flames and gas—and took them back to Bedeque. John Wright had a shoemaker friend in the town and searched for him but found his cottage only smouldering ruins. As he gazed at the desolate scene through the smoke haze he was startled to behold his shoemaker friend sitting on the hearthstone in the ruins and making signs that his Bedeque friend should take up the stone. After which the form vanished. Greatly disturbed by what he had seen, John Wright waited until he could approach the hearthstone, then heaved it out and found a pot of gold coins. He took it with him but his conscience told him he should try and locate the shoemaker's daughter who had married against her father's wishes and left the place some years before. So Wright advertised extensively for the missing heir but there was never a response. The coin treasure was kept for many years and eventually was divided among the daughters of the household as part of their doweries.

Our friend might have gone on until noon quoting from the book, but we wanted more information about the present and he said the district was like other Island communities, losing many of its younger folks and having it hard enough to hold its own.

"Our hope is a causeway," he declared. "In the winter and spring it's often hard to get to the mainland on account of ice. They've spent millions without number up on the St. Lawrence Seaway to help a country already rich. Why can't they spend a few dollars down here and build us a causeway?"

That was one we couldn't answer, so away we went to Albany, where people were emerging from their houses and walking about like hens coming out of the pen after a frosty night. The sun was getting stronger by the minute and the views all the way from Summerside had been remarkable. All the new drive from Borden on fine pavement is through a most pleasing countryside, with many farm houses in silhouette against the skyline, and hayfields, crops and gardens making pleasing squares of varied colour in all directions.

The first three persons we spoke with acted as if they were not ready for the day but the fourth man was ready to talk and told us about a remarkable trip he had had to Alberta on a harvester excursion back in 1913. We asked if he were a native.

"In a manner, I am, but not from choice," he grinned. "I come from over Carleton way when I was about four. My people died and an uncle raised me. In fact he raised me frequently with a barrel stave, his favourite weapon. And he had the chances, too, for his wife, my aunt, was worse than him. She used a birch switch and was always peeling a new one. She gave me a real whipping when I was ten and dared get myself an extra doughnut from the table while she was at the door chatting with a neighbour. Well, I kept thinking about how to get even with that one and all of a sudden it come to me that she was more scared of mice than the devil himself. Out in the barn I had a mouse almost tame as it used to get at the cow feed. One morning I was out very early, pulled out by the ear as my uncle growled that my aunt was not feeling well and I had to do the milking while he got her some strong tea and toast and put the milk through the separator. Well, I caught that mouse easy and put it in my pocket, milked five cows and had my arms and wrists so tired they were shaking. Then I went in with the pails and had a miserable breakfast that uncle had thrown together. He made me tiptoe around as he said my aunt was sleeping and when he went to separate the milk I slipped into my aunt's room, picked up one of her stockings from the floor and put the mouse in it, then tied the top of the leg. Well, I was out in the field when the screeching started and I never heard anything like it before or since. My uncle started to go in the house and aunt come out the door like a fire engine and sent him flying backward into the woodpile. She was in her nightgown and her hair was down her back and she went around the barn so fast the hair stood out straight. Uncle got up and started to run after her and yelled to me to go fetch a blanket. So I run into her room, took the mouse out of the stocking and threw it out the window, then came with a blanket. Aunt was just coming around the barn on the third lap by then and slowing down some but still screeching. Uncle caught her and had quite a struggle but got her to the house. She would not go in her room so he had to take her to the spare room and when she raved about her stocking he took both in to the room to show her but she wouldn't believe him. She said the stocking was going over the floor like a snake. Neighbours had heard and they come, and first I knew I was packed off to another house. Aunt was a nerve wreck for months and gave uncle a hard time, and when he died I went over and told her about the mouse. I thought she'd maybe try to sue me or something but she was the happiest woman I ever saw and grabbed and kissed me. She said that crawling stocking was always at the back of her mind, and now that she knew the truth she wouldn't go crazy. I had to tell her it had nagged my mind, too, and I was ashamed of what I did, but it was her use of the birch drove me to do it. And she owned she'd been a mite mean with me, and all ended well. Well, I can't tell you anything unusual about Albany. It's a grand place to live, and finer people just don't grow. If they'd get that causeway built it would put new life into the Island, and there isn't another place needs it more. How about putting that in your book?"

We said we'd be glad to boost the project, and drove along to North Tyron where we stopped at a small store where people were buying what seemed their breakfast, cereals and bacon and eggs. When I asked some questions of a very friendly man back of the counter he introduced me to a man who had just walked in, Edward Sharkey, and our first amazement was to know he was ninety-one. He didn't look to be eighty, and walked easily as a young man.

"I guess you might say I'm the only 'one of a kind' over here," he smiled. "I doubt that in all the Island you will find another man who followed my line of work. And you'd never guess it."

We made wild stabs and got nowhere. "I'll tell you," he said. "My business was installing burglar alarms."

"Oh, we thought the Island was an honest place? We didn't know you had burglars?"

"Listen, my friend," he kept the smile, "when I was active

there wouldn't be a house door locked here to Summerside. Everybody was free and easy, and, in most ways, honest. But along come the black fox business and some pairs sold away up in the twenty and thirty thousands, and one black fox looks like another. If a man could steal a pair some dark night he'd make more than if he robbed a bank. Farmers and fox breeders had to take turns watching all night for there were dozens of attempts to steal foxes. Finally, somebody invented this burglar alarm for the pens and I got roped in to go and learn about installing them. It was quite a trick and I'm not going to spill any secrets for some day they may use that system again for some other fur animals or something in cages. Anyhow, I went away and took the course and when I had the knowhow I was busy all the time. I'll never know how many burglar alarms I installed on the fox ranches. I was all over the Island and then got word to go to Nova Scotia, down at West Gore in Hants County and as far down the Valley as Bridgetown. Those fellows in Nova Scotia had had their troubles, too, and men with shotguns were on the watch all the time. I did a large number of fox pens over there and made real good money for the times. Sometimes I've wished I could go back and visit there again."

"Did the alarms ever fail?" we asked. "Did any breeder ever lose foxes after your burglar alarms were installed?"

"Not a one." He said it proudly. "You must remember that back in those days the average man knew mighty little about electricity, and fellows who would take a chance at stealing foxes weren't really professional burglars. There were about three attempts after the alarms were installed and that ended the business. Each time the alarms worked perfectly and they nearly caught one fellow or fellows as the breeder got to phoning quickly and if they had had cars instead of horses the constables would have had their man. You know that over here on the Island it was pretty hard to run a car.

For a long time you could only drive them certain days of the week, and the whole countryside was against them."

"Why?" we wanted to know.

"For one thing, the average farmer didn't feel he could afford one, and even if he could afford it he was sure it wouldn't operate on the mud roads we had at that time. A heavy summer shower made the red mud greasy as oil, and a car couldn't stay on the road. I know some farmers made quite a few dollars hauling cars out of the ditches. But above all else, the horses were frightened of cars. Worse here than anywhere. There were six runaways in one day down in Summerside when the first cars were around."

We admired Mr. Sharkey, were proud that we had discovered the one remaining burglar alarm expert, and we respected him that even now he would not give away trade secrets. We said as much as we left him and he smiled once more.

"A lot of money changed hands in the fox business," he said, "but very few became rich. I'm sure that when I quit putting in burglar alarms I had made as much as the average man out of foxes."

# 8

## "Midder," Mrs. Yale, Ghosts in the Belfry, and Skunks

CRAPAUD WAS NEXT and luck took us down a grade to a pretty scene near a long pond. We went to a house at random and luck pranced right along with us for we were admitted to the home of Mr. and Mrs. Thomas Best, who were very elderly citizens and knew the history of the community. We learned that at the beginning there had been many frogs in a quagmire so the place was named "Frogmore." Away back in 1767 Lot 29 included Crapaud and it was owned by Admiral Sir Charles Saunders. First settlers arrived in 1817 when 196 passengers from Hull were put ashore. It was tough going at first for the people who had to start from scratch. They cleared land and found it good, built their homes and managed to exist through hard work and endurance. They found great mussel beds and someone discovered that the beds and silt made excellent fertilizer. Crops improved as much as forty per cent under its influence and at once "Mudding" became a regular winter chore.

"I doubt," said Mr. Best, "you'll find another old-time 'mudder' on the Island. I don't know how I got into such work, for it was about the hardest, coldest, dirtiest job a man could tackle. But I did, and then I was always in demand. You see, we had to wait until there was ice thick enough to carry us as you couldn't hoist mud in a boat or from a raft. And when there was ice thick enough there was always cold weather, freezing winds, blustering snow, ten below days on end. We'd rig a capstan and use a horse to run it and hoist up the mud from oyster beds. It was a steady job sixty-five years ago when I was in my prime. Three neighbours would work together and we'd have a hot breakfast, all a man could eat, wrap ourselves as warm as we could, but not make one's self awkward with bundling, and out we would go at daylight. The ice would be one to three feet thick and we'd have to chop or saw out an opening large enough to hoist through. We used to chop a long cut, say twenty feet, then make an almost square hole and use the scoop. That's where the trick came in—to use that scoop properly. It was hard to set. You had to know the exact way to tilt it and hit the bed. If you didn't set it right you'd only get half a load and it was mighty hard work. And when we had a load up we had to keep it going or the stuff would freeze. We'd haul that out on the land and it was better'n manure. Cold! We'd be so cold back in those days that it would take all noon hour to thaw out. We'd drink quarts of hot tea, hot as you could take it. Everybody was after the mud and so there come a time when we had dug practically all the mud that was of any use and that was the end of 'mudding.' I never was sorry, either, but I guess all that freezing didn't hurt me. I'm eighty-five and going strong as ever. I remember when we used up and down saws here at the mill."

Mrs. Best was as active as her husband, and the historian of the community. Among her treasures are a very old cup that had no handle, and a bowl that came over in 1801. She showed us a prayer book dated 1729 "For the Church of Ireland Under the Kingdom of Ireland." And there was even a special prayer for a debtor held in jail.

"Crapaud was always a good farming district," she said, "and away back in 1820 they had a first exhibition of what they called 'autumn products,' and included about everything raised on a farm. There were very fine oxen, and sheep and geese and ducks, and cheese. Around that time there was quite a campaign to start a community-trading with Wallace in Nova Scotia. Some Wallace farmers were over to the exhibition and there were some trades of sheep and fat cattle and spinning wheels and chairs, but nothing much ever came of it. Spinning wheels were wanted by everyone in those days. The women hadn't much finery but they did wear pretty bonnets. Some of them—the bonnets—were still around in the older homes when I was a girl. It's very different today. All the ladies buy their hats in town. In those days they made everything they wore."

"What did you do for entertainment back in those days?" we asked.

"There was more going on than there is today," she said. "We had pie socials, and singing classes, and debates, and there was skating. The men made a rink on the millpond and Harry Moore got to be a wonderful skater. He had those old wooden skates with a steel blade but he went to Charlottetown and won the skating championship of the Island against men who wore spring skates. All these gadgets they have today, and phones and electricity, is grand, but in many ways the old times were the best."

We asked if there were any handcraft places around.

"No, but you must have come by Mrs. Amy Leard's at Central Bedeque," said Mrs. Best. "She makes everything in pottery. I've seen the cutest shoes, and island potatoes made as salt and pepper shakers. She makes an Island map, too, and lobster claws that look real."

It was fine scenery as we drove along, fine views to right and left, the sea, the rolling farms, the pretty settings. In fact the Island seemed to become more beautiful with every mile and it was easy to understand why cars with American number plates were driving along at twenty miles an hour. They didn't want to miss the scenery. Here and there a car would be stopped and men and women with colour cameras were in fields, on fences, perched hither and yon, trying to get the most effective colour shot.

Then, suddenly, we were in Hampton. An elderly man was coming from the store eating ice cream.

"Maple walnut is my favourite," he said, "and they only get it now and then. What's that? Anything different in Hampton? I reckon not. You like anything funny?"

Certainly, we said.

"Up the road a way there's a fellow my age is quite touchy. I think maybe he's got ulcers or some such ailment. And he's quite a gardener. He keeps his place nice. But there's an old girl who lives with her sister the other side of his lot, and both of them are pretty fat. When they come out to go to the stores or down in the village they naturally don't want to walk further than need be, so they used to cut across his lawn. That made him awful mad but he wouldn't say anything. He's what you'd call 'shut-mouthed.' However when they kept it up and started a sort of path he thought of something. One day all the place was talking about a notice he put up at the edge of his lawn: 'Careful! Cattle Crossing!' Them two old biddies was madder'n wet hens but they didn't walk across his grass any more."

He chuckled and went on eating ice cream with evident satisfaction.

"Isn't there anything different, anywhere, in Hampton?" we asked.

He paused. "I guess maybe there is. Captain W. M. Silliphant, Director of Pathology in the Armed Forces of the United States—I hope I've got that right—was born here in this village. He's a really big shot now in Washington, D.C. And he was a prisoner of the Japs three years in the Philip-

pines. Well, his folks or kin live here, and they rescued the
room where he was born from the old house and moved it
up and butt—ended it into their home. They tell it's a mighty
neat job, too, though I haven't seen it. But many have. And
there's plenty of antiques, too, in the house. You go and
see it, up on your left, where there's dogs. Me, I'm timid
about dogs."

We followed his directions, found the house, and were
graciously admitted. The old man had spoken truly. The
carpenters had fitted the room in so neatly that it looked
as though it had always belonged, and the furnishings were
perfectly natural. Then the hostess showed us other rooms
and the wealth of antiques in them. It is a beautiful home,
and the hostess was charming, and the dogs were quite
friendly. We cannot say that curious visitors will be welcome
there, but we were fortunate to see something very much
out of the ordinary. And when we came away we wished
that others had had such a thought. Many a fine old home
had one special feature, and it could have been saved by
good workmen who could incorporate it in another building.

A little later we stopped at Bonshaw, and there met a
jolly short little man with a huge gold watch chain and a
perpetual twinkle in his eye. He was walking toward a store
when we stopped him and asked if he were a native.

"Yes and no," he smiled. "I was raised hereabouts, and
that gives me the citizenship," he bowed, "but I have strayed
from the fold as it were with sojourns in far places, ever
returning to the home nest, though not as often as the spirit
moves."

His speech was delightful, so unusual, and he bowed
often, sometimes rubbed his plump hands together.

"Is there anything historic connected with this area?"
we asked.

"Not to my knowledge," informed our friend. "Unless
you might call some of the adventures of older citizens

historic. When I was a child, I recall, some of the happenings were almost incredible. There was old Nancy, who wore a bonnet most of her days, and tried to keep up with the times. When the first Yale locks were on the market she insisted on her husband getting one for her kitchen door. One day in the fall when the first snow came in a high wind she had to go to the little outbuilding sometimes called a 'necessary' and the wind caught the back door from her grasp, slammed it shut so heavily that the Yale lock snapped in place—and she was locked out. There were no near neighbours and Nancy kept making sorties to the front where she could see the road for some distance. At long last, almost frozen, she found a ladder by the carriage house and raised it to a bed-room window. But the wind flung it down before she could get climbing, and it was her third attempt before she got up to the window. It was hard to hold on and at the same time raise the window, and as she made a lunge inward the the ladder was whipped away. She was part way in, however, and the window came down across her back and trapped her there. Then the gale played a fearful game with her skirt and petticoat as she struggled vainly, and a great shout from below wanted to know what in the devil she was doing. Her husband had come home and when she screamed loud enough for him to hear, her fury knew no bounds as he calmly walked around and entered the front door. 'Never trusted that new-fangled lock,' he said. 'So I just left the front door unbolted.' Nancy was so mad at him that she crowned him with a stool when he had freed her, and went down and bolted the front door. Her husband had left his horse and rig in the yard as he rushed to help her and the animal was trying to get from the storm and had the cart caught in the gate. Out rushed Nancy—and bang went the door again! She yelled and pounded at the doors but her man stayed upstairs, and she had to get to the barn for shelter. It was nearly dark before he let her in, and the next day he took off the Yale lock, and

Nancy took down with pneumonia. It was a neighbour who nursed her and got the story, and behind her back they always called Nancy 'Mrs. Yale.' Now as far as anything really important goes, I might say that the thrills have passed us by. I remember a Bonshaw pig winning first prize at Charlottetown, and that takes in all the highlights I know."

We kept asking him questions just to hear him talk in his fluent precise English, to watch his twinkle and his hand rubbing. Then he struck a pose and declaimed: "There is nothing like this anywhere else in Canada—a valentine of some two thousand square miles. To find its equal one must go to England and Europe where men have long nursed, pampered and worshiped their earth. No fence, building, no stone, no tree or blade of grass is out of place. Best of all—that is the Island's true secret—no human being is out of place either." He rubbed his hands. "Do you know who said that?"

"No," we had to admit.

"I'm saying it tonight," he smiled. "I have to speak at a meeting farther along, and that's the way I'll start my talk, but I'll not tell where I got the words." He waved a droll adieu, and was gone.

Our next stop was at Cornwall, which looked an interesting place. We asked a woman coming from a store if we could get information about the place, and were sent across the road to a corner house. It was getting near noon and we were glad to be welcomed warmly by a lady who knew the answers as far as Cornwall was concerned.

"It's hard to know who settled here first," she said, "but away back it was called Rye's Corner, and maybe a settler named Rye was a firstcomer. Then some Irish and English came. The Irish wanted to call the place Glenbrow, but there were a few more English than Irish and they chose Cornwall and kept saying it until finally Ottawa adopted the name for us. One of the finest of the early settlers was a very large woman named Mrs. Enoch Drake. She was big-hearted with everyone, and the Indians got to know about her. They were camped over at Bass Cove and would cross on ice from Rocky Point and call on Mrs. Drake to fill their baskets with food. Of course they fetched her baskets and axe handles and things like that, but she had more than she needed, and fed them because they were always half-starved. They could depend on her helping them but they used to travel around the whole area and try to sell their baskets or swap them for old clothing and food. One bad winter Mrs. Drake heard that one Indian family had got an old army tent and put it up on the ice in a sheltered corner of the Cove. They were sleeping and living in it, with the ice covered by a brush floor. One night an Indian knocked at her door and said the Indian woman in the tent was going to have a baby, and they wanted her to come. Mrs. Drake never hesitated. She filled a big basket with food for the Indian woman, took some extra loaves of bread, and a bundle of warm clothing for the woman. Then she went outside, bundled to the ears, and sat on a big home-made sled the Indians had borrowed and they hauled over the ice to the Cove. Mrs. Drake was successful as a mid-wife, they say she brought over one hundred babies into the world, and she left the Indian woman warmly dressed and with food enough for a week."

"A fine story," we said. "Handed down over the years?"

"Yes," smiled the lady. "We've been collecting all the information we can and by 'we' I mean the Women's Institute. We're making up a book on this district. We found that back in August, 1818, the first preacher came out here, so Cornwall must have been founded a short time before. There was no church but the old record says he had a 'preaching exhortation' in a barn three times that summer. Then a log church was built on land granted to the Church of England, that had never been claimed. The Methodists took it over and have had it ever since. The first driving wagon came here in 1878.

The first school was a log building with the desks turned to the wall, spiked there. The boys had to chink the walls with moss when it got cold in the fall. A regular school was built in 1877 and in 1948 it was turned around to let the sun in. The first car was owned here in 1918. The law forbade anyone driving a car nearer than within three hundred yards of a church, and cars could only be driven three days a week on certain roads that were named. It was a long time before they could be used every day."

The lady paused and eyed us thoughtfully.

"I don't suppose you want to print anything that can't be proved?" she said. "You know this is the only place along the coast where a mermaid was seen. Nobody had a camera, then, but if they had it could be proved for the mermaid was seen by at least a dozen different persons. It was big as a small girl and came by the shore the first of July. I've heard the story dozens of times, and one man tried to talk to it. It was shy, though, and wouldn't let anyone get too close. It stayed around for an hour and then sank and swam away."

We said we couldn't promise anything but saw no reason why the Island should not have a mermaid as well as any other place, thanked her for her information and drove on to Charlottetown over the grand new highway that swung up and down and around like a glorious roller coaster. It was noon and we were hungry and the food at the Charlottetown Hotel was very good.

After lunch we strolled around and visited the old delivery room where Confederation was born, inspected the long table around which the planners sat, and wondered what their ghosts would say should they return and find the way in which the terms of Confederation have been carried out. All for one, and one for all, sounded good and true in the preamble to the British North America Act, but the one has been Canada—Upper and Lower. Away back, we were told in the very fine library, Denys de la Ronde and Sieur de Gotteville sailed into the harbour and were so delighted with the situation they named it "Port la Joie." Then Acadians came and made settlements but after the fall of Louisbourg, Lord Rollo with four ships and 500 men came and took possession of the Island, razed the settlements and deported the people, many of them were drowned when their ship was wrecked. Then came the Irish and English and Scottish, and British founders laid out a town on the fine harbour and named it after Queen Charlotte, stylish wife of George the Third.

The town was incorporated in 1855 and up to that time had been rather lax in many ways as old articles tell of streets that looked like country lanes as pigs and cows were allowed to roam at will. There were soldiers in the town for years, a regular garrison, and so there were colourful parades on Victoria Day and on other occasions. In 1840 the Charlottetown Troop of Cavalry appeared for the first time in their uniforms, blue with white facings, and drew wild applause from the throngs of those celebrating the holiday. General Edmund Fanning managed to acquire much land on the Island, felt there should be a proper residence for the Lieutenant-Governor and granted 100 acres as a site for a Government House. When the building was completed in 1835, the furniture and furnishings were sent from England, fuel and light were provided, and salaries paid by the British Government for the upkeep of the place. A Tandem Club was a feature of the town in the early days and usually the Lieutenant-Governor would head a procession of sleighs driven tandem by officers and young blades of the area. This was a regular winter spectacle and the bright trappings of the horses, the merry jingle of bells, made such events something to remember.

In September, 1864, Sir John A. MacDonald, Premier of Canada later, arrived in Charlottetown Harbour on a government vessel to talk confederation with Charles Tupper and other maritime leaders. One town official in a rowboat went out to meet MacDonald. The rest of the citizens of all degrees were attending a circus. Furthermore, the circus folks had taken all the accommodation the town provided, and the future Fathers of Confederation had to sleep on the government vessel. The trend of those times has continued. The good folk of Charlottetown like a gay time. Each year they have their Old Home Week, and each year more and more visitors from mainland America go to the Island and get acquainted with its beauty and its fun-loving people. Down the years there were always parades and picnics, excursions and celebrations of one sort or another and while this meant, in the old days, clouds of red dust raising a regular canopy over the highways, today it means a good time had by all as the fine paved highways lead to the capital from all directions. There was an especially grand celebration in 1955, the 200th anniversary as an incorporated town, and the committee in charge thought of a novel way to attract visitors. Invitations were sent in the form of a legal summons, somewhat startling at first, and then a joke as the receiver comprehended the message. The summons looked so real, however, that the mayor, popular Dave Stewart, had a few headaches when some irate thick-heads wrote, saying: "Since I've never been in Charlottetown, how could I have done anything to get me a court summons?" One lady even phoned heatedly from a Massachusetts city and the mayor only able to cool her by instructing that the long distance charges be reversed. It is doubtful, however, that she attended the celebration.

A gentleman who had heard our many questions in the Library, very politely introduced himself to say that he hoped we would not forget the horse racing.

"They call the Island the Kentucky of Canada," he insisted, "because we have the best horse racing in the east. Charlottetown has one of the finest tracks in Canada and every Islander is a horse racing fan. They even watch their races under the lights. There are thousands who come over for our Old Home Weeks but you can bet your boots the majority come to see the horses."

He got in the car with us and acted as guide as we drove around and looked at Victoria Park, forty acres fronting on the harbour, at Fort Edward built back in 1793, at Government House and its lovely surroundings, at Prince of Wales College and St. Peter's Cathedral.

"Another thing Charlottetown has that few towns, save Sydney, in Nova Scotia, have, is a real ghost story," said our guide. "It happened away back when the ferries to Nova Scotia were sailing vessels. A man was walking into town early in the morning when he heard what he thought was a ship's bell. I sounded so clearly that he peered out into the harbour area and no ship was there. Then he heard it more clearly and knew it came from a church. As he drew near the bell in the spire tolled slowly, giving him shivers. As he reached the building he saw three women in white enter the church, and wondered what was happening. But when he reached the door it was locked. At that moment the caretaker came running to find out who was ringing the bell. He had keys and opened the church door at once. The man with him, and the caretaker, saw the three women ascending the winding stairs leading up the bell tower. They hurried after them but when they reached the top part where the bell hung, no one was there. This was so startling that they hurried down, and found the minister of the church entering. He had been alarmed by some member of his congregation asking about the bell ringing. He violently disputed any notion of the women being in the belfry, and was so angry that the caretaker sided with him. But the man who had first seen the women and heard the bell knew differently, and told his story to any who listened. Before noon a dozen citizens had called to ask about the bell ringing, and the minister and caretaker became mute on the subject.

"Next morning brought the news that the ferry schooner

going to Nova Scotia had capsized in the morning and among the drowned were three members of the congregation of the church—three *women!*"

"What then?" we asked.

"Well, the story was believed whether the old minister liked it or not, and I've heard it all my life though the details vary slightly with different tellers."

We had a look at the map of Prince Edward Island and decided to drive out of the city on Highway 1, and then turn left on Highway 6 and drive eastward along the shore. We stopped briefly at Marshfield and after talking with five persons and being assured by all that no features of any sort could be found, went along and parked again at Mill Cove.

An oldster there said the people were law-abiding, and a man had to be a crook to become known. Then he grinned and told us his own story.

"I belong up Rustico way," he said, "and when I was a kid we had a school teacher who used a switch on any excuse whatever, and often without any. She seemed to delight in hearing us kids yell. Well she gave me a dandy licking one night for nothing at all. My hands and wrists were puffed and ridged but I said nothing. I had made my plans. Next the school was a farm where there was a large black bull, and this animal was savage. There was a very strong fence to the pasture, and a gate opened from it to the lane. I went to school early and opened that gate. The bull noticed it and came onto the road from the lane, saw the schoolma'am who always came early, charged after her. She beat him into the schoolhouse by no more than a nose and before she could slam the door his head was in. There were two inner doors from the porch to the schoolroom, and she got through one and shut it before the bull nailed her. Then she moved seats against the doors, opened a window and screamed for help. Meanwhile the bull was wild as the outer door had swung shut and latched. The animal was penned and he bellowed and plunged about until he struck one of the inner doors and knocked it open. As he rushed into the schoolroom the teacher squeezed out of the window, dropped to the ground and ran for her life. I was hid in a spruce grove, watching, my heart in my mouth. The bull put its head out the open window and gave a fearsome blat. The noise made the teacher jump straight up and when she came down she fell, screamed some more, finally reached a barbed wire fence and rolled under it, tearing her clothing and hands on the barbs. Just then a rig came along. The farmer stopped and got her in his buggy, drove her to her boarding house, and she sure was a sight. Four men went with pitchforks and got the bull out of the schoolhouse and outside of a lot of hot manure splattered around not much damage was done. But the teacher's nerves were shot. She went home and quit that school. We had three holidays in a row before they got a new teacher to finish out the last of the term, and we were the happiest kids on the Island."

The next place was Corran Ban, Gaelic for "white sickle," and refers to the froth-covered shoreline in October. Scottish settlers arrived in the area in 1772 and when we crossed the bridge we tried to locate some original family names but had no luck. We did see a rather odd-looking church and when we asked about it were told that fine plans were made and a great church planned but after the basement was finished it was found that funds were less than the committee had thought. So the work was suspended a time and then impatient ones insisted on a roof so that services might be held. So a roof was put over what had been constructed and so the building remains to this day.

A mile from Grand Tracadie we entered the Island's National Park on fine smooth pavement. It was a delight to swing along the broad ribbon and feast the eyes on beautiful scenery that changed with every mile. The road gently looped around Dalvay Lake and we had a grand view of Dalvay

House, a summer resort, and could see Park Headquarters across the Lake. Out to the right were miles of sand dunes and beyond them the sun glinted and gilded the waters of the Gulf of St. Lawrence. We saw Stanhope Beach Inn, and crowds of guests having all sorts of fun. One group of youngsters sauntered along in gay bathing suits laughing and cheering a lad with long hair and a banjo who was acting a la Elvis Presley.

We reached another bridge, a junction of Highways 6 and 7, and known as Oyster Bed Bridge. Boats were anchored nearby and we saw nets draped over poles and fishermen chatting with each other as if time had no meaning in their lives. Then we reached Rustico, named after a first settler, Rene Rassicot, who came from Normandy. It was one of the most attractive places we had seen for as you approach you see the white-painted houses as if they were actually bordering the beach. When you get nearer you see that this is so. Some wharves jut out into the water and at low tide the reflections of gray weathered buildings ride on the surface of the dark shallow water.

It was no trouble to find the veteran in Rustico. He appeared with an old coat though the day was warm and everyone else in shirt sleeves.

"It's my blood," he said. "She's thin like water."

"Are you Acadian?" we asked. "French?"

"Some, for sure," he nodded. "From what I been told I am mixed, French, Scotch, Irish—all mix, with, maybe, some Indian. Who knows. I hear my old granny say when she was girl there were people with straight black hair who wore moccasins all the time because they were part Indian. Now that kind all gone."

"Is there anything special to see here?" we asked.

"By damn, you look right time there is plenty," came the retort. "You know there is ghost here. That for sure. Some old French officer, they say, with his sword. He is seen at time of the new moon every September. They say he come to take up gold his crew bury, that he was a pirate. Some say, no, he was captain of a ship that was wrecked, and walked around and around, eating berries, all summer, then starve in the fall. No, I have not seen him, but plenty have."

Our man looked around as if he feared some old ghost might be listening, then changed the subject abruptly.

"Right here on this shore was run the first car in Canada, may be all the whole world," he said. "Father Belcourt could make anything. He made the motor car ninety-three years ago, a steam car, a steam engine on her, fired with wood. She had high wheels and a big steering wheel. He worked one year making her, then come out the twenty-fourth of May making a noise like a hundred machines. Everybody's horse ran away, I guess. The car was painted red and she run half a mile without a stop. Oh, she ran from Rustico right down to Charlottetown."

"What happened to it?" we wanted to know.

"Maybe some museum," suggested our friend. "She was here at Rustico long after Father Belcourt was gone. In a granary."

"That old ghost you talked about should have had a ride in the car," we joked. "That is, if pirates will ride in cars."

"There is a burying ground here," almost whispered our friend, "that the pirate used for hide a pot of gold. Away back. He never come for it, and somehow there is talk about it and, six, seven, times, men go to dig but the shovel is tore from them, and the pick. There is noise like someone hurt. Those diggers never talk after or go back."

It would have been nice to stay at Rustico and wander around that ancient cemetery where pirate gold is buried, to board at some quiet little home and bask on the sands, to loaf around and explore the finest scenery on the Island. There were districts running back that had hills or considerable slopes, fields a checkerboard of vivid colours, and trees in long rows as if trained to stand that way.

The mellow afternoon was one we would not forget as we drove through North Rustico and saw many fishing boats, and a car with American license plates parked by the beach, indicating that its owner was out on a hand lining expedition. Cod and mackerel could be taken easily, we were told, and a fishing trip was a most pleasant diversion after you had driven a thousand miles or so. Then we rolled away with the sea always on our right and after what seemed quite a time were at Cavendish. It is no use to try and tell a person what Cavendish is like. You must go and see for yourself, come under the spell. Green Gables had a large number of guests but we did our exploring just the same, saw the house as Anne saw it during her first years there. There was the little parlour organ, the Franklin stove, Marilla's rocking chair, the stereoscope, spinning wheels, iron kettle and other items. We went up the narrow stairs to visit Anne's room, and Marilla's room, wandered around the grounds to see Lover's Lane and the Haunted Wood and the Lake of Shining Water. We have never met a person who did not enjoy reading *Anne of Green Gables,* and it was a peculiar pleasure to relax on the grounds and see eager young teenage girls comparing notes as they walked around. For Anne really lived in the hearts of her readers, still exists in that lovely land of the Island's North Shore. It was easy to stand there at some spot away from the crowd and see her going to school, or going to visit her sworn friend, peering at this flower and that, gathering some to take to Marilla, radiantly alive, extracting the greatest possible joy out of living. In fact we could almost see Matthew come homeward from a hard day in the fields.

Two whispering ladies came to us after they had inspected the registration book we had signed. They had a look of high resolve and asked our purpose in the place. When we had explained they did not venture more details regarding Green

Gables but began to talk about the John Geddie Memorial Church in the village.

"Put the story in your book," they pleaded. "It's a shame the way he's forgotten. He was a rather small man with a gentle manner and he was called to Cavendish in 1838. Soon after he arrived he was married to a girl just sixteen, and the first Sunday she appeared in church her mother was with her. There were many jokes about which was the bride. He was with the church here seven years and then offered to go to the South Seas as a missionary. He prepared for it and learned how to use tools, the medicines needed for average ailments, how to sail a boat. Then away he and his wife went and arrived at a place in New Hebrides where the people had all sorts of superstitions and wives were slaves. His only real asset was his gentle manner and unswerving courage. He learned the language in less than two months and what he did is marked on a tablet there: "When he landed in 1848 there were no Christians here, and when he left in 1872 there were no heathen."

We took notes and promised to tell about little Johnny Geddes, then fell into the hands of a gentleman who insisted on showing us, off Cavendish Beach, approximately the spot where the world-famous sailing vessel, the *Marco Polo,* lies buried in the sands. He also told us about the graves of twenty-one American sailors who were lost when the *Yankee Star* went down off Cavendish. Twenty-two sailors were drowned that fatal day but the father of one lad came to take his son's body home for burial. It was an ill-fated trip for on the way home the ship he was on went down and both he and his son's body were lost.

There was a sign saying some bridge was out on the route we were taking to Kensington, and a kindly man sketched on brown paper a way that would cut off four miles. We drove with the sketch in our laps and saw little glens that were like postcard views, only prettier, a fox viewing us from back of a bush, a dip into a ravine that was almost dark. We climbed from it by a narrow road that ran under evergreens and saw another small valley before us, crossed it and soon were on higher ground, took two right turns and were in Burlington. It was getting toward day's end but we had no intention of missing something we had been told about at Cavendish, so swung into a driveway and parked in the grounds of "Woodleigh," the home of Ernest W. Johnstone, who is a master builder of replicas of old-world structures. He is an army man and held the rank of Colonel, is still known as "Colonel" over most of the Island. He came to meet us as we began our inspection and was a most genial host.

His whole place shows the result of plenty of hard work and a wonderful imagination. There are shrubs where they show best, a sundial, lily pond, bird bath and fountain. When the Colonel had things going as he wanted he decided to build a miniature castle on his spacious grounds, and had encouragement when an Island firm sent him a calendar bearing a picture of Glamis Castle. So he chose a site and went to work from scratch, setting the stones and forming the towers true to scale. That was a beginning, and the Colonel was enthused. Shakespeare's Birthplace was installed, and Anne Hathaway's Cottage. The cottages are of stucco, and in true Elizabethan style. The church and castles are of granite with lead roofs and window-frames of cast lead. It takes an expert hand and infinite patience to make every wall true and every dimension to exact scale. There is a place for visitors to sign, Ye Olde Blue Dragon, panelled in oak, with casement windows. The decorations are unusual, horse brasses, an ancient coach horn and a veteran bedwarmer. The Inn is eleven feet high so anyone can enter without difficulty unless they arrive on stilts. There is a Wishing Well on the grounds and visitors believe in it as proceeds from it go to the Red Cross and the yield to date is over fifteen hundred dollars.

The Colonel took us to see his latest project, a replica of York Minster. The original took 200 years to build, was completed in the fifteenth century. This structure will be twenty-six feet long, twelve and a half feet wide, will have 143 windows ranging in size from six inches in height to four feet, and they will be composed of pieces of coloured glass. And the York Minster will be lighted, will have chimes and organ music. We stood there as dusk came down gently and were very happy that a man should develop such a hobby, a wonderful way to stall old age, a glorious asset for not only the community but the whole Island, a thing of beauty and a joy for a very long time. We could not ask the cost of the York Minster but knew it would run into four figures. Formerly, guests came and went and bothered without paying any fee whatever but today there is a charge of fifty cents per adult. Anyone under fourteen is admitted free. The place is the greatest show for fifty cents you will find anywhere in America.

One of the men standing around inspecting the York Minster, drew us to one side. "It's a pity he didn't tell you about Prince Edward Island's Beautification Society," he said. "The colonel started it, you might say, when he wrote a letter to the paper and criticized people who didn't keep their places looking nice. Soon a lot of such letters appeared and the colonel was asked to go before the Provincial Legislature and explain what he meant by suggesting an organization to clean up the Island's bad spots. Well, the Society came into being, with the Government back of it, and the thirteenth annual competition is on this year with cash prizes that will total three thousand dollars. You'd be amazed to know how many have painted their places regularly since this campaign began, and the number of picket fences that have replaced old wire ones. There are flower beds where there used to be dumps and shrubs hide anything unsightly that can't be moved. The Women's Institutes have helped a lot and two judges of the competition who have been around declare that the Island has the best kept rural homes in Canada."

We thought of it afterwards as we drove through the countryside and soon began to realize that the man had spoken the truth.

We drove on to Kensington, had dinner at a small restaurant and were pleasantly surprised by the quality of the food, then secured lodging for a night at the Delaney Tourist Home. We had clean, comfortable rooms and can cheerfully recommend this Home to any traveller. Mrs. Delaney went out to play bridge but invited us to watch television if we wished. A walk around the village seemed in order as it was a lovely evening and at a corner two gentlemen well along in years were arguing about Sir Winston Churchill. One claimed that if Sir Winston had remained a Liberal he would have been the greatest man in the world. We broke in gently to ask if Kensington had any unusual feature.

"I'll say," offered the Liberal. "It's the first debt-free incorporated town in Canada, is next to Bear River in Nova Scotia with cherry trees. It used to be called Barrett's Cross, because a Mrs. Barrett had an Inn right here at these crossroads."

"I've heard my grandfather tell about the Inn," said the Tory. "The lady could hold her own in any company, had the frills and fan and lace apron and fine comb to meet the snobs, and could join the others and empty her glass with the best of them. Never showed any effect, either. Just a film of sweat on her trace of mustache after two or three glasses. One bedroom was papered with an old Chinese pattern and that used to be for honeymooners. All the heat was from fireplaces and if the fire got down in the night there'd be frost on your blankets in the morning. There was real snow in the old days, and a man got scarecrow thin with the winter between his ribs. Shovel and shovel and break roads all the time."

"Could have been bad," agreed the Liberal, "but I doubt they ever had it worse than in 1905. The train couldn't get through for weeks. Lots of places you couldn't see a fence for miles and in hollows the snowdrifts were right to the top of telephone poles. I mind we had to go and dig out a couple that was sick. Heard his cattle blatting for food and water so we went and tended them. He'd never been sick before in his life and was scared to death. He was one of them big bulky fellows, hairy as a bear, and just like a baby when he ailed. His wife was worn out with waiting on him. She was thin anyhow, and her clothes simply hung on her like as if they were on a peg. She was homely, too, as a sod wall, but friendly. And he was just a bullhead, the kind that wouldn't take advice from the twelve apostles."

We left them by the corner, going over old tales and enjoying themselves, amiable as long as no politics were mentioned.

It was Highway 1 in the morning, and the whole country-side was bright after a wash of night showers. Soon we were at Springfield and as no old-timers were in sight we rang some doorbells and soon were being entertained. We found that the Women's Institute had written a fine story of the area but it was easier to talk with the gracious lady who entertained us as she knew the region and its history. Between 1764 and 1766 Captain Samuel Holland made a survey of the Island for the British Government and in 1767 the Island was divided into sixty-seven Lots which were given to those who presented claims on the British Government for military or other services. The Lots, averaging 20,000 acres each, were drawn by lottery before the Board of Trade in London on July 23, 1767. Lot 67 at Springfield was drawn by Hon. Robert Moore, and was the largest on the Island, about 28,000 acres. Moore paid no heed to notices about quit rents so on November 17, 1781, the Lot was sold and became the property of General Edmund Fanning who was the Governor of the Island, and he paid for it on January 4, 1793. In 1794 he offered one hundred acres to any man who would enlist in the King's forces but no one made claim and it was not until 1826 when a road was opened between Charlottetown and Malpeque that settlers arrived in the district and began buying farms. General Fanning left his property to his wife and three daughters. One girl was named Margaret William Tryon Fanning, as the General had no sons and was determined to name one child after his great friend, Sir William Tryon. On March 2, 1854, the three daughters divided their holdings and after that more and more settlers purchased land. As the fields were cleared many springs of fine water were found so the place was named "Springfield." Haslam's Inn was built in 1829 and soon became a popular place. Regulations said the Inn must provide three feather beds, and stables for at least six horses. Rates were ten cents overnight per person, and twenty cents per meal. The Presbyterians of the district held their meetings in the Inn, and the place was the local post office as the coach stopped there. The road was rough and the coach horses travelled tandem. Six passengers could be carried and the fee from Charlottetown to Malpeque was one dollar and eighty cents. Shelves and desks from the post office days are still in the old building as are a loom and spinning wheel.

"There's a story anywhere you go in Springfield," said our lady. "One boy here grew to be a very strong fellow and won the Canadian Amateur Wrestling Championship in 1923, 1924 and 1925. In 1920 eight pairs of black foxes were bought from Japan and William Haslam of Springfield was caretaker of the foxes on the way to Tokyo. We had one of the first cars used on the Island, and there's a Model T Ford still in use in the village. The winter of the deep snow the drifts were so bad here that the men had to use seven various heights of ledges to get the snow heaved away at the top. And there are many curious things in Springfield, like a gold ring four hundred years old bearing initials A.B.H. on a square representing a Bible which opens to show braided hair. There's a cane that has a concealed sword, and it's very old, a writing desk over 100 years old, a canopy bed, and a book printed in 1703."

"What is there here that's new today?" we asked.

"Not much," sighed the lady. "There isn't even any romance any more, no regular courting. One of our first settlers went to cross the Stanley River and he had no money to pay the young lady rowing the ferry. She agreed to hold his watch as security until he could raise the fare and when he returned he began courting her. She became his bride and he brought her to his new home here mounted on the horse behind him."

Hazelgrove was next along this road over rolling country of real beauty but we did not find a story there and next we knew were descending a long slope into Hunter River. It was coincidence that the first person we spoke to down by a store was from Hazelgrove, and rather indignant when told of our fruitless quest. "If you'd asked anywhere else you'd have got information," he said. "The place was named for an Inn run by a United Empire Loyalist. It's right on the top of a hill and they call it 'the old stone house' now. It's as square and solid as the year they built it. In the old days the mail drivers from Summerside and Charlottetown used to meet there, change mail bags and return to their towns."

After chatting with some of the residents of Hunter River we drove along a mill site, crossed over the bridge and parked alongside a home in which lived a lady who knew the history of the countryside.

"We've one great honour here," she said. "The Archbishop of Toronto, Cardinal McGuigan, is from this village. And don't let anybody spoil our story about how this place was named. They may say it was named after Thomas Orby Hunter, Lord of the Admiralty in 1761, but Hunter River wasn't founded then. And, anyway, our story is much more romantic. Away back in October, 1806, a George Trueman was a first settler here and he had a lovely daughter, Inez. A man by the name of Fred Hunter was wrecked on the north side of the Island and the Truemans fetched him here and looked after him. When he was active again the war of 1812 broke out and when Fred discussed it with Mr. Trueman he was told that a single man's duty was in uniform. So Fred went away and enlisted. He got into action and was wounded in July of 1814. No word came from him after that but a rumour reached the Truemans to the effect that Fred had died of wounds. Then a swaggering cousin, Jack Trueman, arrived on a visit, saw how beautiful Inez was, and made love to her. When he had to go away he promised he would return at Christmas when they would be married. The reason they had not heard from Fred was that after being discharged from hospital he started for home but was captured by a French vessel and it was a long time before he was released. He got passage finally to Charlottetown, took his suitcase and started for the Trueman's. It was Christmas Eve when he arrived at the house and saw quite an assembly. He peered in the windows and saw Inez in wedding clothes, opened the door and walked in. Inez thought she was seeing a ghost and screamed so that he turned and fled. Some of the men came to look around but saw no trace of Fred, and finally the wedding took place. Then Jack made ready to take his bride on a trip to England. As they were leaving someone walking by the stream came upon Fred Hunter's body. He had lain there and died with his head on his valise, and an account of what had happened to him was in the valise. Inez was heart-broken. She was married but grieved so much that she died aboard the ship before it reached England. And that is why this place is called Hunter River."

The village is very pretty, and surely a place of romance. Looking back from the top of the hill, the scene is like that on calendars of vivid colour. Brookfield was an even higher hill than that leading from Hunter River valley, and a man by the roadside said it was the highest ground on the Island.

"It's the prettiest drive, this way," he said proudly. "They've made the other road the Trans-Canada Highway but we've still got the best scenery."

"What's next?" we asked.

"Milton, where Highway 7 comes in," he said, "and English as Kent. You'll see lots of hedges there. The older generations tried to make the village look like it was in England. There's an old Anglican Church there, too."

Time was passing swiftly so we drove through the capital and soon were on Highway 1 and going through Marshfield and then Tracadie. We saw a sign "Scotchfort" and stopped at the first place we saw people outside their homes.

"My girl had to write an essay on the settling of this place," said a mother proudly. "Run in the house and get it, dear." A dark-haired lassie who looked very smart scurried into the house and was back in a moment. It was quite a paper she had, and the gist of her story was that the place was first settled by the French and called by them "St. Louis du Nord-est." These folk escaped the first drive to expel the Acadians but the English caught up with them later and they were all deported. This left their grounds to go back to the wilderness but in 1772 two hundred Highlanders landed in Charlottetown and proceeded up the Hillsborough River to a landing opposite the old French church of St. Louis. There they saw the upland purchased for them by Captain John MacDonald, Laird of Glendaladale and Glenfinnan, and immediately began taking possession. They occupied the old Acadian lands, which were good, and in due time prospered. Many of the clan have become famous in all parts of Canada. We were shown the way to the old cemetery first used by the

French and then by the Scottish settlers, and having a monument to the memory of the Rev. James MacDonald who came with the Highlanders. A marble cross marks the lasting resting place of Captain John MacDonald who led the Scots to the place, and another monument near the river commemorates the Highland Scots who settled in the district.

Mount Stewart was next along the way and it was really warm as we turned in the main street and parked. Hardly a person was about but we saw a man entering his small barber shop and asked him if there were any unusual feature in the place.

"Boy, it's hot," he said. "No, there's not a thing to write about here. It's sort of gone to seed, you might say. Nothing doing. No money. No work. If they'd only spend enough to build that Causeway instead of all them millions up in Ontario where they've wasted more than enough for two Causeways on canals and the like, we'd get some good business over here."

Just then we heard a small rustling noise under our feet. The floor of the little shop was only one thickness. "What's that?" we asked. For it had sounded like an animal moving.

"Just skunks," said our friend, settling in his barber chair and preparing to nap. "Just damn' skunks."

We went outside and gingerly got down and peered. Five skunks were in a small convention in cramped quarters under the centre of the building which rested on stones. They eyed us gravely, then shrugged as if to say "you can't get in here. There's hardly room enough for us."

"Why do you keep those skunks?" we asked our dozing friend.

"How can I get clear of them?" came the response. "They're under every building in town. You bother them and they'll drive us out. As it is, they're not much trouble. They rummage around garbage or the like at nights, and they stay under the buildings in the daytime."

"But-how-why?"

"Well, nearly everybody around was raising them when the price of their fur dropped clean out of sight. So the cage doors and pen doors were opened and the . . . things were free. They wandered all over the countryside and then they found it was better picking sticking around the little towns. So here they are and how we're going to get rid of them is more than I know."

"And you said there was nothing to write about?"

"Well, hell, skunks ain't much to put in a book. And, say, I'd forgot but we had a middleweight, Bill MacKinnon, who fought all the good men who would meet him. Ask Wilfred McClusky of the *Charlottetown Guardian* about him. We did just that and were told that MacKinnon took up residence in Roxbury, Massachusetts, after finding he could have more fights in that area. He took on a heavyweight for his first amateur battle and lost the decision, then won twenty-nine bouts in a row. He weighed between 160 and 170 pounds and in 1907 entered a boxing tournament at Cambridge, Massachusetts, and won both the middleweight and light heavyweight titles. Two weeks later he took the American Middleweight Championship at Boston. He then started professional boxing and from 1907 to 1921 had one hundred and sixteen bouts. He fought the famous Roddie MacDonald when he was thirty-six years of age and gained a draw. Some of his opponents over the years were Sailor Burke, Jack Dillon, Hugo Kelly, Battling Livinsky, Joe Walcott and Mike Gibbons.

After learning about skunks at the barber shop we investigated further and in all located fourteen in the shade under buildings along that very quiet main street. Everyone we talked to simply shrugged and said they had not, so far, found any way to get rid of them, but the winter would fix them. Some said they thought there was a one dollar bounty on the pests but who would be foolish enough to smell up a town for one buck?

# 9

## Moon Lore, Nose Bleed Cure, Champion Spitter, and "Six Ships a Year and More to Follow"

OUR NEXT STOP WAS ST. ANDREWS and a man in overalls got from under the wheel of an aged car to tell us we were just about on holy ground.

"You're in the place where the first Roman Catholic Bishop of the Island, the Reverend Angus MacEachern, built the first Catholic Church. And there was a college here to which all the Catholics came until St. Dunstan's was started down in Charlottetown. No, I'm not one of the faithful, but it's quite an honour this place has. Are you sticking to the main road? Well, like lots of others, you'll miss things. You should have gone out to Savage Harbour. Not much to see, but a mighty lot of history around it. It was there the Island Indians met with a big bunch from the mainland that were invaders, and all hands went at it for keeps. With so many killed, they couldn't go in for all the rites that used to follow the death of a brave, so they just dug holes and put them in, and anybody who goes to make as much as a cellar out there will dig up a pile of bones. No, I guess the place ain't haunted. Never heard so, anyhow. And you could have gone right on to Derchoe Point where the ponds make good feeding grounds for wild ducks. No, I'm not a duck hunter. I'm just a farmer, but if you're ever out to the

242

Harbour ask them who can tell weather best, and you'll get my name. How do I do it? Just watch the wind and keep the moon in mind. That's all there is to it. Trouble is, so many never think of the moon, and it has more influence than anything else we've got on earth. You just stop and think what it does with the tides. What makes a dog bark at a moon? Or a fox? Specially when the moon's in the full. And you take midwinter full moon and listen where there's a woods. You'll hear owls hoot. Why, me, I've knowed about the moon since my grandfather taught me. I courted with the moon in mind, and the girl said 'yes' in the full of the moon like she couldn't say anything else. If fellows only knew they could get any girl when the moon is right. You watch the moon when it's mowing time and cut your grass right and it'll never mildew. Plant squash and beans according to the moon. Any granny can tell you the time to wean a baby rests with a change of moon. And watch the moon for pig-killing time. Sure, I know there's them college fellows will try to tell you not to take stock in such things, but I take no stock in them, or the weather broadcasts, either. Lots are leaving the farm, but I've made a fair living on a farm, and not one of the best, either, because I use my head and keep the moon in mind. And next time you're on the Island come down to the Harbour."

We promised we would and drove on to Morell. A man who came from the post office plainly had time on his hands and as we looked around the settlement he told us the place was named after a Jean Morel from St. Malo, France, one of the first settlers. It is a prosperous-looking place.

"You'll find one thing here," said our friend. "No farmer fishes, and no fisherman farms. You look beyond the village and see how the land is going back to bush. When I was a lad there wasn't a bush in a mile, and all fine farms and growing shiploads of produce. This was a great place for lobsters, too, and many a bucket of them have I bought for thirty cents. In my house I've got old spool beds the first settlers used, and a vinegar cruet about 200 years old. One of the first storekeepers here had a share in a schooner and he run a good general store. So he put up a sign that read: 'I'll Buy Anything the Farmer Can Produce.' The week after a woman from the district arrived in his store with a queer-looking cheese. It had the wrong colour. The merchant said he couldn't take it. The woman asked him to take down the sign, then, as the cheese was a product of her farm. Sooner than get a reputation for not keeping his word, the merchant took the cheese. The schooner was taking a load of produce to the West Indies and the cheese was in that load. When the schooner came back it carried a request for as much more of the cheese as could be bought. The merchant was amazed. He talked with the woman and found the cheese had been pressed by green planks. This gave it the certain flavour so favoured by the West Indies. Before the year was out the merchant had almost every woman in the place making green plank cheese."

It was grand talking with our friend, as Morell is a pretty place and the gardens were filled with flowers. He talked of all the changes he had seen, of a farmer who fed a pumpkin with milk until it was almost big as a barrel. Then a flock of pigs got loose at night and ate and trampled the prize pumpkin. The man was so mad that he got his gun and shot the biggest pig.

"Soon as he saw the dead pig he knew what a fool he'd been," said our friend, "for that pig was a prizewinner who belonged to a neighbour. So what to do? No one had heard the shot, apparently, so he got a drag and rolled the pig on it, hitched his horse and dragged the carcase over to the far side of the cemetery. There he dug a hole in the corner and buried the pig. That neighbour searched the country backwards and forwards and never did know how his pig vanished."

Driving along the winding turns of Highway 1 brought fresh vistas with every mile and at St. Peter's the route joined Highway 16. Everyone seemed either in the cellar to keep cool or away to the beach. Not even a youngster was in sight. We wandered into a canteen where the usual juke box was silent and a girl looking as if she were up too late at night leaned listlessly on the counter. She seemed glad we did not want an icecream or anything that required effort, and said she did not know a thing about St. Peter's. Outside again, we met a woman who was flushed with the heat and walked as if she were angry. But she stopped when we addressed her and gave us some information.

"The place was named after a first settler, Saint Pierre," she said, "and they say it's been settled since 1721. People used to dig up arrow heads and stone axes at one time. One story is that the first settlement was made by shipwrecked sailors who brought timbers ashore and built homes and planted beans and potatoes from the ship. I don't know if it's true, and if you'll excuse me I'll go looking for my little girl. She broke a water pitcher and ran out for fear I would punish her."

We asked her to be lenient and left St. Peter's languid in the heat, the only living, moving thing we saw as we swung away was a dog lying sprawled in the shade of a cart. We saw signs—Five Houses—Farmington—Dingwell's Mills— and then we were entering Souris and we parked opposite the Town Hall, thinking of the woods we had seen along the road, of the red dust that hung lazily in the air, of the friendly people everywhere. We had given a man a lift of two miles and one would think it a great favour to hear his thanks. Now we roamed around and visited many of the stores. Business seemed to be good but there was no hurry anywhere. We had icecream sodas and heard "Good Night, Irene" in wheezy tones from a machine somewhere. There must be a story about prosperity here, we felt, but the oldtimer, when we located him, would talk of nothing but the plague of mice the Island had endured. "Up this way we got it worst," he vowed. "They come all at once, eating every solitary thing that grew. You could kill them till your arms were tired, and still they came. Millions of them. They ate every potato that was planted. I've heard the story so many times I almost feel I was there. Generally, it is believed that the plague ran right across this end of the Island and into the sea. That was the end of them and there hasn't been another plague except book agents and the like."

"How is it Souris is larger than the other places along the coast?" we asked.

"Trade," he said tersely. "Souris people used to be great traders and knew all the West Indies and what could be sold there. There was no sudden boom. We had it good over a number of years and now the decline is slow but steady. But when they get the Causeway down at Borden the tourist travel will be our biggest industry. The Americans love it here, because it's cool in the evenings."

At George A. Leard's store we talked with a man who wanted to take us to meet the author of *Johnny Belinda,* but time was pressing and we had to keep on the job so back we went to Dingwell's Mills where we took Route 5 to Georgetown. We had to join Highway 3 to get to George-town and when we arrived in late afternoon it was like finding a forgotten village. There were so many buildings that were boarded up, and grass was actually growing in the streets. A little shop was open and we went in to talk with the old couple who ran it. There were no customers.

"In my day," said the old lady wistfully, "this was the best town on the Island. We have the finest harbour in all the world. You don't need to take my word for it, just look up harbours in any good book. And the ice breakers always fitted out here, and there was lots of trade. Now all the young people have to leave as soon as they are out of high school, for there is no work at all. Just a few fishermen go out at three in the morning, and come back around ten. They keep at it all summer even though the price is low and the catch poor, for it gives them Unemployment Insurance for the winter."

It was a gray picture she painted, something that ought not to be. We did not know why the outfitting of the ice breakers was taken away from Georgetown, but her version sounded dismal. She had it in one word—politics!

"We've one thing here you'll not find elsewhere," she said. "There was a common laid out for the pasturing of the town cows away back, and no law ever changed it. No tax is placed on the pasture and any tax-paying citizen can take a cow there for free feeding. Years back it was a common sight to see the boys leading the cows in from the common, and nearly everybody had their own milk supply. But all that has changed. I doubt that there's so much as one cow at the pasture now."

We looked around the harbour front and it was easy to see what a place it had been at one time but everything was going to rot and the gulls. There were homes along the streets with grass a foot high in the gardens, strangling the flowers. Empty houses everywhere. Building after building with blank shop fronts. Depressing to see day or night, in any light.

Winding around a thread of roads, we returned to Poole's Corner, turned left, and were soon at Montague and there we found lodging for a night with a Mrs. MacGregor who had a nice home. We had dinner at the Hillside Inn and talked with visitors from south of the border who found the Island delightful. Then we wandered down the pretty tree-shaded street and on the left saw the Museum. Everything you could imagine was there from old guns and fans and helmets and yokes for carrying water pails down to apple peelers and crimping machines of a century ago. It was a most interesting place and we went back in the morning to make sure we had not missed anything in the unique collection. Montague is one of the prettiest of the many pretty places we found on the Island, and Mrs. Russell MacGregor was most helpful in telling us what we should see before reaching Wood Island and the ferry. So off we went to Brudenell to see a cairn in memory of Jean Pierre De Roma who came in 1731 to found an Eden of his own making.

De Roma had been sent out by a Company to found a settlement and had with him large supplies, artisans and hardy Breton fishermen. He was a hard worker, was possessed of unlimited energy and was exceedingly ambitious. He planned every building, every project, to the last detail, would brook no opposition or criticism. So the forest was cut down and homes and barns and offices were erected and roads made and gardens planted. For two years the work went on until there were dwellings and stores and stables clustered like a village. Then came the attack on Louisbourg, and its capture, when an enemy cruiser that must have had information about De Roma anchored within easy range of Brudenell Point. Boats were lowered and filled with armed men and as De Roma and his flock took to the woods the invaders looted everything that could be carried off and put the buildings to flames. In a few hours the enemy sailed away and De Roma emerged from hiding to find nothing but smouldering ruins. There was no food nor shelter and the party travelled through the dense forest to St. Peter's, and arrived there almost starved. Five years later when a party investigated the site, it was difficult to tell where the buildings had been. Bushes were growing in the cellars and the cultivated fields going back to the forest.

All was bustle at Wood Island and soon we were on the fine new ferry, *Lord Selkirk,* and crossing to Caribou on the Nova Scotia side. It is a beautiful boat and the day was perfect. A man by the rail gazed back on the Island with our binoculars which we loaned him, and enjoyed himself immensely. When he found where we had been, though, he shook his head.

"All that means nothing," he declared, "unless you've been to Belfast. It was there the great riot took place."

We listened to a long account of clubs and cudgels, Scots and Irish, and a wild time and cracked skulls, and no honour settled, softly murmured that we liked to get items about today, not the long ago.

"And on a moonlight night you will do," he stated. "There's the ghost of Scottie roams around and carries his club. He's been seen by dozens."

The *Lord Selkirk* docked and off we drove and to Pictou but a short way where we had lunch at the Braeside, a fine little hotel perched on the side of a hill. The sky was clouded over when we came from the hotel and within a short time it was raining, a summer shower that ended as it had begun—suddenly. We followed Highway 6 to Shinimicas and then turned right to the shore, reached Northport and saw the lobster boats moored around the dock, and the work begun at a new bridge. The road was under construction and we could only creep along as the going was rough and more stone than gravel was being used. Amherst Shore and its colonies of summer cottages was next, then Lorneville, Tidnish Crossroads, Tidnish with a bridge over the river built in 1892 by Scottish masons and though never used as good as when constructed for the old ship railways. Soon we were in New Brunswick and on pavement again through Port Elgin to Highway 15.

It was quite a run to Shemogue and we saw fine farms and comfortable homes as if it had been and was still a prosperous countryside. Some homes had fine flower gardens showing careful attention, and horse-chestnut trees were more common than the elm. We parked by the road as an elderly man wearing a cap with a long peak came along leisurely.

He looked at our licence plate, spoke cordially and said we weren't too far from home.

He was right, we said, and could he tell us if there were anything unusual about Shemogue. "Yes, just as there is about this fine old Province," he said. "I lived here when I was a boy, and remember how kind the people were at Christmas and other times of the year to the one French family in the place. They were regarded as different, and it was thought to be our duty to look after them. Then another French family moved in on a farm where the last of a clan had gone. We felt it a pity to see the old place in the hands of such strangers, and there was much talk about it so that in the next five or ten years nothing happened. Then a third family came in, by the same way, old folks dead, son in the States. And that's the way it went. There was talk about the French coming in and when the next farm was for sale one of the young men tried to buy it but the price was too high. Next we knew, it was sold to another French family. That was hard to understand but someone got to know the family quite well and were told that the Catholic Church was helping finance the buying of the farms, and that was why the price was paid. Well, to make it short, in about thirty years the Shemogue situation was entirely reversed. Where there was one lone French family whom we all helped, there was but one English family left. And only the Lord helped them."

He sighed and looked around.

"It's that way all along this shore," he said. "They breed big families and are urged to, while the English families have one or two children, and pay the taxes."

There was a lot more in a like strain and we felt sorry for the old man, so did not point out to him that the sons and daughters of the English families should have stayed at home and done with a little less instead of going to the States or the west.

More traffic met us as we rolled along to Cape Bald and

saw plenty of cars parked around and some men putting up what looked like a platform for dancing. We noticed many children about and everyone seemed in gay spirits. Beyond the villages there were lobster traps piled by the beach in many places and fishing boats were anchored off shore. Some homes had American visitors for cars with American licence plates were parked in the yards. Farms looked prosperous, and some stretches along the road boasted lombardy poplars.

Along Nova Scotia's north shore we had seen large colonies of summer cottages but when we arrived at Point du Chene there seemed an immense number. There was not the variety, perhaps, seen in Pictou and Cumberland counties, and none were very large, but they were strewn in lavish abundance, many being painted gay colours. People swarmed everywhere though it seemed near the supper hour. Then we sensed the reason as almost everyone was in a bathing suit. The tide was coming in, in fact was almost in. Smaller boats had all sorts of inflated rubber floats, and the scene would be wonderful for a person with colour film in the camera. There were yellow bathing suits, red ones, blue ones, orange ones, green ones, pretty ones, hideous ones. Some fat ladies waddled to the beach like fat old ducks. Some pretty young things with all their curves in the right places pranced as they had seen Hollywood stars do on television, obviously trying to catch the eye of many young men who were singing rather off-key as they plunged into the water. A dignified gentleman in a black and white bathing suit, wearing a straw hat on his bald head, and a large front, carried a folding chair under one arm. He opened it and sat down when he was a few inches in the water, evidently wanting a foot bath.

We had parked and wanted to talk with someone so when three middle-aged matrons came along carefully guiding a group of youngsters we asked if the cottage colony was growing steadily.

"Yes," smiled one lady. "There are many new cottages since I came here three years ago."

"Then you do not belong here?" we said.

"Oh, no," she smiled. "We are from Three Rivers."

So we bowed an escape and tackled three more before retiring, defeated, to the car. The one gentleman we questioned was from Ohio. The ladies were from Brockville, Ontario, and Fredericton.

We reached Shediac and then were on Highway 11. A dinner at Shediac Inn helped compensate for our defeats along the cottages and, outside on the street, we began looking around and talking to those who looked to be inhabitants. One asked if we had noticed the Foch Bridge.

"When it was opened back in 1919," said our friend who had been standing by a drug store as if trying to remember an errand, "World War One was very fresh in the minds, and the late Dr. J. C. Webster, one of our greatest New Brunswick citizens, thought the naming of the bridge would do honour to the famous French general. After his wish was granted, he felt those who passed over the bridge should know more about its name so he had a plaque or bronze relief made bearing the likeness of Foch, and this was hung within the bridge."

Our man looked elderly, and cultured. He told us what great things Dr. Webster had done for the Province, especially at the Museum in Saint John, presenting portraits and assisting in so many ways.

"It was he who got the government to build the Museum at Fort Cumberland," he went on. "And it has a remarkable collection of relics from the area about such as old tools and farm implements and household articles. He and Mrs. Webster worked very hard to promote anything that was good for our Province."

At that point our friend snapped fingers and remarked.

"I had trouble remembering what I came for, until I

rubbed my left ear. You see in our family it's an old trick we have, all of us. We can recall things after we rub the ear. My gracious, don't start your car now. Just sit a time. Look!"

He was pointing to a black cat that was quietly crossing the road, and we asked him if he were superstitious.

"You can call it what you like," he retorted, "but I know what I know. When I was a lad I had trouble with nose bleed. Mother used every remedy she could think of, and they all failed. Then an old man told me to wipe some of the blood on a poplar chip and drive the chip into a stump. Mother hooted at the notion but I was desperate enough to try anything. So I found a poplar chip and carried it and the first time after when my nose started to bleed I drove the chip into a stump. The nose bleed stopped instantly. I did the same thing twice after and was never bothered beyond that. Mother never believed in what she called 'heathenish notions,' but when she went to our old family doctor about it she got no assurance. The doctor said he had seen so many things that couldn't be accounted for that he would be last to laugh at the poplar chip idea. I don't pretend to understand things, but I never travel if a black cat crosses my path, but go back and start all over again. You can laugh if you like, but I've seen too much to go along with your thinking. My sister was bothered with warts. She had them when she was going to school and tried every remedy she read about but the warts stayed. Then one day we were down to Cape Bald and an old woman there told her to rub a piece of liver on the warts and go out and bury the liver in the dark of the moon. Mother almost forbade her doing it, but she got the liver and buried it in our garden. In the morning there was not a wart on her hands. Those things I have seen, so I know what I know. And I've a cousin who was troubled terribly with arthritis. He got copper bracelets and wore them and has never had arthritis again."

"What about carrying a rabbit's foot?" we asked.

"I never did," he said, "and I've found quite a few four-leafed clovers but I don't think they changed my luck any. But I knock on wood when there's a chance my luck may turn, and I have never walked under a ladder. I had an aunt who was very superstitious about placing three lighted lamps on the table. People knew this and were always careful in her home. Then one night a cousin from England arrived on a visit, and one of the first things she did that evening was light a third lamp for her room, and place it on the table. My aunt collapsed into her chair as if she were sick, and the English woman was worried until she learned the reason, then laughed and laughed and couldn't get over anyone being so foolish as to believe such nonsense. 'Never mind,' my aunt said, 'one of the three who put the lamps on the table will die before the year is out, but it may not be you.' The visitor was careful after that, when she saw that my aunt was really serious, and the rest of us forgot the matter. Then, in November, my aunt had a stroke. She rallied a time, long enough to say she was glad the cousin wasn't the one to go. Then in spite of all the doctor could do she had a second stroke and died. After that the cousin believed the danger of three lighted lamps on a table. Look there." He pointed at a passing car. "See that chain at the rear, just touching the pavement. That's to prevent car sickness. Thousands are using that idea today, and it works, but any doctor will tell you it's impossible. A neighbour of ours used to get car sick within twenty miles, and never travelled much as she did not like trains. Then her husband heard about the chain and put one on without telling her. The next day they started for Woodstock and she was never sick. They came home again, and she wasn't car sick. It was a miracle to her, and they were able to take a trip to the States she had always wanted. Down there her folks saw the chain and joked about it, but after she knew it didn't make any difference. She's never

been car sick again. So I know there's a lot in this world
that doctors and anyone else can't explain."

It was easy to see he would brook no doubting, and we
got him talking about Shediac.

"We've a coastline about five miles long," he boasted,
"and it's all settled with rather nice places so that you might
say our street is five miles long. Shediac Bay is landlocked
and we have yacht clubs. Back in 1933 the Italian, General
Balbo, on his way to Chicago with twenty-four seaplanes, put
down here to refuel. The water's warm, wonderful for bathing, and people from Moncton have summer cottages here.
I don't know exactly when the town began but an Englishman named Hanington came first and bought a grant of
land from a navy officer. They say the grant took in the most
of the townsite, and the Englishman had a sawmill and
prospered. In 1821 people agitated for a church and Hanington offered the site for it free. Ship building was beginning
and money wasn't too scarce and the church was started. Most
of the work was donated and it was called 'St. Martin's-in-the-
Woods.' Bishop Inglis came from Halifax to hold the opening
service and there's a story about one of Hanington's sons
climbing up inside the bell tower during the consecration
service with a bottle of wine in one hand. When he got up
as high as he could go he broke the bottle over a ledge as
those do who christen ships and gave the name in a loud
voice—St. Martin's-in-the-Woods."

"A good story," we agreed. "If Bishop Inglis was here it
must have been Anglican?"

"It was, and is," said our friend. "But they've spoiled
the feel of the old place by taking away the doors of the
pews. They said the old pews were uncomfortable, and two
of the kickers about them would sit two hours on a rough
plank seat at a ball game and never complain."

It was getting late by the time we left and though our
friend insisted we should go around by the shore road through

Acadian villages and see some quaint little coves, we kept to Highway 11 and arrived at Cocagne. It was a lovely evening and several young couples, hand in hand, were out on a wharf running from a pier of the Cocagne bridge. Someone was playing a mouth-organ and one couple was dancing. It was good to be young, we said to the man at the filling station. He looked toward the bridge and grinned. "They work in the lobster factory," he said. "It must be good to get out after a hot day in the plant."

Canteens were offering fresh lobsters but we were tired and pulled up at a motor court for the night. The lady who took our money said we could get the finest lobsters and clams in the world in Cocagne, that the name meant "a land of plenty," and Nicolas Denys had named it so three centuries ago.

We murmured that she knew her history.

"Not much," she smiled. "I had two professors stay over a week-end, and all they did was study history books and talk about this coast. They can have their history. I'll take today and tomorrow."

It was past midnight when we heard her arguing with a carload of very tired young ladies who wailed they had driven all the way from Bangor and would sleep on the floor if necessary. "Not here, you won't," she said. "People like you have got to learn to make reservations this time of year."

"But we didn't know where we'd be," came the protest.

"Then learn to plan," flung back the lady. "You young-sters think the world's your oyster and that you can talk your way into anything."

We were still thinking of the oyster mentioned when we drove into Buctouche the next morning. The night had been slightly cool but the sunshine soon made one forget it, and Buctouche looked a pleasant place with varied greens along the slope of the Buctouche River. A truck loaded with young folks in holiday dress roared past us with a burst of speed, slowed with much back-firing, and turned into a shore road. We stopped beyond the river bridge and asked a jolly-looking woman with a basket what we might find as a feature in the village.

"We've got one," she said, mopping her three chins, "but it's in Saint John. You see all them Irving Oil places. Well, this is the home of K. C. Irving. I see you're from Nova Scotia but you must know that he just about owns New Brunswick and the bus lines and oil companies and anything else he fancies. I've heard him called everything from Santa Claus to a hard-boiled boss, but he must be all right and have a head on his shoulders to make a million down in this part of the world. You ever meet him?"

We had never had the pleasure, we said.

"Don't anticipate too much," came the advice as the handkerchief mopped away more perspiration. "But if you want to get in right with him start preaching there should be a Chignecto Canal. My hubby says that's his dream—Irving's, I mean."

"But a Fredericton man, Ketchum, said a ship railway was best across the Isthmus," we debated.

"Humph! Fredericton! Stuffed shirts is all they are." She kept on mopping and waddled away. She had a lot to be thankful for—roughly, about two hundred pounds.

St. Anne de Kent was next and we idled along at five miles per hour, surveying canteens and homes and filling stations, dogs and children, flowers and hooked rugs for sale. Then a little man with a brick-red face waved at us cheerfully from his seat on the back of a stopped truck.

"How do you like our weather?" he wanted to know.

"It's tops," we said, getting out to talk with him. "Are you a native?"

"Off and on," he grinned. "What are you selling?"

We explained we had nothing to offer but were looking

for anything outstanding, a story that could be put in a book.

"I've heard some good ones by our fishermen," he said, "but you couldn't print them in a book. I guess the best claim to fame we have was settled here in the hungry thirties. And you'd never guess in a million years the champion we had in these parts."

"A boxer? Wrestler? Swimmer? Singer?"

"No, sir, none of them common stunts. Joe LeBlanc was the champion spitter of the whole North Shore."

"Spitter! Did they . . ."

"Sure. Joe could spit twenty feet when he was just a kid. Then he started to chew tobacco and got better all the time. At a picnic down the Point du Chene he beat six fellows and won him a two-dollar bet. They tell he did twenty-six feet there. After that his name was known and I dare say he won bets in half the towns from here to Dalhousie. There was a six-foot-four lumberjack, lean as a clothes pole, come up along from Sussex way, and he could spit tremendous. But Joe trimmed him by a foot, and on a windy day at that."

We wanted to get away from the subject and asked what he did for a living.

"A fair question," he shrugged. "I do anybody I can. I been half around the world, and I've been in jail. Now I'm going to visit cousins I've got over Minto way. If they lived here you could write their grandpa up. He was a stubborn old fellow and when he built his house he made the plans himself. Got the timber and nails and spikes and hired a chap to help him. He'd clean forgot about the stairway and the hired man pointed it out to him. That made him mad, and he kept on with the plan, leaving just a three-foot hole in the upstairs floor. He made a good ladder and fastened it to the wall by the hole. Well, when they moved in and his wife saw the ladder she said she'd never go up it—and she didn't. She had her bed in what he intended for the dining-

room, and put another bed in there for her girls, two of them.
The two boys slept overhead with the grandfather. The neighbour women always said old granny was foxy in not going
up the ladder. She got rid of making beds and cleaning
overhead. Too bad the old place got burned. It used to be
called 'the ladder house'."

How much was fact and how much fiction we could not
know, but said good-day and drove on to Rexton, that had
even prettier tree-shaded streets than some of the others. In
the centre of the town we saw a monument and parked nearby.
The inscription told us that the Rt. Hon. Bonar Law, Prime
Minister of Britain, was born in Rexton, and as we read the
plaque a man came up to us with his thumb hooked under a
suspender.

"There ain't another Province got a claim like this," he
said proudly, pointing to the memorial. "You can go out and
see the old house, if you want, for it's only five minutes in a
car. But it's just another white farmhouse. Right beside the
place is where Senator David Wark lived when he was young.
Likely you wouldn't know about him but he was the white-
haired lad around here in the old days, and he was over one
hundred and two when he died. The Hon. Murray MacLaren,
who was Lieutenant-Governor of New Brunswick, was born
here, too. He's made his pile and he give Rexton a new
Presbyterian church. Yes, sir, we've raised a lot of famous
men but—ah—I ain't one of them."

We said that many of us could never be famous, and he
nodded quick agreement.

"One more thing," he grinned. "This place used to be
called Kingston. I don't know why they changed the name,
unless it's because the word makes you think of a penitentiary,
like up in Ontario."

Richibucto seemed quite a large town as we drove down
the long street that is the water front. There were cars and
trucks parked in drives, plenty of people going hither and

yon, some boats by old wharves, and what looked to be a lobster factory. We parked at the first available spot and got from the car to meet a tall, white-haired man, hatless, in shirt sleeves, walking as if he were on an errand. But he stopped when we addressed him, and soon was talking eagerly about the town.

"The word Richibucto means 'River of Fire' in Indian," he said, "and the whole place was on fire back in 1922. The flames cleaned out this section and there wasn't much we could do about it. I have a friend who kept his money and papers in one of those old ships' chests that used to be quite common in any seaport. When the fire started he didn't think about it reaching his house and went to do what he could helping fight the blaze. Then, when he saw his place in danger, he ran back and began carrying out kitchen chairs and the like, just as one does at such a time. He had helpers, of course, and, too late, thought of the chest. He mentioned it to a neighbour who said he had seen someone carrying out the chest and other items from the upstairs. So this started my friend on a search. He told his son about it, and his brother-in-law. Now down that way, beyond where you see that filling station sign, many people had carried articles saved from houses. So finally my friend located his chest there, and carted it to his own belongings. To his amazement there were two more identical chests. His son and brother-in-law had each found one, and brought it back. The same key fitted all three—and not one contained my friend's treasures. He never did find his own chest."

Our friend paused, and looked at something in his hand. "I came out to buy blades for my safety razor," he said. "If I don't get them now I'll forget them, as I did yesterday. Come along to our Court House and look at the pictures in there. I'll join you soon as I have my blades."

As a rule we did not inspect town halls or court houses but we wanted to please our informant so went in and were pleasantly surprised by the fine portraits hanging around, all famous sons of Kent County. There was the Rt. Hon. Andrew Bonar Law, Prime Minister of Great Britain; Wm. John Bowser, Premier of British Columbia; Hon. David Wark, Senator; Thos. E. Holderness, G.C.B., K.C.S.I., Under Secretary of State for India; Colonel, the Hon. Murray MacLaren, Lieutenant-Governor of New Brunswick; Hon. Peter J. Veniot, Premier of New Brunswick; the Most Rev. James O'Leary, Archbishop of Edmonton; S. E. Norbet Robichaud, Bishop of Moncton; James Hannay, lawyer and historian; Rt. Rev. Louis James O'Leary, Bishop of Charlottetown; Hon. Joseph Cunard, one of the Cunards of the famous steamship line. What other county in the east could produce such a platoon of celebrities? We were very glad we had been given such an introduction by our friend who returned in triumph with his razor blades, led us outside to a fine seat in the shade and began talking as if he had been reading up on history while on his errand.

"The first Acadian who came here," he said, "came by boat along the shore and found an Indian encampment here. He stayed the winter with the tribe and in the spring married a pretty Indian maiden, and took a place apart from the main camp where he built a log home and planted some corn. Soon the tribe respected him, not only for his industry and honesty in dealings, but because he got in touch with trading vessels and secured cooking pots and knives and tools in exchange for furs. Then came trouble in the form of a pirate ship needing repairs. It was brought into the river and the pirates descended on the Indian camp and forced several of the husky braves to assist in the repairs and in maintaining the ships' pumps. They also made the Indians fill the fresh water casks on board the ship. As the repairs were almost complete the mates of the pirate decided to take a comely Indian girl away with them, but she refused their advances and fought so gamely that two of the pirates were slashed by her knife. This enraged them so that they killed her, and wounded her brother. Then the tribe vanished into the forest and as night came on quickly the pirates decided to wait until morning before trying to navigate the river mouth. Some of the Indians made their way to the Acadian's log camp and told him what had happened. He was furious, and made plans. Waiting until between two and three o'clock, the dead of night, the Indians drifted in canoes to the side of the ship, climbed on board and silently did away with the guard. Then they ghost-footed below deck and took the captain, his mates and grisly crew by surprise. Most of them were killed before they were fully awake, and the deck was running with blood. The ship's sails were hoisted in the morning and she was headed out to sea with the wheel lashed. But the craft foundered near the harbour mouth, and no one went near it. The hulk gradually buried in the sand but could be seen until twenty years ago. Of course there are stories of pirate ghosts but nobody believes them."

"What about the place where the Acadian had his camp?" we asked. "Is the site marked?"

"No, and I don't think anyone knows exactly where it was. I've heard it was on the north side of the river, but nothing definite. If you think the Acadian deserves a cairn, what about the first Englishman to come here? His name was Powell and he was a Loyalist, a fiery one at that. His biggest possession was a family of nine sons, yes, nine. He settled here and when the war of 1812 started he wanted to do something against those who had taken his farm, but it was one of his sons who avenged the family. His name was Jacob and he was captain of a privateer that captured an American ship, took its big gun and scuttled the craft. Then Jacob met with a French vessel and took care of it as well. He sailed into Halifax with his prisoners and left them there. Legend says he had a cabin boy named Michaud, and that Michauds here in Richibucto are descendants."

"What happened to the nine Powell sons?" we asked.

"They married and settled up and down the shore. I've seen Powells listed in almost all the old militia rolls along this North Shore. You see, many English came here at the close of the War and some of them resented the Indians staying around and begging instead of working. One settler had grain planted alongside a salmon pool and the Indians came and put up brush shelters beside the river. This made the man so angry he loaded his musket and drove the Indians off, tore up their shelter and threw it into the river. That started trouble and some of the Indians made savage threats. I've heard old men tell that guards were kept all night lest the Indians set fire to buildings. Anyhow, during that summer another settler, according to an old story, killed an Indian's dog when it was chasing his cattle. The Indian and some of his friends came in the night and cut the throats of the man's oxen, were surprised by a settler going home late and carried him off into the bush. Word was sent to Fredericton, and out came a company of soldiers. The Indians vanished into the forest but the soldiers chased after them and captured some of the old ones and children. That fetched the tribe out with their hands up, and their prisoner was brought out, none the worse for his experience, and the captain in command made all hands promise to keep the peace. The Indians were told not to camp on cultivated ground and that was that."

"It must have been an exciting time," we offered.

"Probably," our friend agreed. "But I've seen exciting times, too. When I was a gaffer there was man in town who went crazy if he had a drink of rum. Some of the lads used to offer it to him on purpose and one day when there was a big wedding they managed to get him drinking. Next we knew—I would be ten or so then—we saw our man, he had whiskers from ear to ear, riding a bony cow, armed with a manure fork which he used as a prod, and yelling like mad. He came down the road with half the town turned out to watch him, then jabbed his steed too hard and was unseated. They took him away to some institution after that but we never had more fun than that morning."

"What keeps the place going?" we asked.

"It's hard to say, right now," owned our friend. "At one time this was the third largest shipping port in New Brunswick, and I can remember seeing over forty schooners and brigs in the harbour at once. There was a John Jardine who started the ship-building here somewhere around the 1820s and by 1882 his firm had built more than one hundred vessels. Of course that stopped and then came lobster canning factories. I've a paper home with an article saying more than one million tins of lobster had been sent from here. And one canner was a great church man. They say he had rubber stamps made with Bible texts and used to have a text stamped on every tin."

Time scampered by as our man talked over old times at Richibucto and he had us under his spell to such an extent that we waited his getting a book and showing us what the old-time explorer, Nicolas Denys, said about the North Shore:

Following the coast about twelve leagues, one comes upon Cape Tourmentin. It is a great point which advances into the sea, and is only two leagues and a half from Isle St. Jean. This is the narrowest place in all this strait. The coast is only hills and very dangerous rocks, which are far out from shore. In front of it some are visible, while others are uncovered only at low water. This point is between two large bays bordered with hills and rocks. All over the top is hardly anything but Pines and Firs, and some few other trees. Having doubled this point and made about ten leagues along this coast, one comes to another river into which longboats enter. It is necessary to keep close in the channel, and having passed a little island, one is well under shelter, and finds water enough. The anchorage is in front of a large meadow which makes a cove of reasonable extent where one is placed in shelter. I have named this river the River of Cocagne, because I found there so much with which to make good cheer during the eight days which bad weather obliged me to remain there. All my people were so surfeited with game and fish that they wished no more, whether Wild Geese, Ducks, Teal, Plover, Snipe, Pigeons, Hares, Partridges, Salmon, Trout, Mackerel, Smelt, Oysters and other kinds of good fish. All that I can tell you of it is this, that our dogs lay beside the meat and fish, so much were they satiated with it. The country there is as pleasing as the good cheer. The land is flat and covered with trees which are very fine, as well in their stoutness as in their height, of all the kinds which I must have already named. There are also great meadows along the river, which runs about five or six leagues inland. The remainder is only navigable by canoe, and many more Pines than other trees are found there.

Continuing our route we went into the river of Richibuctou, which is about ten leagues from the latter of which I have just finished speaking. This river has great sand flats at its entrance, which extend almost a league. In the midst of them is a channel for the passage of vessels of 200 tons . . . The Chief at Richibuctou, named Denis, is a conceited and vicious Indian. All the others of the Great Bay fear him. He has upon the border of the basin of this river a rather large fort of stakes, with two kinds of bastions; inside is his wigwam, and the other Indians are encamped around him. He has had a great piece of wood placed upright to the top of a tree, with large pegs which pass through it in the manner of an estrapade and serve as steps for ascending to the top. There from time to time he sends an Indian to see if he can perceive anything along the coast. From this place one can see far out to sea. If any vessels or canoes are seen, he has his entire force brought under arms with their bows and arrows and their muskets, places a sentinel on the approach to ask what persons they are, and then according to his whim he makes them wait, or has them come immediately. Before entering it is required that they make a discharge of their guns, as a salute, and sometimes two. Then the leader enters, and his suite after him. He never goes out from his wigwam to receive those who come to visit him. He is always there planted upon his haunches like an ape, his pipe in his mouth if he has any tobacco. He never speaks first. He expects that he shall be paid a compliment; and some time later he replies with the gravity of a magistrate. If he goes to the wigwam of some

Indian, on arriving he has a musket discharged to inform the other Indians, who come out from their wigwams and go to meet him with their muskets. Then he lands from his boat and sets foot upon shore, and all the Indians who are there discharge their muskets. Then they accompany him to the wigwams, and when he goes inside they again fire each one a shot from his musket. Such is the manner in which he makes them receive him, more through fear than through friendship. They all wish for his death; he is not liked by a single one. If they are delinquent in their duty, he beats them, but not when they are together, for in this case he could not do it with impunity. But when he catches them alone he makes them remember their duty. If the Indians make a debauch, he is never of their number, but he hides himself; for in drunkenness they are as great chiefs as he, and if he were to say to them something which made them angry they would murder him. At such times he is wise and never speaks of his greatness.

We said we were glad that Denis was not there to receive us, and thanked our friend for his great kindness.

Away we went and after a time crossed the Aldouane River, then reached St. Louis de Kent, with a fine church at the top of the hill on the right. There was also a grotto under a bank with a statue and when we enquired of a passerby were told it was a replica of the grotto at Lourdes in France. The name of the river intrigued us as we spelled it out—Kouchibouguacis —and a monument nearby marks the site of a college destroyed by fire. On we went and found the first cousin of the "Kouchy" river — Kouchibouguac — with a village that did not offer anything unusual.

Then came quite a drive through scattered farms and small dwellings and bush. We met many cars, more foreign than New Brunswick, and at long last arrived on the outskirts of Chatham, saw a fine large air station on our left and took quarters for the night in the very fine motel, on the left, so new it was not listed in the Where to Stay booklet we had been issued at the Border. Down the hill we went into the town's main street and after a few wrong turnings found a fine restaurant with an abundance of mirrors and an abundance of good food. Then we began exploring and talked with a stout man who looked as if he might have been a sailor. He was a bit short of breath but not of knowledge.

"This town was just the end of the coach road from Halifax," he wheezed. "Then a man named Peabody come along and set up shop as a trader in fish and lumber and a few others joined in and for over fifty years the place just had the usual slow growth one could expect. Then along came Joe Cunard, sent here by his brother, Samuel, of Halifax, who founded the Cunard Line. He had with him here his brothers, Henry and John, but they were soon forgotten. This Joe was a regular he-man, full of beans and plans, smart as a whip most of the time, and a number one go-getter. First thing the settlers knew there were mills and brickyards and stores and shipyards going full blast, and they say Joe had thirty clerks in his counting-house. He moved into Richibucto and Bathurst, too, with his ship-building, and woodswork and you might say he about owned the whole North Shore. He was the kingpin in ship building and fishing and lumbering. He made Henry his agent and Henry, the quiet type, built a fine home over in Woodburn, just a few minutes drive from here, made a tidy pile, enough to see him through, and then pulled out of the firm. It's likely he'd had all he could take of Joe's ways."

Every once in a while our informant had to pause and regain his breath. He mopped his face and neck occasionally and said he was glad we were not in a hurry. He hated hurry and always had, which was why he had never got along with a boss or mate.

"Joe had no notion of letting Henry out-shine him," he went on, "so he built right here in town. It's no use to look at the place now as all the trim is gone and it's just a wreck. But he lived in real style. He had his own coach and four fine horses. He had a coachman and footman in livery, and when he went to church on Sunday it was quite a show. His garden took up a whole block and he had all kinds of flowers and shrubs and peacocks strutted around. He had a man hired to do nothing but cut the grass and hoe. He had everything in his house from carpets inches thick to grand pianos and when they put on a spread it was the real thing. Joe was six foot tall and weighed two hundred and dressed in broadcloth. He had a black horse that weighed fifteen hundred and was built like a thoroughbred. I've heard more stories of what that horse could do than I dare tell but I know he rode around from one wood gang to another, and from one place to another. He had gangs of men everywhere and horses and oxen. Some of the people liked him but most of them were more scared of him than anything else. But they boast about him to outsiders for he always was a show-off and nobody could ever call him a pinch-penny. Twenty years after he came to Chatham there would be over a hundred square-rigged vessels at Chatham almost every week of the summer."

Our man got to coughing and had to rest a time.

"Joe went full blast for nearly thirty years," he continued. "He got to going to the Old Country nearly every year and the story is that when he came back the town had to salute him with church bells and cannon. The day would be declared a holiday and the folks would line the street down by his house and yell their heads off when he showed up. Sometimes, quite often in fact, he would land at Richibucto and send word ahead. This gave Chatham time to organize a real humdinger of a reception, and the bigger the better for Joe. He was in England when Samuel got the mail contract that put him on easy street, and of course Joe let it be known he had a finger in the pie. So when he came home that time Chatham just about outdid itself. They had signal fires to be lit as he came nearer, an escort of thirty men on horseback, and ten cannon to fire three rounds each. But that wasn't all. The next day they staged a huge parade that seemed a mile long made up of mechanics and woodsmen and carpenters and caulkers and hammermen and shipwrights and sawyers and riggers and blacksmiths and joiners, all sorts of workmen who drew their wages from Joe, and who carried banners and emblems and axes and saws, tools of their trade. This procession escorted a deputation in silk hats that presented Joe with an address, and nothing written ever outdid the praise on the roll of paper. It listed then things he had done for the Miramichi, the foresight he had showed in all his planning, the accomplishments to his credit, his untarnished honour, his unheard of vigour, his fairness to all men, and the wonderful results the world over now that steam was in use. It must have been ironical to some less excited listeners. They would surely know these paraders were celebrating their own finish. Steam meant iron vessels, and they couldn't build those on the Miramichi. But they milled around and cheered and cheered and it was a big holiday and drinks were free and some tried to sing: 'Six ships a year and more to follow, he built in the yard at England's Hollow. Ships of spruce and hackmatack, at Richibucto and Konchibouguac. And the ships that he built in the Bathurst Yard made another fortune for Joe Cunard. Lumbering in winter, in summer the trade, that's the way the money was made. Fifteen hundred men, they said, looked to Joe for their daily bread. Then the whole works busted. The shipyards shut down. Joe was a goner but more'n half the people still admired him and talked about him. I've heard my old grandad talk about those times and I never got tired of hearing it. But they'll never come again. They can't. And the timber's almost gone. D'ye know that if a man could have a choice, I'd sooner have lived in them days when Joe was king than the best times there'll ever be ahead of us. It's all machinery now. Them days a man was a man with a saw and axe and canthook, on a log drive or in a rigging. And he had pride in what he could do, in the job he could do. Today it's all unions and union bosses and everybody doing as little as he can, and crying for more pay. I tell you the world is in a hell of a shape."

Our man was getting excited, and his breath was shorter, so we tried to calm him by talking of other things. Finally he grinned. "I know I make a fool of myself," he said. "A man never learns. I was seventy-four my last birthday, too. The old age pension is a big help and I've done a lot of reading the last year or so. It helps pass the time. Mostly I'm in Saint John, but I like to come back here every summer for a few weeks, though there's mighty few I know. My wife left me years ago. Went back to England. I married her over there in the first war but when we got here she said I'd misled her. I'd told her about the Miramichi same as I tell you now, but she said it was a dump, and the more I tried to show her what a fine country we have the more she said I was crazy. So away she went. I got to thinking about it afterward and realized she, being from Leeds, wouldn't see things like I did. So I wrote and told her so, asked her to try it again. She didn't write but she sent one of them old mugs of Leeds, made away back in 1789, to celebrate the King's recovery from madness. I sold it for ten bucks in Saint John, and that was that. Hope I haven't bored you."

We assured him he had not and made our way out of Chatham by a road on the left and crossed over and came down the other side of the river to Newcastle, up from the pretty square and along the highway until we reached the Beacon Light Motel, a fine place to stay, far enough off the road from traffic, and clean and bright and new. Down the hill a distance we saw a sign pointing down the slope — ANTIQUES — and went down a path and to a home where fine old books and antiques of all sorts are on display. Miss Louise Manny is the proprietor, and luck was riding right with us for she knows more about Newcastle and the Miramichi than any other two persons in the country. She whisked us away to the Old Manse Library, the massive square house where Lord Beaverbrook lived as a boy and developed a love for this North Shore area that has never abated as the years go by. He was William Maxwell Aitken then and he did like many another native son, pack up and travel to greener fields. But when he had his fortune and all the power and prestige one man can wish, his thoughts were still back in New Brunswick and he has ever remembered the North Shore. Later in the year we drove again to Chatham to witness the North Shore Regiment receive its colours, presented by Lord Beaverbrook. It was Thanksgiving, and a cold and windy day, but the veterans of the unit, proud of their great record in Europe, never complained in the slightest but stood to attention and marched and paraded like a Guards regiment. And out on the small platform swept by the icy wind stood Beaverbrook, the Honorary Colonel of the regiment, carrying out the presentation as if he truly were a soldier.

Mingling with those who had looked on, we heard again and again warmest praise and admiration for the grand old man who had gone from the Miramichi to the very top of the world.

"You can't beat him," said an old sweat, when the parade was over. "He was in touch with the North Shores all the time we were overseas and when the war was over and we were on our way home he had a train take the whole outfit up to London and he gave us a dinner with all the trimmings. It was no do for a few officers but for every lad in the unit down to the poorest rear-rank private. All you could eat and all you could drink, and fun for everybody."

## 10 | Miramichi Fire, Folk Songs, Bull Moose, and "The Coffee Mill"

"MIRAMICHI IS THE OLDEST place name in Eastern Canada that is still in use," said Miss Manny. "It's an Indian word taking in the whole district around the river. The first English-speaking settler here was William Davidson who, with a partner, got a fishing grant of 100,000 acres. He exported fish and furs and masts for the King's Navy. In 1773 he built a 300-ton schooner, the *Miramichi*, which was the first sailing vessel built entirely of new materials in New Brunswick. Loyalists flocked here in 1784. Then there came Scottish shipbuilders from Dumfries, out of work after the Napoleonic wars, and others from Ayr and Moray and Inverness. There were waves of Irish, and then Americans came for lumbering, and stayed. Everything seemed to be going well until tragedy struck on the afternoon of Friday, 7th of October, 1825. People outdoors saw a dense column of smoke rise in a vertical direction a considerable distance from Newcastle. The wind was moderate, but shifting, and appeared to carry it to the leeward of the river so no apprehension of danger was entertained. It was supposed that an extensive forest fire was raging and there had been a long period of dry heat, but, strangely, not a person seemed to be alarmed. In the evening the breeze smartened and all at once ashes and cinders showered down and almost suffocated those outside their

272

homes. An hour later a loud roaring was heard and the falling ashes darkened the area and nothing could be seen. Then the wind blew a hurricane and the roaring noise became tremendous. Flames burst in masses from the darkness and then the whole sky was illuminated by an immense sheet of fire that in a moment enveloped Newcastle and Douglastown. Within three minutes from the first appearance of the flames most of the houses in the area were on fire.

"The night became a hell on earth. The screams of the burned, mingled with the cries of domestic animals, was terrifying. Men helped the sick and aged, women ran with infants in their arms, as all tried to reach the river. The majority plunged in up to their necks but others got into boats or canoes, on rafts or floating logs, and drifted with the current. Hundreds took refuge on marsh lying near the river half a mile from Newcastle. There was little more than dried mud in the area and proved the safest retreat. Eight thousand square miles of forest were consumed by the fire. Three vessels were burned. Between one and two hundred persons perished and three to four hundred were badly burned. Two thousand were left destitute. Many cattle reached the river and submerged in it, avoiding death, and a large bear was in their midst. Most of the wild animals of the district perished. Immense numbers of salmon, bass and trout were found on the shores after, suffocated from substances which fell into the water. Snakes tried to escape to clearings and were found dead in twisted heaps. Moose ran for their lives and many reached settlements forty miles away, still in panic. The magnificent pine forests which had furnished masts and square timbers to Britain for over fifty years were gone, and the masting industry was at an end, but trees in the unburned areas, and juniper which sprang up after the fire, furnished material for shipbuilding."

"Were there any outstanding ships built in this district?" we asked.

"Most certainly." Miss Manny was emphatic. "British emigration to Australia demanded big fast-sailing vessels, and we built them. The *Sword Fish* held in her day every possible record for the run between Bahia and Liverpool. Gilmour, Rankin and Company built the ABC ships, named in alphabetical order, *Annie Laurie* to *Vigilant*. The *Indian Queen* rivalled the *Marco Polo* of Saint John. Then there was the unlucky *Queen of Hearts* that killed a man on every voyage. Her figurehead was a lady dealing cards and that, the old-timers say, was the reason for her bad luck. Another legend is that wood from the demolished St. Andrew's Presbyterian Church in Chatham was used in her construction, which 'put a curse on her.' The *Golden Light* was launched after the river was frozen over and a gang of men had to cut a channel eleven miles through the ice to get her out. Well, to make it short, I have a list of five hundred ships built in the Miramichi area and I'm sure I've missed several."

"You are doing a grand work in collecting the legends and history of this area," we said. "It's lucky there was a person like you to do it."

"I love the work," said Miss Manny, "and I have another hobby as well. In 1947 Lord Beaverbrook got me a helper and sent me out to collect folk songs of the Miramichi. I thought it an impossible task at first and then became more and more amazed as I travelled around and found a dozen or more folk song singers in the Miramichi zone. One from Black River knows over one hundred songs, and Sarah Ginnish came from the Indian Reservation at Eel Ground and sang five songs in Micmac. We got on so well we were soon on radio and people without radios would walk miles on Sunday afternoon to listen to our programmes. We found that Larry Gorman was a traditional figure, the greatest song-maker that ever lived. He'd go into a camp at night, and by morning have a song about everybody in it. There were street songs brought out over the years from the old country, playing up tragedies, shipwrecks, disasters, hangings, and the most popular among them were the "goodnight' songs supposed to have been written by criminals as they waited to go to the gallows. The Come-ye-alls of the Miramichi lumber woods are the direct descendants, in the form of their stories and their tunes, of the folksongs of a thousand years ago, and the oldest local song we have in the Lord Beaverbrook collection is "The Miramichi Fire.' The most popular is 'Peter Emberley' the sad song about a young man who met death in the lumber woods. One man, John B. Stymiest, was eighty-seven when he sang for us 'The Gull Decoy.' It's been real fun collecting these songs and meeting the fine people who can sing them."

Highway 11 skirts the northern shore of New Brunswick all the way from Newcastle and for miles the scenery is much the same, forest and farm and shore, in mingled doses of scenic beauty. We saw many American cars parked by picnic places but the populated places were few and we did not stop at Bartibog Bridge or Neguac and would not have stopped at Tabusintac had not a fox run from cover into a field, probably in search of mice, and a man come from his barn with a gun.

"It took two of my hens," he said, "and is getting too bold, coming out in broad daylight." He took a shot but missed and the fox raced back the way it had come and the man sighted and uttered some North Shore words that sizzled in our ears. Then he looked at us and grinned mournfully. "You just pleasurin'?" he asked.

We explained our mission and he shook his head. "There ain't much up around here," he said, "except an old story that the Indians made their peace — the Mohawks and the Micmacs—over there at Kirbin's Point."

"Did they bury the hatchet?" we asked.

"According to the old story, they did." He shrugged. "They did a sensible thing. Sent their two chiefs out to settle their differences. The rest just looked on. And the Micmac outlasted his man, got him fagged and then slammed him 'gainst a big rock and buried his hatchet in the Mohawk's head. Now if only this here mean Russian and the head of the Yankee army or navy or something, would meet and fight it out, that would be fine. For they'd postpone that meeting until they were very old and we'd have a mighty long peace. In fact, if they could make it law that the heads had to fight, there'd be no more war."

We had to agree to such an idea, and that pleased him. Then he asked the time, was surprised when we told him. "My woman gets meals according to her figuring," he said. "She has an old eight-day clock in the kitchen which is twenty minutes slow, and an alarm clock in the bedroom that's fifteen minutes fast. So she tries to cal'late between them and half the time she's away out. But she won't touch them. She says tinkerin' with clocks is what puts them off."

Away we went and parked in Tracadie, found it had a leper colony, and many fine citizens, then reached Upper Pokemouche, paused briefly and talked with three people, who figured we must be some income tax persons or as bad, and evaded our questions, then drove on and reached Caraquet. A legend said its main street was twenty-two miles long—the longest village in North America. We stopped and talked with many people but did not get any stories. At long last a barber admitted that some income tax officials had been around asking questions of two or three citizens, and no one would trust strangers.

This seemed a natural attitude, we agreed, but we offered credentials to show we had no evil intent, and he loosened a trifle. "I might tell you a few things," he reckoned, "but here everybody is related, more or less, and you can't say much without getting into someone's fur. But don't let anything make you feel these aren't all good law-abiding people. You won't find any better anywhere. I've not much education and I haven't travelled much, and don't want to, but some from here have been to sea and far places. I was talking

to a chap who worked on a ship out of Saint John. One time
he was in New York and a fellow took him down into the
underworld."

"Down?" we echoed.

"Yes, sir, down. He said they went down stairs right
under a building and away down there they even had train
cars running. That's how big that underworld is you read
about in the big cities."

"What is your trade?" we asked. "Were you always a
barber?" He looked to be sixty at least and he had the hands
of an outdoor man.

"I was a farmer," he admitted. "But my health kind of
give out and I had a son-in-law who was a barber and said it
was much better pay than farming. So I took a course and
—well—that's what I do now. The man I sold my place to
used to work in a town and now he wants to go back to it.
He sent me this piece of verse last week."

Our friend took from his purse a folded paper, and we
copied the lines:

I long for a cow of modern make, that milks five days for
    leisure's sake,
That sleeps on Saturday, snores on Sunday, and starts again
    afresh on Monday.
I wish for a herd that knows the way to wash each other day
    by day,
That never bothers to excite us, with chills or fever of mastitis.
I sigh for a new and better breed, that takes less grooming and
    less feed;
That has the reason, wit and wisdom, to use the seat and
    flushing system.
I pray each weekend, long and clear, less work to do from year
    to year,
And cows that reach production's peak, all in a five-day
    working week.
I look for officials by the mob, to guide the farmers at their
    job,
And show these stupid breeders how to propagate a five-day
    cow.

We handed back the paper and allowed that in this old world it was every man to his choice.

"Not by a darn sight," our man exclaimed. "I wanted to be a blacksmith. When I was a youngster I was fascinated by the blacksmith shop just beyond our place, and was in there every chance I got. When I got big enough to be allowed to pump the bellows I pestered my mother to let me work there, but to her it was a place where the usual loafers gathered and bad language was frequent. It was an old, low building with a pile of junk outside the door, the windows darkened with cobwebs, the floor littered with hoof parings. Most of the time there was a plow or spring tooth harrow that needed fixing, and overhead, by the forge, was a pole hung with horseshoes. No matter how many times I watched old Sam work the bellows and heat a shoe red hot, then pound it on the anvil and send red-orange sparks in all directions, I was always wanting to watch again. It was a thriller to watch him plunge the hot shoe in the tub of scummy water always by the window and see the heavy steam roll upward. Then he'd take the horse's hoof up and test the fit of the shoe and often bitter smoke would rise but of course I knew it never hurt the horse. Then Sam would drive the nails and twist off the ends. I never got to try any of the work because we moved away, but for years I just lived for the day when I would be a blacksmith."

There was real wistfulness in his voice, and it was in our ears for some time after, as well as remembrance of his thick, strong fingers and hardened hands, and we wondered what sort of a barber he was.

The drive from Caraquet to Bathurst was one to remember. We saw so many ancient pole fences crossing the fields, fences of peeled and split timbers, weathered and gray, that we stopped and I struck a top pole with a stone. The timber rang almost like metal, and we wondered how many years it had been there. At some places crows sat on the top pole like black trimmings, bobbing and cawing as we drove past. Robins would run along the pole and drive at a bug that alighted. Traffic had slowed for the supper hour and at one spot a huge raven was pecking at a dead porcupine. It raised itself on heavy wings and merely circled overhead, then alighted again behind us. We slowed as we crossed a bridge as a blue heron was ankle deep in water alongside, so intent on its fishing that it never looked up. It's indifference was so incredible that we stopped, and still it did not look around or fly so we went on and left it in peace, noticing a farmer by his fence who had watched us. He waved a hand so we stopped and told him what we had seen.

"That old fellow has been around the last month," said the farmer. "Twice he's been in our dooryard, and I don't ever mind another heron like that. It was eating from the hen trough when I come home one night and just walked around the barn, hoping I'd go away. It must be pretty old."

The farmer leaned on the fence and in a moment was recounting experiences he had had in watching birds, from an owl's nest in an old wagon shed to a heron colony he had discovered back in the woods. He appeared eager for someone to talk with, and we wondered as it was the supper hour.

"Don't think I'm dippy, talking like this," he grinned. "The missus has some women in and I know there won't be anything ready for me till they're gone, so I kind of intrude on your time."

We looked at the gray unpainted farm house with an iron pump in the yard and felt it must be quite an afternoon for the farm wife when she entertained. It would be nice, we suggested, for him to go in later and sample the cakes and doughnuts left over.

The man shook his head. "I never took to sweets. We never had much of them when I was raised, but one thing we did have that I miss and that was baked beans. We used to have them Saturday night, rich with West Indy molasses and bits of pork. Then they'd be warmed up for breakfast Sunday morning, dried crunchy on a frypan, with brown bread and lots of butter. Mother made the best pot of beans I've ever eaten. She used to say a bean pot was no good till it was five or six years old, that you couldn't get the flavour in a new one, and she was right. But the wife hates baked beans so we don't have any, and canned ones is worse than none. Are you going far?"

We were going to Bathurst, we said.

"Good town," our man commented. "The papers print stuff about it being in the heart of a great metal find or the like, and you'd think the whole country would be rich overnight. Then time slides by and nothing happens. I guess a man ought to have sense enough to take them stories with a pinch of salt."

It was evident that our friend would talk politics or anything in order to keep us with him, so we said good-bye and wished him luck.

Long before we reached Bathurst we could see the tall smoke stacks of the paper mill, and once we were in the place it seemed built around the Bathurst Pulp and Paper Company. But we kept going and climbed a long grade and, somewhat away from the centre of the town, found a fine motel, like those we had located at Newcastle and Chatham. Then we went downtown again and had dinner at a small hotel. The evening was still and warm and we wandered around and found a monument bearing an inscription about Nicolas Denys who, three hundred years before, had built his home and trading post on what is now a main part of Bathurst. We were trying to visualize the place as it had been in Denys' day when a group of six persons arrived. It was evident that half of them were visitors from distant points, and an elderly gentleman was the guide.

"Denys was governor of all the country between here and Canso and Gaspé," he said. "He was a farmer, and he traded in fish and furs, was a friend of the Indians, and very observant. He was a naturalist, too, and wrote a book about the natural history of his domain. Tomorrow I'll show where Denys is buried at Ferguson's Point. After he was gone it is likely his place was abandoned. At any rate a century later a Scottish trader came here and set up quite a business. He bought fur from the Indians and traded with them, but had to get out at the time of the American Revolution when privateers were along the coast acting as pirates. And Cartier was here away back, looking for a route to the far east."

"What about the Acadians?" one of the party asked.

"They would be up here, too, no doubt of that," said the guide. "This was too fine a country to be overlooked. The Indians liked it and the salmon fishing in this country is hard to beat. Maybe we can arrange a trip up to the Nepisiguit Falls. There's a drop of a hundred feet, something to see, and that's where the power is developed for this town. Another thing we've got is a fine beach at Youghall. I'll take you out there. The water's warmer than you can think, and there are lovely drives. You haven't seen the half of Bathurst yet and I'm telling you it's the finest town in the east."

We strolled on as the gentleman was telling his guests that Bathurst has a French-speaking mayor one year, and an English-speaking one the next, by popular arrangement, that a new town hall was in the building. Next morning we came down again for breakfast at the small hotel and afterward found our way to where the building was going on, saw a sign and got to talking with the town engineer, Major M. H. Rogers. Soon we had discovered another side to the area. In both World Wars the men of the district had enlisted in large numbers, and though the ranks of the North Shore Regiment had been filled with woodsmen and fishermen and others of like nature, the unit had proved one of the finest in the Canadian Corps.

"These fellows along the shore," the major said, "are

resourceful. They can take care of themselves in the woods, walk miles with a heavy pack, find their way where another would be lost, know the sea and can adjust themselves to any situation. Many of them own old trucks and are their own mechanics. They're hard and wiry and intelligent and when they'd had their military training were tops in their brigade. In fact, A Company of the North Shores won every competition in England as the finest company in the Third Canadian Division. Their baseball team won the Divisional Championship, and their hockey team won the Brigade Championship, and was only defeated by a team of imports who did little else. No other battalion team beat them. And the North Shores was chosen as one of the battalions to spearhead the landing on the Normandy coast. It proved as good on the battlefield as it was in sports, and made a great name when it captured Carpiquet and held on through terrific counter attacks and days of heavy shelling. Its losses were heavy but it set a great record as a first-class fighting unit."

There had been a shower during the night and the sun had quite a struggle before it was clear of clouds and then the day warmed rapidly. We passed through Beresford and Petit Rocher and Elm Tree and Green Point, seeing many hooked rugs displayed for sale and men busy in the fields, but did not stop until we were at Belledune Point. We talked to two different men by the filling station but they said there was no story to be found in the village and were going to leave when an old woman who had heard our queries came alongside the car, shaking her head.

"Those men are stupid," she hissed. "There was Joe LeBlanc and his race with a moose. He had a bicycle and was coming home. The new pavement was just down that summer and he had won two prizes for racing and was going pretty good when a bull moose come from the woods after him. Joe made his feet churn the pedals and he said he was going faster than ever he had in the races but the bull

kept gaining and Joe could not do better. There was not a
car in sight, nothing, and he was near to give up when he
reached a corner and run into rain. You know how in the
summer a shower will go so far, and no further. One minute
he was on dry pavement—the next it was wet. So he come
around fast on a wide curve and heard what he expected. A
big thump! The feet slid from under that bull on the slippery
pavement and it went down hard. Joe said it made a noise
like swearing, and when he risked to look back it was limping
away into the woods."

That was real luck for Joe, we said.

"And another story is better," hissed the old woman. "A
ship with horses and cattle on board was caught in a storm
and driven in the Bay. There was much damage and the
settlers pushed their cattle and horses from the deck as many
had broken legs and everything was confusion. One horse
was not hurt, however, and that one swam ashore here and
was on a farm for years as no one ever came to claim it."

"That is a good story," we said. "Do you know any other?"

"Not of here," she said, "but I am from Caraquet and I
am one of those who has seen the Phantom Ship!"

We immediately poised our pencil, and asked what she
meant.

"A long time back, away back, some say three hundred
years ago, one July there was a sudden thunder storm and a
ship in the Baie de Chaleur was struck. It was quite a distance
out but the sky had darkened as it was just sundown and
people along the shore called to one another and they watched
the flames begin aft and slowly work forward. The sails blazed
and made a sight that could be seen for fifty miles as the
flames leaped a hundred feet into the air. The ship kept drifting, driven by an onshore wind, what there was of it, and then
the stern was one big furnace and the people watching could
see the crew running forward and some threw themselves into
the sea. After a time those left started climbing into the

rigging but the ropes had charred as the sails burned and they saw figures tumbled back in deck. Then the fire burned higher and higher and soon there were no more figures on deck. All had jumped into the sea. And that ship kept burning right to the water line and the hulk ran aground at Green Point. There was a lot of talk about it and then it was forgotten until the settlers were on the coast another night some years after the fire and another thunder storm came and everyone saw another ship struck and then the sails flamed high and figures jumped into the sea and the people were so alarmed that they manned a boat and put off and all at once there was not a sign of the burning ship. They reached the spot where it had been and there was not so much as a charred stick on the water. I don't know how many times it has been seen since then but when I was a girl we were going home from church one Sunday night in July when it was warm and close and there was lightning and then all of us, there must have been twenty or more persons together, saw the burning ship as plain as I can see that house across the road. The flames roared so high we were sure we could hear them. Some men ran down and got into a boat in their Sunday clothes and all but before they were two hundred yards from shore the burning ship vanished. One minute we saw it plain as could be, saw the men jumping from the deck and splashing into the water, and the next minute it was gone. I know many down at Caraquet who have seen the ship, but don't think I'm a foolish old woman. Because I don't believe in ghosts. But I know what I see, and I don't care how you try to explain it, or what anybody says—I saw the ship, and that's that."

We assured her we were not doubting her word in the least, for she was very much in earnest, then made our farewell and drove along to Jacquet River. There was a small group by a filling station but they said nothing ever happened in that area and when we talked with two men working in a field they said the same thing. Then one man said he had read in a book that the river, and two others, had been named after three trappers from Quebec who came and lived together till snow came and then ran separate trap lines and got much fur. A man in a dooryard honing something on a grindstone was no source of information and we were just giving up when we remembered the lady who told us about the Phantom Ship. So at the next place when we saw a woman in a rocker on the porch we just naturally went up to her with the notebook at the ready.

"Only two people really knew about this place," she sighed, "and they're both dead. I'm sure there's a lot of history here but nobody knows it."

We murmured that a man three farms back had said the same thing.

"Him!" She brightened. "He didn't give you any other kind of a story, did he? No. Well, he could, if he wanted. They had a bony old cow and he couldn't sell her, and she was too old and tough to eat. So last fall when the hunters started coming around he loaded his rifle and hid out in the pasture bushes and the first time a hunter shot near there he fired and killed the cow. Pretty soon a man come out on the wood road and next he knew my neighbour was waving his arms like a windmill and telling him he had shot his prize cow. The fellow wouldn't believe it but when he saw the cow with a bullet through her skull he began to stutter. Then he looked toward the woods where he had fired at something he hadn't seen, really, and took out his wallet. He paid fifty dollars for that cow and got a promise that no word of it would go further. That farmer's always so smart that I just couldn't help telling you about him, and I could tell worse than that if I wanted."

Thank you, we said, but one story would be quite enough, and we hurriedly got away and soon were at New Mills. The second man we talked to told us the name came from back in 1827 when a man named Flemming built a saw and grist mill at the place and forgot he had no grease or oil. It was the first day of May, our man said, but a lad walked across the ice to Carleton on the Gaspé coast and borrowed a gallon of oil.

"He walked by way of Heron Island," said the man, "and you can figure how cold it must have been when I tell you that during the average winter the Bay doesn't freeze."

Heron Island was named because a large heron colony had been there when the first settlers arrived. "I guess too many went to see the nests," said the man, "for the whole colony moved out and there hasn't been a heron's nest over there in years. I found the colony they use now, and it's about nine miles back in the woods, and you can smell it about a mile away for bits of fish and frogs they don't eat fall from the nests, and dead youngsters get pushed out to rot on the ground. People settled on Heron Island and some ships were built there."

Charlo Beach must be a popular place as there were young folks in bathing suits as we passed through and as we drove in to Dalhousie some boys had pails of clams they were trying to sell. We parked in a main square and municipal buildings, built of stone, faced us from three sides. A monument was there and we discovered it had been erected more than a century ago in honour of the town's first merchant—Captain John Hamilton. On the fourth side of the square is the paper mill and a man who strolled over as we studied the monument told us the biggest achievement of Hamilton had been the building of St. John's Presbyterian Church. He said the town had been laid out in 1826 and named for the Earl of Dalhousie.

"You'll notice as you drive up from Moncton that most of the people are French," he said, "but Dalhousie was never French. It's been a town of tough old Scottish gentlemen, mostly Presbyterians, hard workers, good hearted, and believers in predestination. I've got a neighbour who is a nice old lady but is almost stone deaf. I tried to interest her in a hearing aid, but she said the good Lord must have intended her to be deaf, and she was not going against His wishes. I'm not one of them, but I grew up with five families like that. Not one of them took any special precautions in any matter. They would say what is to be, will be. So why fuss over it? One of the boys went to war and got the Military Medal for bravery. He didn't duck because he knew that if there was a bullet marked for him it would get him, and if there weren't he needn't be scared. The deaf old lady was on the train coming from Campbellton when a man she knew, a young lad who chews gum, got on and sat facing her. After a time, watching him chewing, she tapped his arm. 'It's nice of you to try and talk to me,' she said, 'but I can't hear a word you're saying.' He had to take his gum out so he wouldn't bother her."

We wandered around the town a bit, and realized the dignity imposed by those stone buildings, met four ladies coming along with large shopping baskets and were interested to note two of the baskets neatly painted in tartan colours. Then we drove on and soon were doing no more than thirty or forty miles an hour for the beauty of the rolling hills in the distance, the sea and river catching the sun's glitter, and the fleecy clouds drifting overhead to chase shadows across our way, made a combination simply fascinating. One wished for a camera with a lens large enough to encompass the whole scene, and we were not surprised to meet American cars travelling at a slow pace. We saw many summer cottages, and some smart sports cars, some very attractive summer visitors in shorts and sun tan, then we made reservations at Doyle's Motel, a fine place to stay and serving good meals. After which we drove in through quite a stir of traffic and almost got bumped while looking at Sugar Loaf Mountain raising its hoary head above the town. Pulling to one side of the street, we parked, and soon were talking with a pleasant little lady of some eighty summers who said there was nothing as nice as

the old horse and buggy days. There was the occasional run-
away, she said, but not the car accidents we have today.

"I could talk all day about Campbellton," she said. "I was
here when the big fire of 1910 burned most of the place, and
I remember when some of the older people thought it a foolish
thing to have a swimming pool right here in the town. How
ideas change. We had better times, too, than the young folk
today who have to have them noisy juke boxes to fill the night
with noise, and they all act like they suffer from St. Vitus
Dance. What kind of items do you want? You can tell in
your book that we get our elecricity from Metisse, Quebec,
that we have the finest scenery in New Brunswick, that people
on trains change their watches here, that you can cross the
river on a ferry boat and see a few timbers they call an old
French battleship. You can get booklets on Mission Point
which tell about a sea battle fought off shore between French
and English ships. You can climb Sugar Loaf if you're one
of them kind that likes climbing, and you'll see a cross that
marks the spot where two girls fell and were killed. No, sir,
we didn't do any climbing when I was young. Us girls were
hampered by long skirts, and they were foolish, no doubt of
that, but so are some of the rigs women wear today, like them
fat ones in slacks. Oh, that some power the gift would gie
'em, to see themselves as ithers see 'em. And we're keeping up
with the world in other ways. Even the men who take off
storm windows or do odd jobs talk about unions and union
pay. My brother wanted a fellow to paint his one-car garage,
and the man said it would cost thirty-two dollars. My brother
is rough-tongued and he said he wouldn't pay Michael Angelo
that much. The man got mad and said if Michael did the job
for less he would get his men and picket my brother's place.
Now if you want stories about old river drives, Jim Murphy
would be your man, only he's dead. I can think of at least
four others who used to be river men and guides and had
grand stories but they're all dead. I guess you have come

around too late. Everything has changed and they're doing
most of the work today by machinery. Even do the house
work. My daughter lives in Montreal and, bless you, she even
has a rig to pulp up garbage and wash it down the sink, and
another button to push that takes away all the cooking odours.
She wanted to know if I didn't wish I lived in a push-button
age, and I said all the button I knew when I was her age was
a button that turned—and it was on the outhouse door. I don't
know what this world is coming to, and am just as glad I
don't. The papers and radio and TV would scare the living
daylights out of you if you believed one-quarter what they
said, and people do the craziest things. I'll be watching for
the book but don't let them put the price too high, for you
can't do anything with a book after you've read it."

She might be talking yet if we had not gently eased ourselves into the car and driven away. As it was she followed us,
walking by the window, until we were into traffic, and though
she never raised her voice we heard every word and she simply
didn't draw a breath. It just flowed from her like a small
torrent.

Away we went across Highway 17 to St. Leonard and it
was a drive through forest most of the way. Now and then
we came to a small settlement but very seldom and there was
not much traffic. Ravens and crows and squirrels showed
themselves and sometimes there would be a rabbit in a ditch.
When we were a little more than halfway through we came
upon a small car parked by the roadside. It was at least twelve
years old and the man standing by was at least seven times
that age. We stopped and asked if anything were wrong.

"Everything," he sighed. "I've a flat tire, and no jack."

We assured him that was not a tragedy, produced our jack
and quickly hoisted the rear of his veteran. He produced a
spare from the back seat and carefully slid it into place,
tightened all the nuts with vigour, inspected the tire critically

as we let it down, wiped his hands on his overalls and said he was satisfied.

"Not likely you're a boy scout," he said, "but you've did your good deed for the day. I waved to eleven cars in a row when I stopped an hour ago and not one of them as much as slowed down. Worst of all, seven of them was New Brunswick cars. That's human nature for you. And I wouldn't be here at all if it weren't for an accident."

We said we were sorry to know he had had misfortune.

"Worse'n that," he pronounced. "My wife's mother lives at White Brook and her health's not good. She got on the phone first thing this morning and I've driven forty miles for nothing. We thought she'd broken a leg or the like, and couldn't make sense to anything. So I just got out the car and let the work go. When I got there the old lady reminded me of a story I heard about a preacher who'd used up all his sermons and couldn't get any new ideas. So he wrote away to a publisher and asked for help, and got word that a sermon a week would be prepared and sent him for one dollar per week, but he would have to sign for the year. The preacher signed and got the first sermon and was delighted with it. But he couldn't think up anything for the evening service and was still sweating on it when Sunday come. He give the sermon at the morning and it went over good but he was worried stiff about the evening. Then his wife said there would only be a handful who had been at church in the morning, and most of what he said sounded different when he had his false teeth out. So the preacher slipped his teeth out before he started to preach and used the same sermon and nobody knew it. That's what happened to our old girl. She broke her false teeth and over the phone it sounded ten times worse'n that."

He gave us a hearty handshake, adjusted his police braces over his faded blue shirt, climbed in his car and after a few minor explosions was away on high gear. We went on feeling it was nice to help someone and had our reward as a doe and fawn calmly emerged from the bush and crossed the road ahead of us as if it were a daily performance. After that we met more cars and dipped into hollows and over slopes and small hills and around turns, seeing trees and trees and trees and ferns. Finally, at long last we arrived at St. Leonard and threaded our way through a jumble of traffic, saw some signs indicating a workshop or store of the Madawaska Weavers but cars and trucks milling about kept us crawling to safety and at last we were on our way along Highway 2 to Edmundston. There was cracked pavement now and then that kept us at a slower speed and then Green River appeared as centred about a sawmill that must have taken all the trees around into its maw as the land was flat and there were very few trees.

A car with a New York licence passed us doing about seventy miles an hour and jumping bumps as if it were a game and then we were at St. Basile though the American car never recognized the speed zone at all but roared through. There were some shade trees and large buildings, one a hospital, and then we began to see the outline of Edmundston. Its wide streets looked inviting but we quickly learned to be extra careful. We parked and went into a modern-looking jewellery shop and asked for a good place to eat.

"Keep on the way you are going," smiled the clerk, "until you see a new motel. There is a very good restaurant."

We thanked him and went on, stopped at red lights on the crest of the hill and watched in amazement as three cars raced through, narrowly missing cross traffic. We saw no police and drove with the utmost care thereafter. The restaurant proved as he had said, and we had a fine lunch, drove back into town and cautiously parked near a handcraft shop. The clerk was very kind and showed us a card bearing the name "Madawaska Handcrafts d'Arts Domestiques 60 Rue Canada." There were fine samples of weaving and hooked rugs and paintings, crochet work and jewellery—all excellent products of expert handcraft. We were shown necklaces and earrings that seemed unique and were told that they were cut from sea shells by tiny saws and that the saws were so fine and so expertly handled that imitation flowers were made from the sawn shells. There were samples on display—the finest work we had seen.

As we came from the shop a fine mist was beginning and we were in and out of a dozen buildings in a search for a story of the town. Then a man in a light gray suit joined us in a doorway as a shower began and after a few words joined us in our car.

"We've got the greatest story in New Brunswick," he said. "That is, I mean this part of the Province. In the beginning we didn't belong anywhere. Quebec claimed us and so did the States and New Brunswick, and that state of affairs existed for fifty years. I guess you might have called us the Republic of Madawaska, and there were no boundaries named. Quebec used to have officials come down and tell us this was all Quebec territory right down to Grand Falls. Then the Americans would come over and say we were a part of Maine. They got mad when anybody differed and at one time called out their troops. New Brunswick got its dander up and it took all Sir John Harvey's goodwill to save a scrap. He was the governor of New Brunswick and a very able man when it came to using the old oil of friendship. Lumbering was going on and two firms from here cut what they felt was their land and Maine loggers came over and tore out their dam. It was a Saturday night and the New Brunswick fellows went looking for the Maine raiders but found their camp empty so tore it down. There was a small war for a time but in the end things were ironed out and now the Maine lads are our best friends. In fact I think we have more in common with them than our own men down at Fredericton. We're doing all right, too. The Fraser Pulp Mill is the main employer hereabouts and the pulp is carried across the St. John River in a pipe to a mill in Madawaska, Maine where it is made into paper products. Our Rotary Club has put up a monument to Archibald Fraser who was the founder of the Fraser Companies for it was his great work that put this town on the map. We have a good town, a fine town hall, community centre, and everything to help along sport. Of course most of the people are French, but they speak both languages, especially in the stores. We have a very fine cathedral, too, and good bands, good handcraft."

We told him about the earrings and flowers made from seashells and he said we would find some very fine wood carving for sale as many in Edmundston were very good at carving. Then the shower let up and away went our friend on a sprint through the traffic, and away we went back on Highway 2 heading for Grand Falls. There was another shower and then, as if by miracle, the sun was shining and we felt the whole countryside had been washed for our benefit as all the fields and trees and lawns took on new vivid colour.

It was not a long drive to Grand Falls and after we made a sharp turn right and crossed the bridge we stopped and had a look at the Falls. They present a fascinating picture and there were about twenty of us taking camera shots and studying the sheer drop that provides power to quite a section of the Province. At the base of the Falls there is a rock on which the water strikes in such fashion as to send a column of spray upwards and adds much to the picture of wild frenzy. Then the water tears furiously through a gorge in solid rock and at the narrowest point a mass overhanging is called the Pulpit Rock. Another big boulder in the middle of the channel is known as the "Camel's Back." A native told us stories about the Falls and said there were Wells near the gorge that were sixteen feet across the top and thirty feet deep, that steps lead down to them. We did not take time to explore but listened with interest as he talked about a whirlpool known as the "coffee mill" where the action is so rough that if a log goes through it is unfit for the market.

It was easy to park along the wide main street and after a few futile efforts to get a story we met a prim lady armed with an old-fashioned green parasol who overheard our questions and swung about.

"I am ashamed that you have to ask such questions more than once," she exclaimed. "When I was teaching school every pupil in my room could have given you the history of Grand Falls, and the story of the Indian maiden who saved her people. Do you know the poem?"

Without waiting an answer she began to recite and a dozen persons had gathered before she reached the second verse. This seemed but to add to her effort and she really declaimed in platform manner, telling about the Maliseet Indians who had a village above the Falls and were forever at war with the Mohawks. Then came comparative peace:

> But buried was the hatchet, they went to war no more,
> And little children gambolled about each wigwam floor;
> Around each savage village were maize fields waving green,
> Mid such sweet peace one scarcely knew that war had ever
>   been.

However it seems that the Mohawks were not to be trusted and when an old chief, Sacobie, and his daughter, the dark-skinned Malabeam, went upriver on an excursion they were ambushed and the old man was killed by the treacherous Mohawks who had, apparently, only pretended peace in order to lull the Maliseets into relaxing all watch and sentry go. The Mohawks told the chief's daughter that at sun down she was to guide them to her village, and her reward would be marriage with a Mohawk brave. If she refused, they would torture her and make her a slave for life. The girl agreed to act as guide for the three hundred warriors who were to make the sneak attack and told them that as there were many turns and the stream widened at places she wanted all the canoes to keep close together. This seemed a reasonable request and away went the Mohawks down the river chanting their war song as they descended on the doomed town. The moon hid behind a cloud and it was very dark and the singing stopped. The Mohawks heard a faraway thunder and asked the girl what it was. She explained to them that another stream joined the river below the village and at the place where it joined there was a considerable fall. Thus heartened and rid of forebodings, the Mohawks drove on and at the last instant the Indian girl gave a shout of triumph and cried that never should any of the three hundred have a grave in the earth nor a widow to mourn over his remains. The whole three hundred went over the Falls in the twinkling of an eye and for days after the Mohawk dead drifted to shore far below, battered beyond recognition. But the body of the girl who had saved her people was never recovered. This story has been told for five hundred years and is generally believed.

When the lady who had once taught school had finished, she turned to us with a regal gesture and began reciting a history lesson for our information.

"There may have been many Indian villages in this area," she said, "but the first white man's establishment was a military post placed here in 1791 by the first governor of New Brunswick, Carleton. Settlers came in slowly and found very good land and by 1815 money was voted for a road between Grand Falls and Aroostock. There had been some trouble, of course, as there generally was with settlements. When the Loyalists came up the river in 1784 they found Acadians living on land that had been given to them, and the authorities had to move fast to avoid bloodshed. The Governor hastily made a reservation for the Acadians of sixteen thousand acres between Grand Falls and Edmundston, and gave them deeds to the land they had cleared as squatters, so they might sell to the Loyalists and so have something for their work of clearing and cultivating. This seemed a very fair deal and all was fine until the international boundary was established. Then the Acadians on the south side of the upper St. John River found they had become Americans overnight and were living in Madawaska County, Maine. The town was laid out in 1842 and has never stopped growing. One of the first coach drivers was John Curran, who was always called 'Count Curran' because he wore a tall silk hat that came to be called a 'stove pipe'. He ran a boarding house and one night a drunken customer upset his candle under the bed and the place was burned to the ground. The Count built again and the town called his place 'Castle Curran', but the feat by which he is remembered was his training a big black horse he owned to make a sound like 'I want my oats.' Some declared the horse could talk but that is far-fetched. As the soldiers of the military post had a parade ground it was soon enclosed by homes and you are standing on it now—as our main street. It is called 'Broadway' and is the widest main street in eastern Canada. You said you wanted word about something different. Well, this place is different. It's the capital of the potato country. Nearly seventy thousand acres in this Upper St. John River valley are planted in potatoes, and if you were here in the fall you could see the machines that grade and sort for crates going to South America and Africa. The ones for home use are put in bags. This was quite a game country at the beginning and many moose were shot, and many bears captured by deadfall. The story is that two men caught bears and sold them as pets. They would get a cub and tame it, and at one time there were bears in town, kept in a barn. They would do tricks, if anyone paid the owners, and drink beer just like chained bears drink pop today at some of the canteens. There were towboats on the river in the old days, about seventy feet long and eight feet wide, drawn by horses which were used in relays. They took supplies upstream for the big logging operations. The tow lines were two hundred feet long and fastened to a mast in the middle of the boat. A man steered with a sweep and there was a cookhouse at the back of the boat. After that came the steamboats and they ran excursions up from Woodstock."

The lady paused for breath. Her audience had melted to three. Beside ourselves a youngster eating icecream avidly was absorbing every word.

"How did they get across the river?" we asked.

"That is a sensible question," approved the lady. "They had a footbridge at first, made of heavy ropes with staves or boards across the ropes. It swayed badly when one travelled on it but barrels of flour could be rolled across. Then a suspension bridge was built in 1851, at least it was started then but was a long time in construction and the builders were painting it when the whole thing collapsed as two men with a horse and wagon were crossing. One man and the horse fell to the rocks and were killed. The other man was badly injured and died two weeks later. The same contractor immediately went to work to replace the bridge with a stronger one that lasted until 1914, when we got the steel bridge that is here now. Of course there are some superstitious people who always talk about the fact that the St. John River is crossed by thirteen bridges, and that is bound to bring bad luck. It even reached the railway bridge for it crashed down in 1900 when a train from Edmundston was crossing, but nobody was drowned. And back in February, 1887, there was a snowstorm that lasted three days and the drifts were so deep it took the train six weeks and one day to get from Grand Falls to Little Falls. Put that in your book for a 'Believe It or Not.' One hundred and sixty men had to be hired to shovel the road out."

"It's four o'clock," said the child licking last nourishment from her icecream cone.

"My goodness!" said our lady of platform poise. "Why didn't you tell me before?"

She left so fast that we felt she wanted to gather up her skirts and run and the child vanished before we could learn the identity of our informer. We turned to go, scanning our hasty scribbling, and a man came from the store behind us. "I guess you got the town history okay," he said. "She gives talks on it. But I bet she didn't tell you about the rum that was sold here in the old days or about the time they were digging for a sewer at the head of this street and uncovered an old powder magazine with three kegs of gunpowder still in it."

"Phone!" someone shrilled from the store.

Our man left us hurriedly and after waiting five or ten minutes we went to the car and got in. We felt we had really obtained enough notes for one town.

It was not long before we were in a little village, Aroostook Junction, and asking questions of a man who was tinkering with a potato sprayer.

"Here's where the Aroostook War was fought," he said. "At least that's what I was told since I was kneehigh to a grasshopper. The governments of Great Britain and the U.S.A. was poking along as they most always do and nobody knew where the boundary would be so a man named Baker got mad over being put off for five years in a row and said he would go along with the State of Maine's idea to settle the question without the two governments. So he put up a flag on a pole in front of his house and it was the American flag. Somebody went and told the constable down at Woodstock or somewhere and he came and took away the flag. But Baker went and got another one and put it up and this time the constable took both Baker and the flag and they had a trial and Baker was put in jail for three months. That cooled him off but the Maine fellows kept getting ugly over some timber land and decided they'd go to war. So two forces came over to this neck of woods, with the Maine chaps under their governor and our lads under the New Brunswick governor.

The President moved fast and sent a general who cooled off the Maine fellows and talked an agreement with the New Brunswick governor and the upshot was the Ashburton Treaty which fixed the line. Poor Baker found himself in New Brunswick after all but he took it like a hero and got on all right with his neighbours. There's some of his clan living now over at Baker's Brook."

"Do you belong here?" we asked. "Were you born here?"

"Not me. I married this place, in a way, got it through me wife's relations. No. I'm from another part of New Brunswick where it ain't so good for farming. I was back a while ago and there are five or six more vacant farms. It makes a man feel bad just to walk around the back road and find nothing but overgrown cellar holes caved in, the farm road just a gully, and old lilacs and apple trees about all that's left alive. There was some apples on the trees, little scabby ones, and deer had been eating them. Three farms there in a row had been going good fifty years back, but now there's nobody. Down here it's different. We have the potatoes. But prices are bad and it's tough enough. A man has to go all out just to get by these days. The human race is the toughest I was ever in."

He grinned and you could tell he was not a mourner.

"You hear the one about close races?" he quizzed. "One fellow said he was at a horse race so close that the winner got the money by putting its tongue out. The next man said he saw a boat race so close that it was won by the thickness of its new paint. Then the third fellow piped up and said that was nothing. The closest race in the world was in Aberdeen, and he knew because he had lived there five years."

We asked if he were a Scottie.

"Not even a wee drappie in me," he grinned again. "Most of them are pretty shrewd, though. We were into town for the 24th and it was hard to get a parking place. I had to leave our old lizzie in a back street but my Scotch neighbour drove in and parked by a bus place. Then he took an old parking ticket out of his pocket and put it under the window scraper, and walked away. It worked. The cop saw it and just grinned, sure the fellow had been tagged by the chief or someone. It takes nerve, of course, but Jock has it."

# 11

## Big Cat, Longest Covered Bridge, "Thumbs-Up Church," and Brigham Young's Father

A FEW MINUTES LATER we had reached the twin towns of Andover and Perth, looking at each other across the river. We parked and went into a store in Perth and asked for a story.

"Too bad the paper's gone," said the lady back of the counter. "It had lots of stories but it was on the wrong side of the street, across from this shop. The whole row of buildings were moved away when the Beechwood Development began. And the same thing went on over there in Andover. Having a deed to your property didn't mean a thing. You were moved, your place taken down, and the most of them just quit. I guess the Development's a good thing but it hurt a lot of good people, and I doubt we ever have another paper."

The good lady would not talk of anything else so we went out and wandered around a bit, saw where the buildings had stood and could understand a certain bitterness resulting. Progress always makes changes and there are those of us who dislike drastic change in anything. We went along the street to the end and back again and found no one with a story and were about to leave when a car with a lady at the wheel pulled up next to ours and we saw a large cat hop to the back seat and get up to look out the window. It was a curious tawny colour and much bigger than average.

A woman got from the car and noticed our interest.

"Joe likes to watch the people," she said, "just as he likes to ride in the car. We always bring him when we come in from camp to shop."

She went on to explain they had a summer camp somewhere up the river, had been there for some years. "One night I was washing dishes and heard something that seemed demanding. I looked all around before I saw a big yellow face pressed against the window and round yellow eyes staring in at me. I was so sure it was a wild cat at first that I looked to see if we had the shot gun in the closet. But Joe stayed and eyed me and asked to come in and I opened the door. He trotted in and stood around expectantly so I got a saucer of milk and he lapped it up, had two refills. Then my husband came home and our dog, a boxer, was with him. He took a look at Joe and started to chase him out. Joe didn't growl or raise a hair. He merely stood and looked at the boxer and the boxer backed away. We had the impression that Joe has been used to tangling with bears and wild cats. He ate and ate, and then sat down and washed his face and then we saw what huge paws he has and that he has no tail. We were still unsure but when I sat down he came over by my chair and hopped up on my knees heavy as a dog, put his head down to be stroked and purred loud. You should hear him. Some times he will sit on the floor and rock forward and back as if he were in a rocking chair, purring his loudest. Now and then he goes into the woods for a few days but he always comes back and we know that someone must have had him as a pet before he came to us. We never had a cat before, and don't like them, but we are really fond of Joe."

We took another look at Joe and decided we would never want that much cat around our home or camp or anywhere else, thanked the lady for her information and got into our car, never knowing until we were forty miles away that we had missed a cottage studio where the Gillett sisters use native flowers to create beautiful souvenirs. Before we were gone a block we saw two Indians carrying a basket as if they had something to sell, but traffic took us some distance before we could park again and the native sons had vanished. As we peered and pushed our way around corners we met a man in a faded yellow sweater and jeans, carrying a bucksaw.

"Don't be in a rush," he advised, running his tongue along the edge of his upper lip. "It don't pay. You got any wood you want bucked?"

We shook our head and asked his rate.

"Depends on the wood, hard or soft, dry or green, but I'll gamble you won't get cheaper any place. My father told me he used to buck wood at a dollar a cord when he was young, and you know how times have changed. I'll do a cord to fire-place size for five bucks. Ain't that fair?"

We admitted it was very fair, but said we were only passing through.

"You might say the same about myself," he sighed. "Work ain't plenty, and I'd as lief do any other chore this hot weather. You take in winter a man just naturally enjoys bucking wood on a sunny day and no hurry. I like the smell of sawdust and I like the way a good saw bites into wood. January and February are my good months."

"Did you see two Indians go this way just now?" we asked.

"No," he grunted. "They looking for scalps?"

He peered around in mock fright and right away we knew we had a character for he said he figured the Indians had been driven from the country years before.

"Into their reservations, I mean," he explained. "Oh, yes, they do come into town now and then but they've faded out till you can hardly call them redskins. Too much white blood's got mixed with them. Pardon me, if I sound a bit bitter about them, but I've had my experiences."

He led the way to a space before a filling station and there we stood, he fingering his bucksaw lovingly as he related his adventures as a young man.

"It was a mighty good ways from here," he explained, "and I was a young cub who thought he knew all there was to know. There were some Indians up our way and I knew most of them like I know most people, from the face. But this day I see a girl around that is a knockout. Mister, I'm not handy with words so I can't make you understand, but she was really constructed, not built. And the way she walked you didn't see anything else. She was looking at store fronts as if in a strange land so I strutted up and said if I could help I'd be delightful. She took a look and said her feet were weary and she were looking for a place to sit. The look said more than her tongue and I guided her to benches in a place where the band played Wednesday nights. She sit down mighty thankful and the least surprised party was me when she asked me to sit with her as she was nervous of town fellows. Then she indicated that all we would do would be innocent and she hoped I had good home training. Her talk took all the freshness out of me and all we mentioned was the weather and store prices. We sat about half an hour when a guy a little more'n my size come in the park and looked us up and down, said some ugly words and went away. The girl got nervous then and said she must be going and would catch a ride in the mail cart which was just coming by. She climbed over the wheel like a boy and I didn't know whether to peep or go blind I was so exaggerated by then, but I found my tongue enough to offer to take her any place in a livery rig. She smiled real sweet and said she had a previous predicament with another fellow and when I stumbled away the guy who had come into the park caught me with a haymaker and when I woke up he was gone. Later I went west on one of them harvest excursions and learned to box out there. When I was home again some years later I met the lad and had my revengance. He wasn't half the man I had thought but when I was through with him along come a hellcat who clipped me over the head with a stick and darn near put me out. I rassled the club from her while she spit fury and then saw she was the one I'd set with back when, only her teeth were mostly gone and her knees were kind-a sprung and she'd turned colour, was real Indian. That's how come I've never risked hitchin', and my old dad told me often that sooner or later all wimmen go sour. Well, I don't want to hold you up, and I can see you've had better luck than most."

We slipped a dollar into his leathery palm and wondered why some enterprising radio station had not got him for an interview. Such as he are the real thing when it comes to professional entertaining.

It was pleasant driving along Highway 2 but night was coming along and we did not stop at Upper Kent. At Bath, however, we saw a typical man of the woods surveying the river pools and stopped. We asked him if there were good fishing places in the area. He glanced at our car license.

"You're in the finest salmon fishing there is in New Brunswick," he asserted with the warmth of a native son. "Don't let them talk to you down in Hartland or over on the Miramichi. Any time you want real good fishing, you come here, and I'll show you a pool that hasn't an equal in this Province. This is really the greatest game country you can find. There's deer and moose and bear, everything and lots of good camps and guides. Ain't it nice country just to drive through?"

We assured him it was.

"And now they're talking of putting a road through over the hill back of here that will cut off Bath. I know a sight of places they could cut off easier, and do more good. What's here? Why this is where they make all the potato barrels for shipping. It's a steady place, hasn't so many ups and downs, though it's generally more down than up. And if you're wanting stories just slip across to Greenfield on the other side of the river and ask about Mammy Hopkins of the 104th. She was born in the States somewhere and was married to a John Jasper who was a marine sergeant when they fired that shot that was heard around the world. Well, Mammy had the right stuff in her and went on a brig with her man, helped with the guns. However they were captured and Jasper was sentenced to be shot. Mammy was sharp as a steel trap and got away and rigged it so Jasper and twenty-two more got away at the same time. The sentries did some shooting, though, and Mammy got a bullet in her arm. The sentry who fired the shot was on horseback and Mammy got hold of a gun and shot him and took his nag and got away. Her man died soon after and Mammy married a man named Woodward, and got taken prisoner again. They held onto her and Woodward till peace come and then they set out for New Brunswick but the ship was wrecked in the Bay of Fundy and nearly all hands were drowned. But Mammy and Woodward got to shore and later Woodward died. I guess living with Mammy took a lot out of a man. So next she married a Hopkins who was a soldier with the 104th Regiment and they had twenty-two children, eighteen of them being boys. Almost a platoon. Five of her boys and a son-in-law joined the 104th, and around here there's a hundred stories of what she did raising her family. If we had had a thousand or so like her this here country would be really populated today. There's some of her descendants over in Fredericton, I've heard."

Away we went with memories of Mammy dominating and enjoyed the river scenery all the way. It had been a beautiful drive all the afternoon and when we reached Bristol we parked beside a store surprisingly large for the village. E. R. Marich, the sign said, and we went in to find a bigger surprise for on display was the finest selection of china and glass we had seen outside of Halifax. Only Saint John could offer anything in competition to the stock we saw that included **Hudson Bay blankets and a hundred items tourists look for.**

There was wonderful showing of Spode and items from all countries even Israel. The store has been operated by five generations and is known far and wide. We saw three parties arrive, two from Ohio and one from Michigan. The Michigan man said it was his fourth trip east and he always shopped in Bristol. There were three ladies in one of the cars from Ohio and they got out lists as if they were going to fill the car. We talked with a clerk who said it was nothing out of ordinary to sell five hundred dollars worth of glass and china to one party.

There was a tearoom that looked inviting but time was pressing and away we went through Florenceville, reached after a drive through hardwoods that must be a wonder in colour during October. There were elms and pines to shade the road after Florenceville, and Stickney and Peel were very small hamlets. Then we arrived in Hartland and saw the longest covered bridge in the world—1,282 feet long. We parked and visited the town paper briefly, asking about the bridge for we saw construction work started on another river crossing. We were assured the covered bridge would remain as a tourist attraction but that all trucking and heavy vehicles would use the new bridge when it was ready, which might be a very long time as first efforts to build river foundations had met with failure.

We saw a car parked not far away with a Connecticut license and an elderly man was in the back seat alone, leaned forward and gazing at the bridge. We paused and asked him if he had seen anything like it elsewhere.

"I've seen many covered bridges," he smiled, "but none as long as that one. When I was a boy seventy-odd years ago there were many in Pennsylvania and Ohio and Vermont. I've heard all kinds of arguments as to why they were covered and never heard the real reason. In the old days there was generally a good fishing hole under a covered bridge and they tell me there is a salmon pool inside the town limits, the only place that has such a thing."

"Not so," we demurred gently. "Middleton in Nova Scotia has a salmon pool within the town limits."

"Anyhow," responded the old man, "there's something here I bet you haven't got in your Middleton. Did you ever see the fishermen sitting in chairs to fish? You come here early in a good morning or just before dark and you'll see five or six men sitting in chairs and fishing. They've told me a lot of stories in this place about salmon. One they tell is that some fishermen planted a lot of fish vitamins in a pool down below on the way to sea and that a big salmon that fed there a week took a jump that sent him sailing right over the covered bridge. Mind you," he grinned, "I'm only passing this story along as I got it at the hardware store. Two or three other fish noticed the jump and they give it a real go. A pair of them sailed over the bridge, and the other almost did. So the fishermen fixed themselves up with a balloon fly, that is, a salmon fly tied to a balloon string. No one says they actually hooked any jet-propelled salmon going over the bridge, but do you know of any other place where salmon jump that way?"

We had to admit that we did not know of any other such place, but knew that New Brunswick salmon were the greatest jumpers in the world.

"That's interesting," said the old man. "I've never been around this country before and I don't want to miss anything. I remember in Ohio they had lattice work along the sides of many of their bridges, and all of them had signs like 'Walk Your Horse or Pay a Two Dollar Fine.' When you come to think of it, maybe towns and cities should put up signs like that. 'Slow down or you will pay a fine.' The heart attacks and ulcers are the fines. They tell me, too, this bridge used to be a toll bridge, ten cents per team."

We had a long chat with him, then left him to his dreams and made our way through the bridge and away we went to Woodstock and were fortunate to get accommodation at Hill

View, which was all one could ask, clean and new and very comfortable, with the adjoining Home Town Tea Room serving delightful meals. It was good to roam down the long main street and back in the evening as robins were singing a goodnight, and there was a heavy scent of flowers and shade trees. Only the occasional terrific rush of some youngsters in cars disturbed the peace.

In the morning we began to explore and drove out on the river island where crowds of youngsters were having fun and picnics were in the making. The buildings of a race track and exhibition are there and it was on the island that the famous North Shore Regiment did its training back in the early days of World War Two. We heard many tales of men getting back to camp late and wading the stream to avoid the sentries. Then, as we looked around and talked with some men who seemed to have the day off, we learned that Woodstock had its one hundredth birthday as an incorporated town in 1956, and that a short history had been published. So away we went to the town hall to interview Colonel Calkin, the Town Manager. He was absent at the time but his assistant was most courteous and helpful showing us framed pictures of former mayors and explaining many points. She showed us the quotation at the beginning of the history: "Tell ye your children of it, and let your children tell their children, and their children another generation." Joel 1: 3.

The history was very entertaining. We first learned that Woodstock was not named for an abundance of trees but by some settler from the ancient boroughtown of Oxfordshire made famous by Sir Walter Scott's novel *Woodstock*. First grants of the site of the town were given to discharged soldiers of the First Battalion New Jersey Volunteers who came to New Brunswick following the close of the Revolutionary War, and their common complaint was that their lands were all length and no breadth. Two Smiths—father and son—acquired the greatest portion of the land on which the town was later built. The son married Judith Jenkins, and the account continues:

He died about 1833, and within a year she married Captain Frederick Morehouse. Richard Smith had left her all his property to enjoy the income derived from any leases she might give. A curious inclusion in the will, is the warning that if anyone interfered with the peaceful enjoyment of his widow's estate, all his property should then revert to her in fee simple ! She was, however, given permission to sell enough of the land to pay his just debts and funeral expenses. Evidently the lady, not being able to sell any of the remainder, decided that none of her husband's relatives should derive from the property any more than she was allowed to enjoy under the terms of the will, and forthwith, to any who wished to build houses or places of business, she gave leases for terms of 999 years. Only three such numerals are as famous (at least in Woodstock) namely those of a well known wine!

When bulldozers were excavating a site for a present plant in Woodstock hundreds of chipped flints were uncovered, proving that centuries before the spot had been a campsite for aboriginal craftsmen taking time out to create weapons of war and chase. Three large oaks were prominent features of the town and when progress in the shape of telephone men cut them out of their way the trunks measured nineteen feet in circumferance. The rings were counted which denoted the growth years and the oaks were found to be 435 years old, had been good trees when Champlain discovered and named the St. John River in 1604.

The growth of the town was slow until a first bridge spanning the Meduxnekeag was built in 1826, the piers being of massive hemlock timbers. By 1847 there were 600 inhabitants and ten years later the population was 1581. The first mayor was Lewis P. Fisher, who occupied the post for the next twenty-four years. The first supplies that reached the town came by towboat but after that came steamboat service. Four times fire devastated the town. The first big fire was April 16, 1860, when a Farley Hand Engine was all the citizens had as fire fighting equipment. The town was scarcely rebuilt when, in 1867, came another big blaze and after that a steam fire engine was purchased, though many citizens resisted the idea and the majority vote was only twenty. Surely they learned a lesson, the resisters, for in 1877 again came a terrible fire. The fourth was in 1881 when fifty-three buildings were destroyed and sixty-one families left homeless.

Woodstock was fortunate in having a fairy godfather, the first mayor, Lewis P. Fisher, who practised law and, like his kind today, made a fortune. At death he left the bulk of his estate to the town for educational purposes. His money built for Woodstock the first Vocational and Agricultural School in Canada. It also built the fine town school and the Fisher Memorial Library, finished within with solid mahogany, the pride of Woodstock and unique among Maritime libraries. Add to these the Fisher Memorial Hospital, and you have some idea of what one man did for one town.

A watchmaker and jeweller of Woodstock, H. V. Dalling, in 1866 made and installed two telephones; one in his store and one in his residence. Main Street was then known as The Great Road and the wire was strung from trees. The Bell Telephone Company heard of the happening, came to investigate, and opened a small exchange in Mr. Dalling's store, with Mr. Dalling as manager. There was no night or Sunday service so Mr. Dalling built and installed a miniature switchboard of eight lines in his residence in order to answer important calls after hours. This unique switchboard was donated to the Pioneer's Museum by Miss Edith Dalling, daughter of Mr. Dalling. In 1900 Woodstock had another "first," the first automatic dial system in Canada.

We wandered around the town all the morning, meeting many people who were cordial and friendly but could not give us much history. Five different persons we accosted said they had not been in the town ten years, and one had come from Newfoundland. We were about to give up the hunt when a reserved-looking small man of uncertain age listened to our plea, backed into the shade of an alley as if we were carrying on some illegal transaction, and began to talk.

"I've been hereabouts the last sixty years," he said. "What have you got so far?"

We told him and he nodded. "That's about it," he said, "except you ought to have it in about old Charlie Connell. We've a street named after him and he was postmaster-general before Confederation. Back in 1859 the pound sterling went out in New Brunswick and Charlie went to New York and arranged for the printing of a lot of new postal stamps of the new money, like five-cent, three-cent and so on. When they reached this Province it was found the five-center carried Charlie's picture and the government ordered the stamps destroyed. The order was obeyed, of course, as far as the government knew, but a good few of them that kept post office hung on to the five-centers and today they're worth a fortune. I don't know as we have had many of them you call characters in this county. I do remember a man downriver who was handy with tools, and his wife was sickly. So one winter when she was bed-fast most of the time he built a coffin for her. When he had the last paint and varnish on it and it was ready for an occupant, the good woman died. This made the chap so conscience-stricken that he built one for himself but his health stayed good and that coffin stood in what had been his wife's sewing-room for more'n seven years. Then he married again and wife number two made him sell it. Say, watch that lady getting out of the car."

We watched the lady climb from a car and then go to the trunk which was not locked. She took out a jack which she adjusted under the rear at almost one motion. Then she pulled an old tire from the trunk and placed it on the pavement well back of the car. Following which, she primly walked away.

"I saw her do that two or three times," said our friend, "before I talked to her and found she'd had her car hemmed in so tight two or three times that she'd had to sit and wait for the ones who'd hemmed her in. So she thought of the tire and jack trick and now when a man sees them he parks a good way back and she has no trouble whatsoever."

We thought there must be some pretty smart folk in the Woodstock area and took our departure, or started to, but the little man followed us to the car.

"Can't you put in something about Confederation in your book?" he pleaded. "You know us down here were seduced into Confederation. Our natural market is in the States, especially New England and Ontario and Quebec stuck up tariffs that have strangled us and paralyzed our trade. We ought to belong to New England, then we wouldn't have to pay hundreds of dollars more for a car than a man living just ten miles away—in Maine. Look at us now, our forests wasted, our salmon rivers leased, our taxes high, and half of them going to build that St. Lawrence Seaway which will finish us off, specially Saint John. Even K. C. Irving can't do anything about that Seaway business. Them at Ottawa think they've give us all we need down in Gagetown, wasting money in the woods and putting folks off their farms. This training business is foolish when everybody knows that if there is another war it will be a matter of who gets off their atom bombs first. What can infantry and tanks do against guided missiles? Did you ever hear of more foolish waste than Gagetown?"

We started the motor for it was easy to see he carried a heavy grouch, and he was still shaking his head as we drove away and inhaled a beautiful morning, one that had no room for a growler.

Our next stop was Meductic and we parked to read the inscription on one of the usual monuments erected by the

National Historic Sites and Monuments Board. All look the same, are generally by the roadside and often enclosed with a fence. Not once in all our travel around the Provinces did we see a car of the Province or a visitor stopped by such cairns. It is a pity that there is no imagination within the Board and means taken to erect something that will catch the interest of a passerby.

The particular cairn at Meductic has a tablet on three sides. On the north side we read:

On the River St. John half a mile eastward stood Fort Meductic, chief Maliseet stronghold in Acadia in the 17th and 18th centuries. Near it was a village with a church and burial ground. The church was built by the French in 1717 and a replica of the dedication stone is incorporated in this monument.

On the southern side we read:

Ancient Indian portage. The portage from Meductic to Eel River led to the waters of the Penobscot and formed part of the main route of travel between Acadia and New England. During the French regime military expeditions against the English settlements travelled by way of this portage.

On the western side was the replica of the dedication stone of the church, and as we studied it a man in shirt sleeves came from nowhere, inspected our car and asked if he could be of help. He said it in a nice way and we asked why there was not a memorial at the actual Maliset fort instead of half a mile away.

"Because there is nothing to see," he said. "A few years back you could still trace the wall but I doubt that can be done now. The Indians had an earth wall carrying a stockade of timbers driven in the ground with the top ends pointed, and a ditch outside. The traces of the wall show that it was a big place and they had a cabin of logs inside that was about thirty by forty feet, was more like four cabins joined together.

They were quite builders, the Maliseets, and quite warlike, too, always having trouble with the Mohawks. I was brought up on a book my father had that told about John Gyles, a white lad the Indians captured when he was only ten years old. The redskins took him when he and his brothers and father were working in the field and they fetched him this way and held him until he was sixteen. He had a good word for some of them but the most were a bunch of snakes. Over in that direction there is a spring of fine cold water that is called Gyles Spring, and tradition has it that the Indians made him carry water to them in the hot summer. One account says that he and another young prisoner carried endless buckets one very hot day and the distance was more than half a mile. They were fagged by night and planned to do something before they were completely exhausted. So the night became very dark and when they got at the top of a hill they put the kettle down and the older lad ran back to his Indian master and said he and Gyles had heard noises and thought there were Mohawks around. The Indian jeered at them but went to the hill where Gyles pointed to some stumps vaguely seen and said they were Indians. In the poor light they could imagine the stumps moving and as the Indian started to run the older lad kicked the bucket and sent it clattering down the hill whereupon the Indian ran as if the devil were after him, alarmed the camp and the whole crew piled out into the night and didn't stop going until they were miles away. It was two weeks before any of them ventured to return and by then the hottest part of the summer was past. If you want a book that's mighty interesting if it was written two centuries ago, get the story of Gyles."

We told him we would remember to do so, and he talked about a chapel the French had built for the Indians at Meductic but it had been taken down and another built farther down the river.

"The original chapel had a bell they say was sent from a

church in France that was interested in Acadia, and I've heard the old people tell it could be heard for twelve miles on a fine day, and the Indians simply loved to hear it rung. No, I don't know as there is much else to see around here. Some find old Indian arrow heads and stone axes, but I've never had such luck. Oh, yes, there's a man here that does good wood carving, if you want a souvenir. It's bird-eye maple he uses, and pretty nice. When I was a youngster nearly everybody did some jackknife carving, made wooden chains and the like. The crop growing up now don't know much beyond juke boxes and comic books."

He said it sadly and we couldn't take time to explain that his grandfather had probably lamented that the country was going to the dogs as the young fry showed no signs of progress, but it was too much of an effort so on we went and pulled up at Pokiok when we saw five American cars parked beside the road. We soon saw the visitors were following a path up a bank to the left from where they could get a fine view of the Pokiok Falls, and when we reached the spot it was certainly worth while. It is a fine view and several cameras were clicking. Others went exploring far beyond and we heard one man shouting to his wife that he was going to get down to the water's edge. It was lovely under the trees, listening to the Falls, and we imagined what a spot it must have been when the white men found it. We walked back to the highway and discovered a path going down to the stream on the far side of the road. A young couple saw it, too, and away they went, camera in hand.

At the narrow spot the gorge was twenty feet across and there were walls seventy-five feet high, of what looked to be dark red granite. We couldn't guess how many steps there were in the stairs going down to the river but it was quite a distance.

On we drove along the river and after half an hour came to a stop as a car had been in collision with a truck and a dozen vehicles were stopped and it looked as if it would be some time before we could get through. A farmer in a field had come to the fence with a timothy stem in his mouth, studying the situation.

"Same old story," he said, edging along the fence to where we stood. "A creeper going as if he owned the road, and a man trying to get past him when he didn't have a clear view. These fellows that drive thirty-five and forty on through paved highways should be fined on the spot. Put the police on them for a month and we'd have no more such nonsense. All the signs should say 'Drive 30' or 'Drive 50', instead of saying that many miles is the limit. Tell the cars what speed to go and if everybody drove fifty—which is fast enough to get any place you're going—then there'd be no passing. And if any can't drive that fast, or a big truck or the like can't, let them travel the roads between twelve p.m. and seven in the morning. Any country could stop half the accidents if they made everybody drive fifty out clear of towns. It's the passing that makes accidents, and people pass because there are crawlers in the way."

"What's the name of the place around here?" we asked.

"Long's Creek," came the answer, "and Kelly's Creek is just over there, only them ain't the names the Indians used. They called them the Skoodawabskook and the Skoodawabskooksis. Quite a mouthful, ain't it? You ever hear the DeMille poem? I know the first and last verses, and it's called 'Sweet Maiden of Passamaquoddy':

> Sweet maiden of Passamaquoddy,
> Shall we seek for communion of souls
> Where the deep Mississippi meanders,
> Or the distant Saskatchewan rolls?
> Ah, no! in New Brunswick we'll find it —
> A sweetly sequestrated nook—
> Where the swift-gliding Skoodoowakskooksis
> Unites with the Skoodoowabskook.

Then never of Waweig or Chamcook
I'll think, having you in my arms;
We'll reck not of Digdeguash beauties,
We'll care not for Popelogan's charms;
But as emblem of union forever
Upon two lovely rivers we'll look;
While you'll be the Skoodoowabskooksis,
And I'll be the Skoodoowabskook."

We had to applaud, for he handled the jaw-breakers with great skill, and it was easy to see he was proud of his accomplishment.

"When you go on there isn't much before Fredericton 'cept Kingsclear," he said. "It's an Indian village and the chapel has the bell that used to be at Meductic. Beyond it you'll see the Snowshoe Islands in the river. The story is that Glooscap was traveling up here one spring when it come out real warm and the snow melted so fast it was soon bare ground. So Glooscap just kicked off his snowshoes as he crossed the river and there they are to this day. There's lots of old Indian yarns around but I never know which was really remembered or which was invented, and that makes me think of a big doctor from town who got himself one of them big gowns they wear in operating rooms and he got called out to a woman going to have a baby. Well, he wanted all to go right and so he give her plenty of chloroform. She practically passed out just as he was getting his gown on and he was a mite worried but all went well and the baby was delivered. The nurse was an old hand and so after mother and baby were fixed for the rest of the night the doctor left. When he come back in the morning he started to ask the woman about the way she faded. 'Did you go right out, black out?' he quizzed. 'Could you hear us talking?' 'Doctor,' said the woman, 'I never knowed a thing you did to me after you put on your nightshirt.'"

The man rocked and chuckled over the fence at his own story, and we asked him if the chapel bell was rung often.

"No, not much," he said. "Some think it's quite a bell but over where I was a boy we had a farm bell nearly as good. Never hear of a farm bell? Well, did you ever see a surrey with a fringe on top, a buckwheat cradle or a dash churn? Back in that time people had farm bells. I remember ours cost about two fifty and we had it on a post by the woodshed. Mother or sister would pull the rope at noon and you could hear it a mile. It was our dinner bell. We had bells on the oxen then, bells on pasture cattle, bells on horses in the winter. If we had a caller or a stranger come, sister went out and pulled the rope just three times. That told us somebody was at the house. I guess many used some kind of a code in those days. Well, they've hauled that car off to one side and I guess you can get through. Good day, and don't be a crawler."

The river widened gradually and then our attention was taken by road construction as we neared Fredericton and it took all care to edge along past trucks and equipment. A car from New Jersey was at our rear too close for comfort and followed us right in to the Beaverbrook Hotel. We got a nice room, had a fine lunch and then went out to roam around Fredericton. It was a still day except for traffic and the river was like a sheet of glass. There seemed to be trees everywhere and some almost met overhead. In no time we had decided that Fredericton was the prettiest place we had found in the Maritimes. A church spire caught our eye and we learned it was one hundred and ninety-eight feet high, and saw it had an eight and a half foot hand and four-foot index finger pointing heavenward as a guide for an erring flock. A passerby, and the notice board, said it was the Wilmot United Church. The passerby said it was dedicated back in 1852 and was named for a one-time governor of the Province. Only one other church in all North America has a spire topped by a finger and that is in Mississippi. The things that caught our eye after hearing the information was a lightning rod on the tip of the index finger. We never had much faith in such contrivances but the passerby said the church had been damaged by lightning and the insurance people had suggested the lightning rod. He also told us that the soldiers in garrison in the old days called it the "thumbs-up church."

Farther up the slope we saw the buildings of the University of New Brunswick, and a man on the grounds told us the Arts Building was the oldest university building in use in Canada, dating back to 1828. We said the beautiful surroundings must be an inspiration to the students of today, and the man peered at us as if he thought we were trying to pull his leg.

"You couldn't inspire the crew that goes to college today," he said. "They come in cars, and too many of them have cars. They park every which way and any place no matter how many signs are up. All they think of is jazz and TV and getting drunk and staying up all night. Leastways, that's the idea you get if you are around. I'm not saying all them are like that, but far too many are. Over there is a monument to three Fredericton poets, Sir Charles G. D. Roberts and Bliss Carman and Francis Joseph Sherman. Yes, some of the students know about the monument and some write poetry. They have a college paper called *The Fiddlehead*, that has good stuff in it. Now come over this way, up here, and look around."

It was amazing, as if we were in a fine woods. We could see some church spires but nothing else to tell there was a city under the sea of green tops. We came around and to another point and had a great view of the river. The afternoon went by on wings. There was the Dominion Experimental Station, a farm inside the city limits with an entrance decorated with flowers and shrubbery. There were lovely flower beds and lawns and we were much surprised to know that picnickers were welcome to go there with their baskets and make the best of the shade trees and surroundings.

We went down to the Provincial Parliament buildings,

and a man in the lobby told us the stone for the buildings came from almost every county, making it really a provincial structure. At the front entrance we saw Queen Victoria carved in stone, and inside over the front arch was Prince Albert. We were escorted into the Legislative Library and found it intensely interesting. There is a Domesday Book, a copy of the original compiled on order of William the Conqueror, and published by King George the Third. We saw the famous Audubon books of bird paintings purchased by the New Brunswick government from Louis Philippe of France in the 1850s. One of the plates, that of a pine finch, was painted in the woods around the Government House when Audubon visited Fredericton in the 1830s. The wood in which he rambled is preserved in its natural state, with bridle paths and rough stone fireplaces for those who like the fern-lined paths and picnic places. And a man we talked with assured us that there used to be a regular "Lover's Lane" at a part now taken over for building purposes. The city's only park is Wilmot Park, and opposite is the old Government House which was used from 1828 until 1893, and where the Prince of Wales (King Edward the VII) was entertained in 1860. The building is now the provincial headquarters of the R.C.M.P.

At the lower end of the city we saw Christ Church Cathedral and were told it was the first cathedral founded on British soil since the Norman conquest. It is a beautiful building in pleasant surroundings, and three huge white birches add much to the scene.

Everywhere we turned that afternoon we saw beauty and quiet and we were tired and glad to browse around in a very fine bookstore before going back to the hotel. Hall's Bookstore is one of the very few better sort in eastern Canada. Soon we were at the hotel and relaxing. We came down to dinner in the long cool dining-room and saw it well-filled. It was a quiet place, though, and dignity seemed to rule. We began thinking about New Brunswick and what a mixture it was of French and English but anyone just arriving by plane in that city and dining in that hotel would never have dreamed there was any French influence whatsoever. We did not hear a word of French spoken. We had not heard it all the afternoon. And afterward, in the lobby, when we were in conversation with a man from Saint John, we asked him when the French would take over.

"It might be later than you think," he grinned. "I get around a lot as I'm a commercial traveller and I feel there are two points you'd do well to consider. In the first place the average Acadian is no longer the serf of his church. He is doing a lot of thinking for himself and a lot of them, the majority, I think, are no longer going along with the breeding drive of the church. They are beginning to be like the Protestants, have a family they can afford. They're seeing the difference education means, and I know dozens of families with only two, three or four children. I'll bet money the birth increase in Acadian families has slowed by forty per cent the last ten years. Secondly, a large number of the young men are leaving New Brunswick. I'd say that, now, in proportion, just as many young Acadians go to other parts of Canada or the U.S.A. as do the English-born. And I don't think the average Acadian wants to take over New Brunswick. He can see the grief there is for whoever runs the government, and knows it's going to be tougher when the St. Lawrence Seaway gets in operation. That is really the final straw and no matter if they dig a Chignecto Canal for K. C. Irving, it won't go very far to replace the damage the Seaway is going to do. You'll call me rabid, and maybe I am, but I see no future for the Maritimes as long as Ontario and Quebec set the tariff to suit their industries and to hell with us. Until and unless we can repeal Confederation and set up free trade with the States, get back our natural market, we are going to be just like we are now, APEC or no APEC."

"What about some parts of New England that aren't much better off than we?" we asked. "What's hurting them?"

"Tariffs, perhaps," grinned the traveller. "I say, take down the whole wall and let's get to trading with each other. The Maritimes would gain far more than they would lose."

We had to leave him as such ideas could become headaches and we wanted to be fresh for Highway 9 the next day. The morning was dull until we had threaded our way over the bridge against the morning traffic and began driving along the new pavement with the occasional river ferry on our right, and many cattle everywhere made it appear a rich farming district, which it is. Presently we were in Maugerville, where we came to an abrupt stop as a lady backed a very large sedan directly from a dooryard across the road. Then she struggled with the gears, stalled the car, started and stalled, and a man arrived at the far side and slid locked tires many feet in screaming protest. Then he was out of his car and the lady slid from under the wheel, he took her place and soon the sedan was out of our way, back in the yard it had come from. A split second later an R.C.M.P. car came along, slowed a trifle to get past our parked cars, and went on.

"Twice this week," we heard the man's voice, "you've risked getting killed. Now, will you leave the car alone."

"No, I'm going to learn to drive," said the lady, "and nothing is going to stop me." There was no mistaking the determination in her tone, and the man turned and bowed as he left her.

"What kind of flowers would you like me to send?" he asked.

There was no reply and we hastily got away as the gears in the sedan began to grind once more.

A few hundred yards and we saw a man with a tractor. He was at the edge of his lane, peering the way we had come. We slowed, then rolled into his lane beside him.

"Looking for the big black sedan?" we asked.

He nodded. "How did you know?"

"She blocked us just now, and a man got the sedan back in the yard, but she's in it again."

"Well," said the tractor man, shaking his head, "I guess I better wait a bit. It don't take her long to get into a ditch or something."

We began to talk with him about Maugerville, and he smiled.

"There's lots of history around here," he said, "and there's just my family and one other that are direct descendants of the first settlers who came from Massachusetts. I guess there was about two hundred came, and it was at the time when what they called the New England Planters were going to Nova Scotia. Down there they had put messages in New England papers—there used to be one in our family—but my ancestors felt that all the rush would be to Nova Scotia and it woud be better to go to New Brunswick. The main thing they wanted was to get away from the religious fanatics who made life a misery. Every family watched the other and you've read about the witch hunts they had in Salem. Our people got land here in 1762 and found it much better than what they had left. There were two brothers and both settled here. When that Eddy from Nova Scotia was trying to get Nova Scotia to join with the rebels he sent a man here and some of the people went along when his party went to attack Fort Cumberland. But as far as I can make out by old stories there were only two or three young fellows went. Over in Sheffield they were not so satisfied as our ancestors and more of them went along with Eddy. The main one who was against the British was their preacher and he was in touch with the folks back home and after the war he got the United States government to grant he and some of his crowd land over in Maine. Away they went and others jumped right in to take the land they left. The story is that the preacher had a favourite hymn, 'Bangor,' and that where he settled is the town of

Bangor. Anyhow, it doesn't matter now. This has always been good farming country though it's a bit flat when the river gets in flood. Back when I was a boy it came over the banks and filled our cellar. Mother had always lived in fear of such floods and knew what to do. She had the parlor rug upstairs so fast it seemed nothing to do, and she even thought of the wood and kindlings for our Franklin stove. I remember that at night all the hens were roosting on top of the pen, which had about a foot of water in it. Our cattle wandered all over the place and were the biggest worry as there was a foot of water over the pasture. The water ran off soon after, however, and the biggest job we had was to pump our cellar dry. Father wanted to build brick walls outside the cellar windows but mother told him not to bother. There wouldn't be another flood in his time—and there wasn't."

He talked a lot about the various floods and told about getting women from a tree in a row boat, of cattle drowning, of calves being put up into haymows, and then we asked him if those first settlers had found the religious freedom they wanted.

"There was no more witch trouble, anyhow," he said, "but they couldn't get over being severe right off. One elder lost his wife and although he was sixty he married a girl just twenty years old, and there was a lot of scandal about that and they had him on the carpet and condemned such a move because his wife had only been dead six months. He told them it was a free country and they were hypocrites, and they tried to have him arrested when he said that a good half of them were really wishing they were in his shoes. Nothing was done about the matter and the elder had a family of three. He had had none by his first wife, and he used to say it was proof that he was in favour with the Lord. Then there was a French girl from Quebec married one of the farmers here and joined the church. As she had come from an unholy land, in the eyes of the elders, they watched everything she did and the story is that they accused her of roasting beef on the Sabbath, and she proved them wrong. Then they made a fuss about a bonnet ribbon, and she stumped them again. After that they let her alone and when those old stiff-necks died out there was no more such nonsense."

The sedan had not gone by, and it was a glorious morning. The farmer was more than willing to talk but we had to be on our way and soon were in Sheffield but did not stop. The broad flat fields, the hay barns, the river, made us think of the Tantramar marshes, and the new highway was perfect. We met cars roaring at terrific speed but it was too nice a day for such folly, and we arrived in Jemseg, parked and talked with a lady who was working in her garden.

"Mother used to tell me that when she was a girl many people saw ghosts over where the old fort used to be where the Jemseg River joins the St. John. You know the first fort was built there in 1659 by the English and was a trading post, and then the French got it by treaty. The Indians went there from miles around to trade their furs and then a Dutchman came in 1674 and captured the place and everybody in it. One prisoner was the governor of Acadia who was making the place his headquarters. The Dutchman seized all the stores and carried everybody off to Boston after naming this whole district New Holland. At Boston they let the governor send word to Quebec about what had happened, and the ransom the Dutch wanted. It was about ten thousand dollars in our money, a huge sum in those days, and the French had to get in all the furs from their trading posts and send down to make the payment. This was a great centre for fur buying then, and when the French were back here old stories say that one Indian party alone brought in over one hundred otter pelts. The legend is that the governor was not frightened in the least at what had happened but came back to Jemseg with his family and carried on the trading. Maybe he was trying to make up some of that ransom of one thousand beaver skins, or maybe all those officials were accustomed to danger. Anyway, his rule was not troubled after that for some years and he had a daughter, Louise, who spent her childhood at the fort, then was sent to a Convent in Quebec to be educated. She married the Marquis de Vaudreuil, and it was her son who was in command at Quebec when Wolfe captured the place. You might wonder how I have such a memory, and I'll explain. We had a teacher who was almost a fanatic when it came to local history. She gave prizes for best essays on Jemseg, and she drilled us on all the old records, told us all the old legends. I've never forgotten the gist of it."

We were glad she hadn't and told her so, admired peonies and heard how she nurtured them, protected them in winter, then made our adieu. We rolled along to Young's Cove and at a filling station asked if there were any historians around.

"No," said the man. "They've all died off."

"Too bad you hadn't come around before Bill passed away," remarked another who was standing by. "He carried a history book in his head."

"And made more'n half it up out of clear wool," retorted the man with the hose.

"But it was better'n most of that dry stuff they cram into you at school," protested the onlooker. "Bill could tell you all about Brigham Young having lived over alongside the lake."

"The Mormon!" we murmured.

"Sure. Bill could prove this place was named after him. He said Brigham's father had the idea first as back where he lived there was a man married to three sisters. This man had a big property and wanted a son to hand over to when he got old. The first sister had no children and agreed he could marry the second one, which he did privately. No one asked questions when the number two came to live at the house but she had no children either. So the third sister was sent for and she joined the harem. No luck with her, either, no children. There wasn't a fourth, Bill used to say, but the three wives give the man such a good time he forgot all about a son and then up and died suddenly of a heart attack or the like. With that, the first sister married again—and had a son right off. So did the other two, and Bill could really tell that story. He said Brigham's father got so envious of seeing that man with three fine-looking wives that he dreamt up the scheme that Brigham used afterward. Bill even wrote to the government and wanted them to put up a marker at the site where he said Brigham was born. But he never so much as got an answer to his letters as Brigham wasn't born in New Brunswick. It's just a story that's told."

We left feeling thankful that Bill had gone to his final reward before we arrived and paused at Coles Island but could not find any story of interest although we talked with several people. Then we had a long ride down to Sussex, a sort of roller coaster effect with very long slopes and dips and woods and field and cars streaking by. Sometimes there was such a panorama at a hilltop that a car would be parked there while people with cameras tried to find a correct site for taking a picture. It was all a real thrill, the wonderful new paved highway, the warm sun and the fragrant breath of the forest. We reached Sussex at last and were at journey's end.

As we had lunch we talked about the many impressions we remembered, and marvelled that we had not known the difference that exists. Nova Scotia seems very like New Brunswick until you drive through all of it, north, south, east and west, and get a finger on the pulse of the people. Then you discover it is different. Even the people tell you their stories in a different manner. On the main routes they listen to you and accept you much as they do through Maine. In Prince Edward Island they have more time for you, are more courteous, live more in the past, want very much to be of help. By and large they did not seem to be readers like Nova

Scotians, did not bother too much with world events. Island events mean much more in their lives. We cannot forget the villages along the new highway to Charlottetown, the friendliness and helpfulness of the members of the Women's Institutes. Nor the grand sweep of shore line and new paved highways along the north shore, the sheer beauty of the surroundings at Cavendish, the warm friendliness of Kensington, the roller coaster old road into Charlottetown with Hunter's River so lovely and sheltered in the hollow, the serene way of life along the way to Souris, the gentle resignation of Georgetown, the liveliness of Montague, the varying colours of Canada's "million-acre farm," the picturesque villages that spring up regularly out of peaceful valleys, the slowly winding turns in the road that in themselves express serenity.

It had been so different driving up the east coast of New Brunswick, stopping at small canteens for lobster or oysters and sensing the blend of Acadian background that makes the Province different. Chatham, Newcastle, Bathurst, Dalhousie—give another impression, one of work, hard work, river and lumber and virility. And from Campbellton across to St. Leonard is another experience, a fascinating reminder of what the country was like in the beginning. The drive down Highway 2 creates new impressions for Grand Falls is tremendous, and Woodstock a delight, the gorge at Pokiok picturesque, and the covered bridge at Hartland something to remember. Fredericton is a city of sheer beauty, a must for anyone touring New Brunswick, and Saint John is in a class by itself, so rugged, so sea-worn, so gray and strong and so constructed as to make one think of a fortress on a hilltop. Then there is delightful St. Andrews, the blessing of saints you get before the meal of scenery and folklore and history that is yours, and don't ever omit a side trip to Fundy National Park or a drive down Magnetic Hill near Moncton. Oysters—lobsters—pulpwood—shore line—forest—waterfalls—handcraft—covered bridge—pottery—park—tree-shaded streets—all have a different flavour from the sunny, serene rolling Prince Edward Island countryside.

And Nova Scotia is no more than a country cousin with the dyked lands and Grand Pré, ancient Port Royal and lands-end Yarmouth, the swarming Pubnicos, Loyalist Shelburne, *Bluenose* Lunenburg, the gallant old lady that is Halifax, the Causeway, the Angus L. Macdonald Bridge, Cape Breton Highlands National Park, Louisbourg—all rugged, flavoured with the Gaelic Mod and Highland Gathering, Highland Games at Antigonish, tinged with the quaint drawl and Dutch idiom of the South Shore.

Three Atlantic Provinces, all salty to the taste, all slightly old-fashioned in many ways, all offering a difference that so often captivates visitors from other lands. These are the Maritimes.

# INDEX